The **Institute of Southeast Asian Studies (ISEAS)** was established as an autonomous organization in 1968. It is a regional research centre for scholars and other specialists concerned with modern Southeast Asia, particularly the many-faceted problems of stability and security, economic development, and political and social change.

The Institute's research programmes are the Regional Economic Studies (RES, including ASEAN and APEC), Regional Strategic and Political Studies (RSPS), and Regional Social and Cultural Studies (RSCS).

The Institute is governed by a twenty-two-member Board of Trustees comprising nominees from the Singapore Government, the National University of Singapore, the various Chambers of Commerce, and professional and civic organizations. An Executive Committee oversees day-to-day operations; it is chaired by the Director, the Institute's chief academic and administrative officer.

History of Nation-Building Series

Malaysia
The Making of a Nation

CHEAH BOON KHENG

ISEAS

INSTITUTE OF SOUTHEAST ASIAN STUDIES
Singapore

First published in Singapore in 2002 by
Institute of Southeast Asian Studies
30 Heng Mui Keng Terrace
Pasir Panjang
Singapore 119614
<http://www.iseas.edu.sg/pub.html>

The five-volume series of Nation-Building Histories was made possible
with the generous support of the Lee Foundation, Singapore and the
Chiang Ching-kuo Foundation for International Scholarly Exchange, Taipei.

All rights reserved. No part of this publication may be reproduced, stored in a retrieval
system, or transmitted in any form or by any means, electronic, mechanical,
photocopying, recording or otherwise, without the prior permission of the Institute
of Southeast Asian Studies.

© 2002 Cheah Boon Kheng

*The responsibility for facts and opinions in this publication rests exclusively
with the author and his interpretations do not necessarily reflect the views
or the policy of the Institute or its supports.*

ISEAS Library Cataloguing-in-Publication Data

Cheah, Boon Kheng.
   Malaysia : the making of a nation.
   (The State and nation-building)
   1.   Nationalism—Malaysia.
   2.   Communalism—Malaysia.
   3.   Pluralism (Social sciences)—Malaysia.
   4.   Malaysia—Ethnic relations.
   5.   Malaysia—Politics and government.
   6.   Malaysia—Economic policy.
   7.   Malaysia—Economic conditions.
   I.   Title.
DS596.7 C51   2002

ISBN 981-230-154-2 (soft cover)
ISBN 981-230-175-5 (hard cover)

Typeset by Superskill Graphics Pte Ltd
Printed in Singapore by CMO Image Printing Enterprise

Dedicated to

TONY REID
friend, teacher and scholar of Southeast Asian history

Contents

Glossary

Berjasa	Barisan Jemaah Islam Se Malaysia
Berjaya	Bersatu Rakyat Jelata Sabah
CPM	Communist Party of Malaya
DAP	Democratic Action Party
IMP	Independence of Malaya Party
ISA	Internal Security Act
MCA	Malaysian Chinese Association
MIC	Malaysian Indian Congress
NEP	National Economic Policy
NCC	National Consultative Council
NOC	National Operations Council
PAP	People's Action Party
PAS	Parti Islam Se Malaysia
Pekemas	Parti Keadilan Masyarakat Malaysia
Pesaka	Party Pesaka Anak Sarawak
PBS	Parti Bersatu Sabah
PN	Party Negara
PPP	People's Progressive Party
PSRM	Partai Sosialis Rakyat Malaysia
SCA	Sabah Chinese Association
SNAP	Sarawak National Party
SF	Socialist Front
SUPP	Sarawak United People's Party
UDP	United Democratic Party
UMNO	United Malays National Organization
UPKO	United Pasok-momogun Kadazan Organization
USNO	United Sabah National Organization

Acknowledgements

I wish to thank Professor Wang Gungwu of the National University of Singapore for inviting me to participate in the project on "History of Nation-Building in Southeast Asia" and the Institute of Southeast Asian Studies in Singapore for funding the project and my research fellowship at ISEAS.

The numerous discussions and conversations that I held with Professor Wang and the other five research fellows in the project — Charnvit Kasetsiri of Thailand, Reynaldo Ileto of the Philippines, Taufik Abdullah of Indonesia and Edwin Lee of Singapore — contributed in no small way in the formulation of ideas and the shaping of the monograph in its present form.

The first drafts were written in 1998 and 1999 and presented in contributors' seminars. The discussions served to bring about a common awareness of some identical developments in nation-building of the first five ASEAN nations and the deep problems of our subject.

Others at ISEAS who shared their ideas on the subject of nation-building were Lee Hock Guan, Leo Suryadinata, Lai Ah Eng, Christopher Wee W.-L., Patricia Lim Pui Huen and John Funston. Thanks also go to the ISEAS library staff under Ms Ch'ng Kim See, to the secretariat under Mrs Y.L. Lee and to the Managing Editor, Mrs Triena Ong.

Cheah Boon Kheng
Penang
28 March 2002

Introduction

Wang Gungwu

The Series

This volume is the first of a series of histories on nation-building in Southeast Asia. The idea of having such a series had its beginnings in Bangkok at the 14th Conference of the International Association of the Historians of Asia (IAHA) in 1996, where I noted that nation-building in Southeast Asia began fifty years ago and suggested that it was time for historians to write about that phenomenon.[1] Most books on the region's new nations have been written by journalists and social scientists. I wondered whether historians would tell the story differently. Decades of anti-colonial nationalism came to a climax with the Japanese invasion of 1941–45. New states like those of the Philippines, Indonesia and Burma were born immediately after the war, followed soon by those of Malaysia and Singapore. The independence of a unified Vietnam was delayed by a bitter war and this held back the liberation of the two other Indochina states, Cambodia and Laos, but the independence of all three was only a matter of time.

Many of the protagonists of the early phases of nation-building have described their roles in this new process. Political commentators and journalists provided up-to-date accounts and analyses. But historians of the region have been concerned not to write prematurely about this subject. Many were, like me, fascinated by the first generation of nationalist leaders, men like Sukarno, Tengku Abdul Rahman and Ho Chi Minh, followed by Lee Kuan Yew, Soeharto, Ferdinand Marcos and Ne Win, but hesitant to take on full-length studies about them. These men had offered their different peoples sharply distinct visions of their countries' future. Would historians wait, as they are wont to do, for all sources to be available before they began research on their countries? How long would it be before the story of each country in Southeast Asia is told by the historians themselves?

When I returned from the Bangkok conference, I brought the question to the Institute of Southeast Asian Studies (ISEAS) and was gratified when the then director, Professor Chan Heng Chee, encouraged me to try and find out. With that support, I approached five of the leading historians of the original members of the Association of Southeast Asian Nations (ASEAN in 1968 consisted of Indonesia, Thailand, Philippines, Malaysia and Singapore). They were Taufik Abdullah, Charnvit Kasetsiri, Reynaldo Ileto, Cheah Boon Kheng and Edwin Lee. We met to discuss the feasibility of a joint project to write the contemporary histories of these five countries. They agreed that this was worth doing and I sought ISEAS and other funding to allow us to proceed. The support we received enabled us to meet and hold a series of meetings to define the scope of the project.

We began our meetings by focusing on the common features of the Southeast Asian "nation-state". We knew that there had been attempts to study the early products of new nationalisms in the region. It was clear that some of the peoples of each country were less prepared than others to be citizens of these nation-states. Furthermore, the unfamiliar models taken from Europe have seemed alien, and each of the leaders who advocated using these models often had great difficulty explaining why any one of them should be adopted. We also noted that historians in these countries have closely observed the stresses and strains that were generated, and some have felt the urge to study the actual business of nation-building more systematically. The five historians who met to discuss this phenomenon felt that they would not wait any longer before they began their task. They agreed that they would use their historical skills to take on this project.

We began with questions about what kind of a series we should write. Very early, we agreed that each country had its own story and each author would write a volume about his own country. At the same time, we should try to find out how much the five countries had in common and whether we should adopt a common approach to the subject. From the discussions over several months outlining the main features of the nation-building story in the region, it became increasingly clear that there were several kinds of stories here. Despite their coming together in a regional organization like ASEAN, each of the five had very different experiences inside their countries. While this fact itself was no surprise, it was astonishing how contrasting their respective stories were. The more we surveyed what each country had to do to attain their nationhood, the more it seemed that the ingredients they had to start with forced their leaders to seek very different routes to achieve their goals. We concluded that it would be a mistake for us to try to treat them as if they were different examples of similar models. Although the foreign models that each country used may have appeared to share common characteristics, what each country inherited from previous regimes at the point of independence was so different that we had to think afresh what needed to be done to capture the essence of each experience. We agreed that these differences justified our adopting distinct and separate approaches to each story. Ultimately, each volume would follow the dynamics of change that each country encountered and allow that to determine the shape of the history that the country deserves. This series of histories is the result. The writing has taken somewhat longer than we first anticipated. We are grateful to Professor Chan Heng Chee's successor, Professor Chia Siow Yue, for her sustained support for our project.

In addition, the Lee Foundation, Singapore, and the Chiang Ching-kuo Foundation, Taipei, helped to fund the project and I would like to thank them here for their generous support.

Let me place the series in a broader context. The study of modern nationalism was the work of European historians. The historians of the American and French Revolutions were the first to underline its global significance while others turned back to study the evolutionary stages of earlier nations like Britain, Spain, Portugal and the Netherlands. Later, historians worked with linguists, philosophers and lawyers to shape narrower kinds of nationalisms in Central and Eastern Europe. Their work stimulated social scientists later to embark on theoretical explanations of what the nation-state system meant to the world. The work of historians, however, continued to be influential, most of all by providing ideas for many of the Asian nationalists of the 20th century. Those who studied in

Western universities, in particular, were inspired by these histories to use the ideas in them to prepare their platforms for political leadership.

For the post-World War II period, nationalism was largely seen in the region as a positive development, an organized quest for independence, freedom, and modernization. The Cold War determined that leaders of the newly independent countries could look in at least two different political directions. Some chose to build their nations with the help of capitalism and liberal democracy. These would use the Western European models as the basis for nationhood and, for them, the best way to modernity was through an open market economy. Soon, they found the United States more than willing to help them along that route. Others chose to follow the socialist path either against the capitalist democracies or seeking some kind of neutralism in the Cold War. These were encouraged by the Soviet Union and the People's Republic of China to contest the global economic and military power represented strongly in Asia by the United States. The more radical among them went further to advocate the overthrow of neo-colonial and feudal structures by mobilizing the working poor who were the majority in each of their countries.

The new leaders soon discovered how difficult nation-building was. It was not enough to proclaim independence. They needed outside help if they wanted to modernize quickly. Large amounts of capital were needed to build a new infrastructure for industrial development. Basic literacy was essential, so were the skills that could only come from secondary and tertiary education for the next few generations. But the nation-state as a new kind of polity was more alien than most people realized at the time. Learning from Western and Eastern Europe, or Japan, China or the United States, may have looked easy for the small group of élites who captured power in the post-colonial states, but building a stable and prosperous nation has been much more elusive.

The responses by historians in the former colonial territories of Southeast Asia have varied from country to country, for example, from those in older countries like the kingdom of Thailand to that of the Philippines, and from those in Indonesia, Malaysia and Singapore to those of war-torn states like Burma (Myanmar), Vietnam and Cambodia. Up to now, these different national experiences have largely been studied professionally by political scientists, and the dominance by political scientists, sociologists and anthropologists has continued to the present day. On the whole, there have been few academic historians of the region who have ventured into the period after 1950. This is understandable. The first generation of historians had enough to do to write the story of national origins, often to meet a teleological need, because they realized that the task of nation-building from scratch was a painful one. Some felt it their duty to delineate the contours of the future by giving a new and greater certainty to their countries' more distant pasts.

However, I believe that historians here, as in Europe and elsewhere, will have an important part in shaping future understanding of the phenomenon of nation-building in this part of the world. It is now more than fifty years since many of the new states began making their respective nations. There is now a rich record for historians to study and some official files are open for the first two decades of nationhood. The historians who wish to come closer to the present can now begin to do so. Theirs is a different kind of training, and their intellectual make-up and methodology have much to offer the subject. Therefore, it is time for more historians to take up the challenge and tell the story of the nation-building that many of them have themselves lived through. More than ever, we should not depend on existing theories of nationalism and what they do to the actual task of building nations. The study of each national history should take into account the specific conditions of the nationalism found within its borders. When more historians write their countries' contemporary nation-building history, other social scientists may look at the subject afresh, examine new facts and interpretations, and re-assess the theoretical work done so far. They might find that a new set of theories would be needed to make sense of what the new nation-states of Southeast Asia have achieved. Or, they might find that the simultaneous development of nations in the context of an exceptional regionalism like ASEAN has rendered previous ideas of nationalism inapplicable, if not irrelevant, and a new paradigm is needed.

Until we have done the work, it is premature to talk about a borderless region, least of all a new world order in which nation-states and nationalisms will begin to fade away. From what is known so far of the modern history of "a world of nation-states", it would seem that nation-states are here to stay, if only as basic units of regional groupings that will increasingly play a major role as distinct protagonists. Therefore, the sooner we have the more recent developments of aspiring nation-states fully studied by historians in their regional setting, the sooner we will know how to live with them and even how to make them serve the cause of peace in our region.

Malaysia

Was Malaysia primarily an Anglo-Malay creation or the unintended product of an UMNO-MCA-MIC co-operative leadership that has lasted over fifty years?[2] If the former, we must wonder what was in the British constitutional experience that led hard-headed Malay élites to accept the idea of a multi-racial or multi-communal state. If the latter, we are led to ask what kind of men could have wrought such a lasting compromise? It was, of course, not simply either one or the other, more likely both, together with other powerful internal and external forces. It might even be argued that the other factors were more decisive. For example, within the country, the unique mix of communities of Malays, Chinese, Indians and other indigenous peoples were thought by some to have been impossible ingredients for a new nation, certainly a severe challenge to any idea of nation-building. On the more positive side, this was a microcosm of continental Asia's encounter with the Western world, and could also be seen as an uneasy co-habitation of several cultures whose merchant classes had known one another well for several centuries. Of course, none of the historic cultures they represented had any notion of the nation-state in their pasts. It is a measure of the pragmatism of the leaders of each community at that time that they not only looked within themselves for defensive strength but also faced realities and drew inspiration from other relevant experiences. There were deep fears and widespread skepticism in the 1950s that independent Malaya would be a fiasco if not a tragedy. What a contrast that was to the optimism of the 1990s when many commentators expected Malaysia to become a future economic powerhouse in East Asia.

For historians, international pressures on the region would also have to be taken into account. Throughout Afro-Asia, the pressures of decolonization were as irresistible as those of the ideological war that threatened every country. The coming end of the British and French empires certainly focused the minds of that generation of leadership. The struggle for dominance between the Soviet Union and its satellite states and the Western allies led by the new superpower, the United States, had impinged on the fates of every nation. Malaya/Malaysia in the 1950s and the early 1960s faced the most contradictory of choices. Its Malays looked to an Indonesia that toyed with a radical and left-leaning neutralism in the Cold War. Its Chinese, on the other hand, found their ancestral homes in China tightly under communist rule. As for its Indians, at least the democratic socialism that India represented was still widely admired.

Clearly, the country had to look within itself to find its own way out of an extraordinarily complex position. Looking back, was it merely good luck that Indonesia after 1965 changed direction from neutralism to a form of capitalism and thus offered Malaysia both timely support and also a more rational choice? Was it even better luck that the Great Leap Forward and the Proletarian Cultural Revolution in China turned most Chinese in Malaysia away from the China experience? Certainly it was not merely luck that brought the United States and its Western allies to support all enemies of communism and its collaborators. Taking sides became even more essential when the Vietnam War threatened the future of the region as a whole. Whether luck or not, these dramatic changes in the neighbourhood gave the leaders of Malaysia an opportunity to firm up the ideological direction that they had, in any case, preferred. Thus they turned fully to the capitalist world to find the answers for the nation-building tasks they had taken on.

This volume on Malaysia by Cheah Boon Kheng is the first in the series. Malaysia, with its peoples of very different races and cultures, including many of recent immigrant origins, offers a striking example of the complications that a yet-to-be nation has to face. As the communities were asked to acknowledge a common future nationality, they have needed wise leadership to survive the immense strains to which all of them have been subjected. Cheah Boon Kheng has lived through those tense and exciting years and has drawn on all his historian's skills to tell us what it has been like to make a nation. He has thought deeply about what the people hoped for, the quality of their leaders, and the processes that rendered Malaysia so distinctive. He has written a terse and focused account about the hopes and realities that the country's many communities have experienced. His venture into contemporary history makes an appropriate start to this series.

NOTES

1   Wang Gungwu, "Nationalism and its Historians", *Bind Us in Time: Nation and Civilisation in Asia* (Singapore: Times Academic Press, 2002). That volume of essays is offered as a companion volume to the series.

2   The three political parties were the United Malays National Organization (UMNO), Malayan Chinese Association (MCA) and Malayan Indian Congress (MIC).

CHAPTER ONE

1945–57
Malay Dominance and the Making of a "Malay" Nation-State

With regard to the proposal that independence should be handed over to the "Malayans", who are these "Malayans"? This country was received from the Malays and to the Malays it ought to be returned. What is called "Malayans", it is not yet certain who they are; therefore let the Malays alone settle who they are.

Tunku Abdul Rahman in his inaugural speech as
President of UMNO on 26 August 1951
on taking over from Datuk Onn.

You asked who are these 'Malayans?', and I must admit that this remark really worried me. I regarded this remark as implying that the non-Malays in this country had no right to call themselves Malayans ... in the last analysis what converted not me, but many other Chinese, was your magnificent leadership. It is no exaggeration to say that had anybody but you been at the helm of the Alliance in the early years of independence, the history of Malaya, and later Malaysia, could well have been different.

Tun Tan Siew Sin, former Finance Minister in the Tunku's
Cabinet, in his letter to the Tunku, reproduced in the
Tunku's memoirs, *Looking Back*, pp. 175–81.

W HO WOULD inherit power from the British? Who would receive independence? In the contest for Malaya, these issues were quickly decided in the immediate post-war period. "For the people of Malaya," says a British observer,[1] "decolonisation was a series of profound struggles through which they fought for the welfare of their communities, to secure position and place, and to contest the identity of the nation."

A resurgent Malay nationalism was born during this period. It was manifested in the United Malays National Organization (UMNO) which successfully campaigned against the British Government's post-war Malayan Union plan. Under the plan the British had intended to end Malay sovereignty, impose direct rule in Malaya and create an equal citizenship for both Malays and non-Malays. If this plan had been fully implemented (the Malayan Union was only in force for two years), Malaya would have become more of a "Malayan" nation-state than a "Malay" nation-state. When it withdrew the plan in the face of the strong Malay opposition, the British Government restored Malay sovereignty and Malay proprietorship of the country and thereby ensured Malay political primacy among the various races. This allowed the Malays to set the pace and agenda for the creation of a new "Malay" nation-state. Independent Malaya eventually materialized on 31 August 1957. It formed the basis for the future enlarged federation of present-day Malaysia.

The period 1945–57 marked the crucial last 12 years of British rule, the period of decolonization. In 1948 British officials together with the UMNO nationalists and the Malay Rulers worked out the legal framework for a modern administration, citizenship, the future basis for the construction of nationhood, and a brief, final and meaningful pattern of collaboration and partnership. All three parties had agreed to create a Federation of Malaya comprising the nine Malay states together with the settlements of Malacca and Penang to replace the Malayan Union under a centralized form of government. In order to end colonial rule and achieve national independence for Malaya, the UMNO nationalists were compelled by the British officials to work out a formula of inter-racial co-operation, unity and harmony among the various races in the country. In 1955 and again in 1956 they negotiated and achieved a "Social Contract" with the two major non-Malay political parties, the Malayan Chinese Association (MCA) and the Malayan Indian Congress (MIC), on the basic principles for co-operation, partnership and administration of the future nation-state. The UMNO-MCA-MIC coalition won the country's first general elections in 1955. Two years later, after independence talks had been concluded, the British Government handed over power to the UMNO-MCA-MIC coalition government. It is necessary to assess the major political events which had led to the formation of the new nation-state of Malaya.

The New Malay "Nation-State"

To a large extent, the UMNO nationalists had dictated, and obtained, their terms for the future nation-state when they and the Malay Rulers had secured from the British Government the Federation of Malaya Agreement in 1948. The Agreement had won back recognition from the British Government that Malaya was basically "the country of the Malays". In actual fact, this meant the nine Malay States under their Sultans, although the settlements of Penang and Malacca were still British colonies with larger non-Malay populations. The Agreement, however, also secured concessions from the UMNO representatives and the Malay Rulers that qualified immigrant non-Malays who were resident in Malaya would be allowed to share citizenship with Malays. The British Government had negotiated the terms for citizenship following representations by the non-Malays. But the conditions for obtaining citizenship were made restrictive by both the UMNO representatives and the Malay Rulers.

Although the 1948 Agreement returned political rights to the Malays, the issue of who would inherit political power had still to be settled. In 1948 an armed communist insurgency had broken out, and the British Government found itself fighting a "war" that could not easily be won overnight. Although Malays and non-Malays were found among the ranks of the armed communist insurgents, the majority of its members were actually Chinese. The British Government saw its fight against the communist insurgents as part of the Cold War against international communism. Within Malaya, however, the communist struggle had made British rule untenable as the former attempted to present itself as a nationalist movement and part of a world-wide anti-colonial struggle for national independence. The British

Government was, therefore, forced to adopt a policy of rapid decolonization. It decided to grant self-government, hold general elections and eventually transfer power to a locally-elected non-communist government. One of its conditions before it would relinquish colonial rule was that there should first be inter-racial co-operation and unity among the various races. This triggered off the formation of several inter-racial alliances and political groups among the various communities, such as Datuk Onn Jaafar's Independence of Malaya Party and Tunku Abdul Rahman's UMNO-MCA-MIC Alliance.

In Malaya's first general elections held in 1955, the UMNO-MCA-MIC Alliance won 51 of the 52 contested seats and was allowed to form the government. In the eventual agreement which the Alliance component parties had worked out among themselves and with the British Government, the UMNO leaders had dominated the negotiations and dictated their terms. These terms were eventually spelt out more clearly in Malaya's 1957 Constitution in the provisions for "the special position of the Malays", "Malay reservations", Malay as "the national language" and Islam as "the religion of the Federation".[2] In 1957, as they had done in 1948, the sovereignty of the Malay Rulers and the individuality of each of their respective states were reaffirmed. The rulers were also given considerable powers as constitutional monarchs to "safeguard the special position of the Malays" and reserve quotas for public service jobs, licences, services and scholarships to Malays.[3] In contrast, the non-Malay nationalists in the MCA and the MIC could only secure citizenship rights for those non-Malays born in Malaya or who qualified on residential and other terms. They failed in their demands for Chinese and Tamil to be accepted as official languages on par with Malay and English. But they secured guarantees that "no person shall be prohibited or prevented from using (otherwise than for official purposes), or from teaching and learning, any other language",[4] and that "other religions may be practised in peace and harmony in any part of the Federation".[5] All parties, however, agreed that for a period of 10 years English could be used in the Parliament, in the law courts and for the drafting of legislation and for "all official purposes".[6]

In fact, what had been put into place on Independence Day on 31 August 1957 was a new, inclusive "Malay" nation-state called "Federation of Malaya", similar to the 1948 state. Known by its shortened name, "Malaya"[7] comprised some 5,200,000 million people, of whom about 2,200,000 were Malays and other races deemed indigenous, and the other 3,000,000 were non-Malays. In the Alliance representations to the Constitutional Commission in 1956, "Malaya" was the name preferred by the MCA, while the UMNO wanted the new state to be called "Malaysia".[8] "Malaya" was, however, retained. It marked a continuity with the earlier Anglo-Malay structured Federation of Malaya, which was established in 1948.

The name Malaya continued to be used until 1963 when "Malaysia", comprising Malaya, Singapore, Sarawak and Sabah, was created, but Singapore left Malaysia in 1965. This time, UMNO got the name it desired originally. The Malay name for the Federation of Malaya was *Persekutuan Tanah Melayu* (literally Federation of Malay States or Federation of Malay Lands). Malaya in the English name "Federation of Malaya", as well as in "Malaysia", reflected the Malayness of the nation-state and the Malays' racial identity. Malaya's citizenship in the 1957 Constitution, however, was known only as "Federal citizenship". "Federal citizenship" meant membership of a nation, like a membership of a club with rights and duties. Nationality, however, meant a national identity, which was something else. The Alliance parties failed to spell out the features of Malaya's nationality in the Constitution because they were uncertain how to define its national identity.[9]

"By *Merdeka* [Independence] the Malay community had been elevated into a nation, and it seems that to Tunku Abdul Rahman the nation was a political and cultural entity based on the concept of original sovereignty. Non-Malays could be admitted to the nation, but Tunku Abdul Rahman did not concede that nationality should be the basis of citizenship. Citizenship had a different foundation: it was merely a legal guarantee of specified privileges. This distinction was played down in the interests of unity, and in so far as the term 'nationality' was used it was used in its restricted legal sense, almost synonymously with citizenship — but the Tunku would not allow the term *bangsa* [race/nation] to be used for it. In 1951 Tunku Abdul

Rahman had asked rhetorically who the 'Malayans' were: his answer was that there could be a Malayan nation, but the Malay *bangsa* [race/nation] would exist as a distinct core within it."[10]

This constitutional arrangement represented a compromise and a dilution of the UMNO's Malay nationalism and its initial stand of an exclusive "Malaya for the Malays" nation-state. Given the strident nationalist appeals of its early days from 1946, its transformation in the 1955–57 period of state formation was, indeed, remarkable. In order to achieve national independence, it had become a "nucleus" of an inclusive, wider, multi-ethnic nationalism which has been called "Malayan nationalism" by some scholars.

The fact that UMNO's leaders did not develop their nationalism into an exclusive nationalism of "Malaya for the Malays" would make the future nation-state always subject to continuous pressures and challenges from its own members and from other Malay nationalists and organizations to realize that goal in the future. This in turn would arouse among the non-Malays strong resistance to such Malay nationalist appeals. These recurring struggles and conflicts would dominate the history of racial politics and nation-building in Malaysia.

UMNO's Malay nationalism had developed in strength during its formative years in the wake of the country's worst inter-racial conflicts between Malays and Chinese in 1945–46 during and after the period of the Japanese Occupation. In this first post-war contest for Malaya, Malays were the "real victors". They had successfully resisted and defeated a wartime armed predominantly-Chinese communist movement which had tried to seize power in many parts of the country when the Japanese Occupation ended. The second time, they defeated the British Government's "Malayan Union" plan to offer non-Malays citizenship and equality of status with Malays.[11]

Both the wartime and post-war interracial conflicts have left long-lasting repercussions on national politics until today. The Malay-Chinese clashes also meant that Malays would resort to widespread extremist violence if pushed. The long-term implications of this extremism were very great: the overall Malayan polity might always be held subject to ultimate Malay recourse to mass bloodshed. If so, then the Chinese would have to either accept this threat perpetually and make concessions whenever demanded, or develop their own capability at least to make the violent Malay option very debilitating. Otherwise, talk of pan-ethnic co-operation would usually be at Chinese expense.[12]

If history could be said to repeat itself, the May 1969 interracial clashes demonstrated once again that a Chinese political challenge could result in bloodshed. The 1969 clashes reaffirmed Malay political primacy which in turn upheld the historic "Social Contract" of the UMNO-MCA-MIC as the "corner-stone of the new Malaysian nation".[13] Much of present-day racial politics and nation-building in Malaysia can only be understood within this wider historical context.

The Problematic "Malayan" Nationality

To ensure that their future nation-state would be Malay in character, the UMNO nationalists had since 1946 objected to the term "Malayan" because this was associated with the detested Malayan Union. In their representations to the Anglo-Malay Working Committee to review the Malayan Union, the UMNO representatives had asserted, "Malayans had come to mean people who had some association with Malaya, but did not include Malays, and that Malays took the strongest objection to being called or referred to as Malayans".[14] Unlike "Malaysian", the term "Malayan", has, therefore, always been problematic. This is due largely to the way it has been used in pre-war and post-war Malaya. Even radical Malays like Dr Burhanuddin Al-Helmy had objected to the term "Malayan" (although not the term "Malaysian"), regarding the former as a "smaller mould" than the term *Melayu* [Malay]. *Melayu* was a "bigger mould" (*acuan yang lebeh besar*) which could incorporate "Malayan" but not the other way around.[15] He said the conflict between "Malayan" and "Melayu" would never end. "Malayan" follows the colonial mould, it belittles and destroys the Malay nation or Malay nationalism that demands the return of its rights, that is wider than the "Malayan" demand", he said.[16]

However, paradoxically, in the past, some Malay political leaders such as Tunku Abdul Rahman and Tun Abdul Razak had not been averse to using the term "Malayan" as a short-hand description of the country's way of life and culture inclusive of both Malays and non-Malays. In their public speeches and statements in English (but not in Malay), "Malayan" had been used when addressing mixed audiences which included both such groups. However, when speaking to only Malay audiences, the Malay leaders would use the Malay terms for the country, "Persekutuan Tanah Melayu". They would also use the term *"bangsa"* which means both "nation" and "race". Delivered to Malay audiences, it would literally mean *bangsa Melayu*, the Malay race. Their usage of the term "Malayan" may be viewed as a "politically correct" term, depending on the audience and the circumstances. Like *bangsa*, it is deliberately vague. Such vagueness was due to their reluctance to define the concept of Malaya's nationality in the early years of Malaya's nation-building.

This ambiguous usage of the term "Malayan" partially followed the colonial usage before independence to mean both a nationality and as a convenient adjective to describe any aspect of life or object pertaining to Malaya. For instance, the term "Malayan" in "Malayan Union" (1945), or in the title of English novelist Anthony Burgess' *Malayan Trilogy* (1956), or in T.H. Silcock's book of essays *Towards a Malayan Nation* (1961). "Malayan" also appeared in the census reports. Some writers, however, adopted the term "Malayan" to mean specifically "non-Malay residents" in Malaya, for instance, British writer Michael Ardizzone in his 1946 book:

A Malay is a member of the Malay race; a Malayan is a person of any other origin who happens to live in Malaya. There are 2,250,000 Malays; and 3,050,000 Malayans.[17]

Given the undefined nature of Malaya's nationality at this time and the problematic meaning of the term "Malayan", the expression "Malayan nationalism" cannot adequately represent the new strand of multi-racial nationalism, especially when Malays were unhappy about it and did not include themselves in the term "Malayan". "If the Malays have the right to continue being Malays first and foremost, what use is there for the term 'Malayan'?" asked political scientist K.J. Ratnam.[18] Historian Wang Gungwu was one of those who had identified this multi-racial nationalism as "Malayan nationalism" and was aware of the problems associated with the term:

> If we were to venture a definition at this stage it would probably be fair to say that "Malayan nationalism consists of two component parts: a nucleus of Malay nationalism enclosed by the idea of Malay-Chinese-Indian partnership". This is perhaps not the way which many Malay and non-Chinese politicians would like to see it. There are some Malay leaders who equate Malayan nationalism with Malay nationalism and prefer to use "Melayu" instead of "Malayan" in every possible context. And many Chinese and Indian leaders who describe themselves as "Malayan" refer to an altogether new political identity and would refuse to consider it as in any way similar to "Malay". But what cannot be denied is that the dynamism, the single-mindedness and the leadership in Malayan nationalism has been ably provided by the present ruling Malay group. These Malays have been supported by both Chinese and Indians, but they have at no time surrendered their claim, or their rights of leadership.[19]

For purposes of discussion and for historical reasons, it might be just as well to retain the term "Malayan nationalism" to refer to its usage for the relevant period or social context.[20]

Historiography of "Malayan Nationalism"

In the 1950s and the 1960s the question of when "Malayan nationalism", or, later, "Malaysian nationalism" had emerged engaged the attention of both historians and non-historians. These writers had apparently not found a more suitable term than "Malayan" to describe this nationalism. They also could not agree on its features. On the other hand, they arrived at a consensus that "Malayan nationalism" had not emerged before World War II. Malaya was said to have had separate strands of nationalism — Malay nationalism, Chinese nationalism and Indian nationalism, each pulling the loyalties of members of the three main communities towards their respective countries of origin.

Clearly, Malay nationalist sentiments were focussed at creating a Malay nation-state for Malaya, although in the pre-war period its form was still unclear. This was clearly recognized in 1946 by the Anglo-Malay Working Committee appointed to review the Malayan Union. In its report it asserted that "as these States are Malay States ruled by Your Highnesses, the subjects of your Highnesses have no alternative allegiance or other country which they can regard as their homeland, and they occupy a special position and possess rights which must be protected".[21] Yet, for a small section of Malays their "imagined community"[22] was a "Greater Malaysia", or "Greater Indonesia", in which Malaya would be part of a large union of the Malay world and incorporate the "Malay" peoples living in the territories of both British Malaya and the Dutch East Indies.[23]

This pre-war ethnic Malay nationalism was aimed at a nation-state exclusively for Malays in which Chinese and other non-Malay residents in Malaya would find no place. The story of "Malayan nationalism", is, therefore, the story of how Malay nationalism, i.e., as an "ideological movement for the attainment and maintenance of autonomy, unity and identity ... of an actual or potential nation",[24] transformed itself into an inclusive "Malayan" multi-ethnic force and movement. This it did due to its overriding need to succeed and achieve complete self-government and independence from British colonial rule. This was a goal that the British Government would not accede to without inter-racial co-operation and unity among the various races in the country.

Henceforth, post-war Malaya's history has seen several Malay nationalists who rose to the occasion by embracing "Malayan nationalism" to make Malaya an inclusive multi-racial nation-state open to large numbers of non-Malay residents, who constituted nearly half of the population of the country.

The climax of these efforts was when the UMNO nationalists successfully joined hands with the MCA and the MIC to forge inter-racial unity and struggle for national independence. The remarkable success of this effort has impressed most scholars of Malaya's political history of this period.

Studies done in the 1950s and 1960s have presented evidence of a nascent "Malayan nationalism" in the immediate post-war decade, 1946–57. The sentiments were said to have emerged when the British Government introduced its Malayan Union constitutional plan which would foster "Malayan nationalism", a "Malayan nation-state", a "Malayan nationality" as well as a "Malayan national culture". The plan aroused the various races to respond and think about Malaya's future. Some of the Malayan Union's basic ideas were embraced by the leftist PUTERA-AMCJA coalition of political parties and social organizations (representing both Malays and non-Malays). Support came in different forms from the British-sponsored Communities Liaison Committee and even from Dato Onn Jaafar, the president of the UMNO who had initially opposed the plan. Later, even Onn's successor, Tunku Abdul Rahman, and his Alliance coalition, the UMNO-MCA-MIC embraced and promoted similar ideas of inter-racial unity and co-operation, the creation of a multi-racial nation-state, a common citizenship and a common loyalty to Malaya.

Some important insights on the crucial 1945–57 period have been discerned by different groups of scholars. Two economists, Ungku Aziz and T.H. Silcock, writing in 1951, commented that while "Malayan nationalism" did not exist before World War II, its sentiments or invocation seemed to have appeared at the time they were writing. "A Malayan nationalism, and a Malayan nation, can be built on the basis of approximate equality of status among the members of all races", they asserted.[25] In 1958 historian Lennox Mills also observed that "Malayan nationalism" had appeared in 1955–57 "among the politically-conscious minority", especially in the UMNO-MCA-MIC Alliance's demands for and eventual achievement of full self-government and independence for Malaya. He added, "The solution of the problem had no parallel in the rest of Southeast Asia. Three communal parties arose in the Federation of Malaya — Malay, Chinese and Indian — and the leaders formed an alliance in order to destroy the only non-communal party. They then demanded complete self-government and arranged a compromise settlement of the principal communal differences...."[26]

In 1962, as already noted above, historian Wang Gungwu, writing on "Malayan nationalism", had claimed that pre-war Malaya's seemingly "three irreconciliable ideas of nationhood" had been replaced by the "unique growth of Malayan nationalism" in 1957. In his view, the "Malayan nation" was born in 1957 when Malaya attained independence from colonial rule. On the other hand, he stated, "Malayan nationalism" in sentiment and in the form of an inter-racial alliance of political parties had emerged only around 1955–57 for the express purpose of achieving independence. Wang described this nationalism as "a modified or attentuated Malay nationalism". It consisted of two parts: "a nucleus of Malay nationalism enclosed by the idea of Malay-Chinese-Indian unity". He referred specifically to the achievement of the UMNO-MCA-MIC Alliance's landslide victory in the 1955 general elections and their successful efforts in establishing "a peaceful, constitutional and democratic basis for nationhood" in 1957.[27] Wang's was the first real attempt to describe the characteristics of the nascent "Malayan nationalism".

Wang's views, however, did not go unchallenged. The Dutch historian, Jan Pluvier, his colleague in the History Department at University of Malaya, where both taught, writing in 1967, without citing Wang's 1962 views on "Malayan nationalism", said that "Malayan nationalism" before 1965 was a "myth". He said that the Malay-Chinese-Indian unity of UMNO-MCA-MIC in 1957 was an "act of opportunism". Pluvier only detected some signs of what he called "Malaysian nationalism" in the period 1963–65 when, according to him, the various races in Malaysia were forced to come closer together to meet the common threat of Indonesian confrontation.[28] In 1972, James Ongkili, another Malaysian historian in the same History Department, claimed that not only "Malayan nationalism" but even "Sarawak nationalism" had emerged in 1946–48. Both these forces were brought about by the British Government's proposals for the Malayan Union and the cession of Sarawak by Rajah Vyner Brooke to the British Crown, respectively. Two years later, and again in 1985, Ongkili reiterated that the most positive evidence of "Malayan nationalism" was that, on 14 September 1952, 1.2 million, or 60 per cent of the Chinese in Malaya, and 180,000 Indians had become citizens of Malaya.[29]

From the different opinions expressed above, it is clear that "Malayan nationalism" or "Malaysian nationalism" had arrived by 1957, if not by 1963. Most of these scholars had acknowledged the British Government's important post-war role in creating a political consciousness among the people towards Malaya for the first time through its constitutional proposals on the Malayan Union in 1945. This represented a major departure from its pre-war policies towards Malaya. What had caused these changes was the wartime Japanese victory over the British forces in Malaya and the three-and-a-half years of Japanese occupation of the country. The British knew that they could not return to Malaya without a post-war programme of political advancement.

Malayan Union: Britain's Idea of an Embryonic "Nation-State"

Britain's post-war Socialist Government, therefore, proposed on its return to Malaya to offer equal citizenship rights to both Malays and non-Malays. The various communities would be encouraged to view themselves no longer as different peoples, but as one people living in one enlarged and centralized state, the Malayan Union. It would comprise the nine Malay states and the British settlements of Malacca and Penang, while the predominantly-Chinese British settlement of Singapore would be detached and administered separately as a British colony in order to inflate the size of the Malayan Union's Malay population. The British hoped the Malays would be weaned from their strong loyalties to their respective States and Sultans and transfer them to the new centralized state, while the non-Malay communities would also be weaned from their loyalties to their respective homelands and transfer them to the Malayan Union.

These proposals were radical in nature because they reversed the pre-war policy of preserving Malaya to the Malays and according them special rights. The Malayan Union citizenship would not be a nationality because the Malayan Union would not be an independent sovereign nation-state yet. But the British Government held out the possibility that this would happen before long and that citizenship could later become the basis of an enduring nationality. Malays would automatically become Malayan Union citizens. Non-Malays had to apply and to satisfy residential and language conditions.

The Malayan Union citizenship provisions have been regarded as "liberal" and "inclusivist" by a later group of scholars. The citizenship was seen as "encouraging and building a new loyalty and identity, and an emerging nation-state".[30] One of its most liberal features was said to be its offer of citizenship on the basis of *jus soli*, i.e., based on birth in the country, to the non-Malays.

The Malayan Union's centralized system of government would replace the three pre-war separate systems of administration in Malaya — the British colony of the Straits Settlements comprising Singapore, Malacca and Penang; the Federated Malay States (FMS) of Perak, Selangor, Negri Sembilan and Pahang which came together in 1896; and the Unfederated Malay States (UMS) of Johor, Kedah, Perlis, Terengganu and Kelantan, so-called because collectively they had refused to join the FMS. Under the Malayan Union, the sovereignty of the Malay Sultans in the FMS and UMS would be transferred to the British Crown. Malay sovereignty had been acknowledged in the pre-1941 treaties between the British Government and the Sultans of each of the respective Malay states, under which the Rulers had to ask for and accept advice from British Residents or British Advisers in all matters except in Malay customs and Islam. But under the Malayan Union plan, the British Parliament would henceforth be empowered under the Foreign Jurisdiction Act to legislate on behalf of Malaya's affairs. The UMNO leaders declared that the plan amounted to complete annexation of the Malay States, an abrogation of the pre-war 1941 treaties with the Malay Rulers and the abolition of Malay sovereignty.

However, the Malay opposition to the Malayan Union spearheaded by UMNO was immensely successful, and forced the British Government to rescind the Malayan Union plan. On the other hand, the non-Malay reaction to the plan was lukewarm. In the case of the Chinese community, various

Chinese organizations appeared to be more concerned about losing Chinese nationality rather than adopting Malayan Union citizenship. In fact, most Chinese in Malaya appeared to have been caught off-guard, unable to comprehend its wider implications.[31] As Lennox Mills rightly observed, "The Chinese showed no interest in the Union and made no attempt to defend a policy which was so much to their advantage".[32] The British Government's change of mind had been brought about not only by the storm of Malay protests, but also by pressures brought to bear upon it from British newspapers, opposition British Conservative Members of Parliament and former British Pro-Consuls who had served in Malaya.[33] In a sense, the non-Malays had lost the contest for Malaya by default.

According to political scientist K.J. Ratnam, "The roots of Malay apprehension [had] now become clear: the non-Malays, having had little if any political authority before the War, were now to be made as much the masters of the country as the Malays themselves".[34] The British Government was held responsible for making this concession. For this reason, UMNO was determined to crush its Malayan Union plan. The future Malay nation-state had to be secured.

Federation of Malaya, 1948: Real Basis of the First Malay "Nation-State"

When the British Government capitulated, it ensured that Malaya would revert eventually to Malay rule. The signs were clear: it agreed to restore sovereignty to the Malays and the Sultans. It would return to the Sultans their pre-war position as the legal sovereigns, respect the individuality of the Malay States and safeguard the special position and rights of the Malays. The Malay rulers and UMNO, in turn, accepted the British Government's need for a centralized government in Malaya by returning to the pre-war model of federation (the FMS) for the nine Malay States and the British settlements of Malacca and Penang. This enlarged territory, similar in size to the Malayan Union, would be called the Federation of Malaya. It would similarly exclude predominantly-Chinese Singapore which would be governed separately as a British colony. This was the second time Singapore was excluded from the other states; but its merger with the Federation would become the subject of nationalist appeals later in both territories right after the independence and establishment of the Federation of Malaya in 1957. It would lead eventually to its merger within an enlarged Malaysia in 1963.

Besides mounting a successful campaign against the Malayan Union plan, UMNO's president, Dato Onn Jaafar, had not only aroused a strong spirit of nationalism among the Malays, but made the Malay Rulers become subservient to the will of the Malay people. He has, therefore, been called "Father of Malay Nationalism", with some justification. It was Onn, an aristocrat from Johor state, who won back British recognition that Malaya was "the country of the Malays". He had used the argument of the historical factor effectively by reminding the British that before 1941 they had treaties with the Malay Rulers but none with the non-Malays. Onn's Malay nationalism was also significant in the "taming" and "demystification" of the Malay Rulers. The Malay Rulers were blamed for "selling out" the Malays' birthright by signing the new treaties with Sir Harold MacMichael, the British Government's plenipotentiary. The new treaties handed over the rulers' powers to the British King, and allowed the British Government to enforce the Malayan Union. The Sultans signed the new treaties, without consulting their Malay Ministers and advisers, but later claimed they had signed under duress.

Malay feelings against the Rulers had first been aroused at a crucial meeting in Johor Bahru convened by the Persatuan Melayu Johor (Johor Malays Association), held on 1 February 1946. At this meeting Sultan Ibrahim of Johor was denounced for signing the MacMichael Treaty in violation of the Johor Constitution, promulgated in 1895, which prohibited the ruler from handing over the state to any European power. Shouts of "Down with Sultan Ibrahim" had punctuated the air. Despite Datuk Onn's intervention, the meeting approved a resolution, declaring that the Johor Malays would no longer recognize Sultan Ibrahim as their ruler. Although Malays in other States did not go as far as this in denouncing their rulers, the repercussions were serious. The Malay newspapers spoke of their rulers' betrayal. The rulers were said to have committed *derhaka* (treason) towards the people.

"The *raayat* [the people] were now the rajas, and the rajas were the people".[35] This was the best example of the full flowering of Malay nationalism. Datuk Onn best exemplified these aspirations of the Malay struggle, when he coined the cry, *"Hidup Melayu!"* (Long Live the Malays), a cry which was picked up by Malays, instead of *"Hidup Raja-raja Melayu!"* (Long Live the Rajas). "From today", he asserted, "the Will of the Malay people is paramount".[36]

The All-Malay Congress, which Datuk Onn convened on 1 March 1946, decided to set up UMNO. It formally came into existence at a later meeting of the Congress on 11 May 1946. However, before the inaugural meeting, at a meeting with the Malay Rulers on 30 and 31 March, UMNO's preparatory committee warned the Rulers not to attend the inauguration of the Malayan Union Governor, Sir Edward Gent. They were told that if they did so, they would no longer be accepted by the Malay people. The Rulers bowed to the advice, thereby showing that they had succumbed to the will of the Malay people. "In those few hours the very basis of the Malay political traditions had been subverted and the trend towards constitutional monarchy had inexorably begun", observed Allen.[37]

The successful struggle of the UMNO nationalist movement in recovering these Malay rights, including the Rulers' sovereignty, had put the Rulers in a position of being beholden to the nationalist movement and to the Malay people. In securing the thrones back for their Rulers, UMNO had also insisted that the Rulers should be their symbols of Malay identity and Malay paramountcy. They became constitutional monarchs to safeguard the Malays' rights and privileges. This was clearly spelt out in the Federation of Malaya Agreement 1948, and in the later Constitutions of the independent states of the Federation of Malaya and Malaysia. Thus, the victory of post-war Malay nationalism in 1946–48 ensured not only the restoration of Malay rights and Malay sovereignty, but also secured constitutional monarchy. In Thailand, constitutional monarchy was achieved through a civilian-backed military *coup d'état*, which has since been called the "1932 Revolution".[38]

Theoretically, however, the Sultans had become "constitutional monarchs" long before 1941, as the British authorities had already treated them as symbolic heads of state. They had to ask for and accept advice from the British Resident or British Adviser and to give assent to legislation which was approved by their respective state legislature. However, legally speaking, only the Sultans of Johor and Trengganu were "constitutional monarchs" within the true definition of this term, as only their State Councils had drafted and approved their state constitutions in 1895 and in 1911 respectively. All the remaining Malay states did not have their own constitutions until 1948 under the Federation of Malaya Agreement.

Under the 1948 Agreement, each Sultan made an agreement with the British Government on behalf of his own state, allowing it complete control of defence and foreign affairs. Each Sultan would govern in accordance with British advice as formerly. The head of the federation would be the British High Commissioner, whose title was different from that of the previous Governor of the Malayan Union. The British High Commissioner's office before 1941 had been in Singapore, but he would now reside in Kuala Lumpur. He was empowered to protect the rights of any state or settlement, the powers and dignity of the Sultans, and safeguard the "special position of the Malays" and the "legitimate interests of other communities". Like his previous counterpart in the Malayan Union, he was to be assisted by an executive council and a legislative council of both official and unofficial members.

However, the Federal Legislative Council would have a greater Malay representation. Of the fourteen official members, nine would be *Mentri Besar* (Chief Ministers of the Malay States); while of the sixty-one non-official members, thirty-one would be Malays, fourteen Chinese, five Indians, seven Europeans, one Ceylonese, and one Eurasian. In addition, there would be one representative each from Penang and Malacca, who could come from any community. A Conference of Malay Rulers would meet whenever necessary. A special provision gave the Rulers veto powers on immigration, apparently arising from their fear of further immigration from China and India. In each Malay state, the Sultan exercised the authority of the state, but he was still required to give his assent to Bills passed by his respective State legislature. It is clear that with the signing of the Federation of Malaya Agreement, which came into force on 1 February 1948, Malay sovereignty was virtually intact. The non-Malays' status had been considerably weakened. They had, in fact, never seriously challenged Malay political sovereignty.

With regard to the terms for citizenship, both the Malay Rulers and UMNO now made them more restrictive. Citizenship on the basis of *jus soli* was withdrawn. Only Malays, who were born in a Malay state or were subjects of the Rulers, would become citizens automatically. Chinese and others had to be British citizens born in the former Straits Settlements of Penang, or Malacca or in the Federation "before, on or after the prescribed date", and one of whose parents was born in the Federation, and satisfy at least fifteen years' residence in the Federation. Applicants for Federal citizenship were also required to have an adequate knowledge of Malay or English. This excluded a large number of non-Malays as very few Chinese or Indians knew English and most had only a smattering knowledge of Malay. The 1948 "Federal citizenship" also was not a nationality as the Federation of Malaya would not be an independent sovereign nation. The general non-Malay position with regard to Malay sovereignty of Malaya was surprisingly one of indifference. At no time did they ever seriously challenge Malay claims to political primacy, or the creation of the Federation of Malaya as a "Malay nation-state". The citizenship proposals clearly reflected the desire of the Malay thinkers that the multi-racial political community should adopt an identical Malay cultural homogeneity, or be assimilated within the larger Malay community.[39] What occupied the minds of most non-Malays seemed to be how to acquire more liberal terms to become citizens of this potential "nation-state", such as citizenship by *jus soli*, and to make Chinese and Tamil official languages similar to Malay and English.

The Anglo-Malay accord created a simmering mood of dissatisfaction among non-Malays in both Malaya and Singapore:

... the Federation of Malaya Agreement 1948 placed certain restrictions on the eligibility of non-Malays for Malayan citizenship and was exclusionary in intent. It was an issue which dominated much of the politics of Malaya in the 1950s and spilled into debates over what language was to be given priority in a national education policy. It polarized the Malay and Chinese communities and posed a major obstacle to nation building efforts. The fall-out from an exclusionary conception of citizenship and its ramifications for language and education spread to Singapore.[40]

However, although the terms for citizenship for non-Malays were restrictive under the 1948 Agreement, the willingness of the Malay leaders to share citizenship with a small category of non-Malays in their new Malay "nation-state" or "Malay nation", in fact, marked a major shift towards an *inclusionary* multi-ethnic nationalist perspective.[41] An awareness of political necessities, coupled with enlightened leadership, had made these new proposals possible. "Although the numbers of non-Malays made eligible were by no means overwhelming", says political scientist K.R. Ratnam, "it should be remembered that, before the War, the Malays would probably have refused to entertain any possibility of such a concession".[42]

In fact, this willingness to accept non-Malays can also be seen in the proposals of the leftwing PUTERA coalition of Malay political parties and social organizations, dominated by the Malay Nationalist Party led by Dr Burhanuddin Al-Helmy and Ishak Haji Mohamed. In putting forward their "People's Constitutional Proposals" as a counter-response to the Malay-British Working Committee's Accord, PUTERA and its coalition partner AMCJA represented the first inter-racial alliance of any consequence in this post-war period. PUTERA-AMCJA urged "equal political rights for all who regarded Malaya as their real home and as the object of their loyalty". The Malay Rulers should become "fully sovereign and constitutional rulers".[43] They also agreed that Malay should be the official language of the country, that the national flag should "incorporate the red and white colours of the Indonesian national flag", and that citizenship should be equivalent to nationality. They even went further and suggested that the federation be given full self-government with a fully-elected legislature. Owing to the insistence of the Malay nationalists in the MNP, the coalition recommended a nationality to be called *Melayu*, the name of the Malay race, and after much debate, it was accepted by the AMCJA led by Tan Cheng Lock. The

PUTERA-AMCJA proposals were, however, rejected by the British Government and by the Malay Rulers and UMNO. Despite this rejection, scholars have remained fascinated by the willingness of the MNP nationalists to compromise and accept non-Malays within their concept of the new nation-state. Commenting on the PUTERA-AMCJA's proposal on the *Melayu* nationality, two scholars Michael Hill and Lian Kwen Fee have interpreted that it would simply connote a common identity and not a "racial identity":

> The new nationality was to be termed *Melayu* acknowledging its historical past and cultural origins. Such an identity was to be conceived as ethnic and transcended "racial" origins. Hence *Melayu* nationality was premised on free will and would be bestowed on all who decided to renounce their ties outside of the Malay peninsula. In other words, "Malays" might choose to reject such an identification or the Chinese could adopt such a nationality if they so wished. A *Melayu* nationality was quite different from *bangsa Melayu*. The latter was defined in primordial terms, in that cultural traits were inalienably bound to a particular people sharing a single and common origin (Nagata, 1981:98), whereas the former stressed a common identity rather than origin and was situational. Hence a Chinese or non-Malay could never be *bangsa Melayu*.[44]

Still, there were many Chinese who feared that they would lose their Chinese identity by adopting the *Melayu* nationality. Tan Cheng Lock, a leader of the AMCJA-PUTRA, assured one group, the Malayan Chinese Chamber of Commerce, that this would not happen.[45] But the fact that there was a section of the Chinese community who were willing to become *Melayu* nationals meant that they did not really mind being accorded an identity homogenous with Malays provided they enjoyed equal rights with Malays, which the Anglo-Malay Agreement, however, refused to hold out.

The non-Malay communities, therefore, bore a great grievance towards the Anglo-Malay Agreement which had worked out a provisional programme "acceptable to Malay opinion",[46] and it would not turn back to what had been offered earlier in the Malayan Union proposals. Non-Malay groups organized a campaign of opposition, including a "hartal" (a combination of both a strike and boycott of trades), but their opposition met with failure, as the British Government stood firm behind the Anglo-Malay Agreement, which had restored Malay sovereignty.

The British rejection of non-Malay demands coincided with a breakdown of law and order on the industrial front, as workers and trade unions fought for bargaining rights and for improvement of wages and working conditions. In June 1948, some four months after the Federation of Malaya had been brought into existence in place of the Malayan Union, the British Government was forced to declare a State of Emergency. This came in the wake of industrial violence by workers and trade unions, which was blamed on the semi-legal Communist Party of Malaya (CPM). The state of Emergency, which was not to end until 1960, was precipitated by a series of murders of European managers in several rubber plantations. The Emergency imposed restrictions on people's movements, food supplies, press freedom, and led to the arrests and detentions of several thousands of people suspected of being communists or communist sympathisers. These repressive measures, which the Government argued were necessary to check the spread of further violence, caused the CPM to launch an armed uprising belatedly, resulting two months later in its proscription.

Communist Insurrection: A Catalyst to Independence

Ironically, it was this communist insurrection which forced the British Government to accelerate its plans further for Malaya's decolonization. Not much recognition has been accorded the communist insurgents for their important role as a catalyst of this development. However, in his years of retirement, Tunku Abdul Rahman, looked back and belatedly acknowledged their role:

> Just as Indonesia was fighting a bloody battle, so were the communists of Malaya, who too fought for independence. With the difference that the communists of Malaya were not the indigenous people of this country and they were fighting to set up a communist regime which the believers in the faith of Islam [i.e., the Malays]

could not support nor could those orthodox people, who believed in democracy and freedom. So the struggle for the independence of this country was carried out by the communists alone and they fought a subversive as well as a shooting war, losing many of their men and at the same time killing many of our men and the Commonwealth soldiers. The battle continued for 12 years [1948–1960] and would have gone on had the British Government not yielded to our demand for a general election as a step towards independence.[47]

Even though the communist rebellion was an ideologically-oriented uprising that coincided with other communist uprisings in Burma, the Philippines and Indonesia,[48] it was also identified as an uprising which involved more Chinese than Malays or Indians because the Communist Party of Malaya was a predominantly-Chinese movement. It would be a mistake to see it as a Chinese uprising, as the targets of the Communists were not only the security forces but also pro-government Chinese supporters and politicians. In 1949 China fell to communist rule, raising problems for the ethnic Chinese community and their nationality in Malaya. Britain decided to recognize Communist China, but not to allow it to set up consulates in Malaya in view of alleged links between the Chinese Communist Party and the underground CPM. Many Chinese were now not keen to return to China. Those Chinese who supported the overthrown anti-communist Guomindang government of Chiang Kai-shek which had fled for refuge to Taiwan, were now anxious to take up Federal citizenship. To the British authorities, the atmosphere appeared to be conducive to wean the Chinese away from their loyalties to their homeland by extending political rights to those "who regard Malaya as their real home and as the object of their loyalty". In 1949, India and Pakistan had achieved independence from Britain, at the cost of a massive racial bloodbath, forcing both the British authorities in Malaya and the newly-independent Governments of India and Pakistan to tighten immigration and citizenship regulations. The Indians in Malaya also seemed to be in a similar dilemma on whether to become Indian/Pakistani nationals or Federation of Malaya citizens. The British authorities, therefore, brought pressure to bear on

UMNO leaders and the Malay Rulers to relent on the citizenship provisions for non-Malays in the Federation of Malaya Agreement.

Communities Liaison Committee

To appease non-Malay dissatisfaction and soften the attitudes of UMNO's Malay nationalists, the British Government appealed to the various races to promote the Federation of Malaya citizenship and the ideas associated with it. British officials reiterated that these citizenship provisions essentially meant the bonding of inter-racial unity and co-operation among the various races in Malaya. Such unity had to be achieved before complete self-government and independence could be granted to Malaya. The British insisted that the "ethnic Chinese problem" had to be tackled. They were alarmed by intelligence reports of increasing Chinese support for the communists, and accused the Chinese of "back-sliding" and insincerity in supporting government efforts to curb the communist insurgency.

To deal with the Chinese problem, they created Chinese Advisory Boards, appointed Assistant Secretaries for Chinese Affairs and Resettlement Officers in the State Governments and officially sponsored the formation of the first post-war Chinese political party, the Malayan Chinese Association (MCA) to organize the Chinese in Malaya.[49] The British Commissioner-General for Southeast Asia, Malcolm MacDonald, in talks he initiated with UMNO's president, Dato Onn Jaafar, urged a moderation of the stand of Malay nationalism. He believed that if some compromises could be reached among the communal parties, a deal or formula could be worked out for Malaya's future. In 1949 MacDonald achieved a remarkable measure of success when he established the Communities Liaison Committee to which he brought Onn and other prominent personalities from the Malay and non-Malay communities, such as Dato Panglima Bukit Gantang, Zainal Abidin bin Haji Abbas, Yong Shook Lin, Tan Cheng Lock (the leader of the Malayan Chinese Association), C. Thuraisingam, a Ceylonese leader, and other community leaders.[50]

Whether MacDonald had made any promises to Onn, such as his possible appointment as the future Prime Minister of a self-governing

Malaya if he was found acceptable to all communities, is not known, but there is speculation that he had exerted some influence over the latter.[51] When Onn was sufficiently won over, he first persuaded the UMNO members to accept the British Government's proposal to offer more liberal terms of citizenship with more relaxed residential and other qualifications. At a special meeting of UMNO on 10 June 1950 to discuss the proposal, Onn was, however, roundly criticized for backing the offer and even accused of "selling out" Malay rights. Stung by the members' criticisms, Onn promptly resigned as the party's president, saying it was clear the Malays did not want to be led by him. Three days later, in an unprecedented display of his popularity and mass support, thousands of UMNO members gathered outside his house in Johor Bahru to appeal for his return. Onn agreed and soon at UMNO's annual meeting on 27 August got the British proposal on citizenship approved, with some amendments. A year later, Onn again advocated multi-racial unity and urged UMNO to open its doors to non-Malays and transform itself into a "Malayan" party.[52] The proposal was first received with a stunned silence, and when it was put to the vote, unanimously defeated. Thereupon, Onn decided not to take up the post of president when he was again nominated for re-election as president.[53]

He, therefore, became the first UMNO president to become a casualty in the cause of "Malayan nationalism". He had transformed himself from an exclusive Malay nationalist to an inclusive "Malayan" nationalist, and when he was disillusioned by "Malayan nationalism" he would revert to being an exclusive Malay nationalist again. His departure from UMNO marked his eventual decline in politics, and is one of the strangest ironies of recent Malay political history. Yet who could have predicted his fate in 1946–47 when he was at the height of political success and popularity? Onn was a hero of the Malays, courted by the Malay Rulers and British officials. In 1951, he formed the multi-racial Independence of Malaya Party (IMP) to work towards multi-racial unity and Malaya's independence within seven years. Since MacDonald had cultivated Onn in adopting "Malayan nationalism", he had, in fact, advised him against leaving the party.[54] However, despite Onn's departure from UMNO, he still believed that Onn had popular support among the Malays. He gave him his official support,[55] which was also endorsed by Henry Gurney, the British High Commissioner in Malaya and the Colonial Office in London.

The British official secret and confidential records, which are now open, reveal that from 1951 to 1955 the British Government continued to endorse Onn and followed closely his speeches and activities in the belief that he still had great charisma and large Malay support. This official support for Onn continued until the general elections in 1955 made it clear that UMNO's Tunku Abdul Rahman was the more popular Malay leader. These official records present an interesting revisionist view that it was not the Tunku but Onn who was Britain's "man" from 1951 to 1955.[56] Since the British stakes were so high, it is little wonder that the British Government had to come to terms with Malay nationalism, first, in the form of Onn, and later in the form of Tunku Abdul Rahman.

The Tunku: From Exclusivist to Inclusivist Nationalist

According to the saying, some achieve success on their own, while others have it thrust upon them. The latter case was certainly true of the Tunku (Malay word for prince). He was catapulted from the relative obscurity of the post of a Kedah branch official of UMNO to that of president at its annual general assembly in 1951, much to the surprise of himself and to everyone else. When Onn stepped down at the 1951 UMNO assembly, the Tunku, who had sided with the faction which opposed Onn's proposal to open the party's doors to non-Malays, was elected as the party's second president. Whether it was due to his princely background or to his Kedah state faction's advocacy of extreme Malay nationalism, the Tunku's open criticisms of Datuk Onn's policies certainly helped ensure his election victory. His election speech, which upset British officials, had attacked the label "Malayan" whose usefulness he had argued had ended with the Malayan Union:

> With regard to the proposal of some of our men that independence should be handed over to the "Malayans", who are these

"Malayans"? This country was received from the Malays and to the Malays it ought to be returned. What is called "Malayans", it is not yet certain who they are; therefore let the Malays alone settle who they are.[57]

Thus, he had begun his career in UMNO by being on the side of exclusionary Malay nationalism. We shall see how, even before becoming Malaya's first elected Chief Minister, the Tunku would follow the path of Datuk Onn and change from exclusionary Malay nationalism to inclusive "Malayan nationalism". This was a trend which subsequent UMNO presidents and Prime Ministers would follow.

The Tunku, in his memoirs, has explained that he had "opted out" of the tumultous years of the nascent post-war Malay nationalist movement in 1946. Although he supported UMNO's campaign, he spent this period in London studying law. In 1948, at the age of 46, he passed the final Bar examination and returned to Malaya where he got a job, first, at the State Legal Adviser's Office in Kedah and then at the Attorney-General's office, as a Deputy Public Prosecutor. He was willing to leave the service and take up politics as a full-time career.[58] On taking over UMNO, the Tunku pursued the policy of Malaya for the Malays, but in order to defeat Dato Onn's new party, the Independence of Malaya Party (IMP), his UMNO formed an alliance with the Chinese communal party, the MCA, to contest Malaya's first ever municipal council elections in Kuala Lumpur.

This came about in an unexpected way, as the MCA leader, Tan Cheng Lock, had agreed to join Dato Onn's IMP by bringing in the MCA as well, but this did not happen largely due to Onn's abrasive personality which led him frequently to antagonize friends and foes. In the municipal elections at Kuala Lumpur in February 1952, both UMNO and MCA formed an electoral alliance to ensure the defeat of the IMP.[59] The Alliance won nine seats and the IMP two. This successful experiment was repeated in later municipal elections, and in 1952–53 the Alliance won 94 out of 124 seats. This led them to formalize their alliance with a view to contesting the general elections which were due to be held in 1955. In 1954, in anticipation of the forthcoming general elections and in view of the dismal support he had received from non-Malay individuals and groups, Onn decided to dissolve the IMP and form another party, the Party Negara.

In 1951 the British Government introduced the "Member system" (akin to the Ministerial system) to train unofficial members of the Legislative Council in various responsibilities. They also became spokesmen of the High Commissioner's administration. Selected unofficial members were appointed as Member for home affairs; Member for agriculture and forestry; Member for health; Member for education; Member for lands, mines, and communications; and Member for works and housing. These special Members sat in the Federal Executive Council. Three were Malays, one was a Chinese, one a Ceylonese, and one a European. IMP and UMNO leaders were appointed to these posts. Although Onn had stepped down as UMNO's president, he was appointed Member for Home Affairs, while Dato Thuraisingham was appointed Member for Education, but Tunku Abdul Rahman was not. It is believed that Onn hoped through his role as Member for Home Affairs, he could build up a public following to undermine UMNO and Tunku Abdul Rahman's leadership. But as it soon turned out, Onn's abrasive personality was a serious liability. He began to lose more and more friends, for instance, Tan Cheng Lock who had initially pledged support for the IMP withdrew when he himself came under Onn's criticism. He decided to throw in his lot with UMNO. UMNO's strategy to sow distrust in his party's inconsistent policies was beginning to bear fruits. The UMNO-MCA Alliance proved that the formation of an inter-racial partnership was more successful than Datuk Onn's single non-communal party, the IMP, which attempted to represent members of all communities. The UMNO-MCA Alliance later enlarged its membership to include the Malayan Indian Congress (MIC). The various communities seemed to prefer communal representation to look after their own communal interests.

Improved Citizenship Terms to Non-Malays

In 1952, given the good work of the Communities Liaison Committee and Onn's strong support, the British authorities in Malaya succeeded in convincing the Malay Rulers to give their assent to the modified citizenship provisions for non-Malays in the federal constitution. A new Federal citizenship ordinance and nine State Nationality Enactments were introduced in 1952.[60] Under these laws, if a Chinese was born in a Malay state he became automatically a subject of a sultan and was qualified to become a Federal citizen; similarly, if one of his parents had been born anywhere in the Federation, he was also qualified to be a citizen. This brought in a large number of second-generation Chinese.[61] It also enabled several categories of citizens of the United Kingdom and Colonies to become Federal citizens. However, an alien who became a citizen by naturalization or registration was required to renounce his foreign nationality. The MCA, however, demanded that citizenship should be based on *jus soli*, but this was not acceded to. "The only answer which could be made was that the law of 1952 was as much as the Malays could be persuaded to concede after about two and a half years of negotiation, and that Britain was not prepared to compel them to go further", observed Mills.[62] By May 1952, 346,935 aliens had been naturalized, of whom about 300,000 were Chinese. Expressed in total numbers, Malaya's citizens were distributed as follows: about 2,650,000 Malays and Malaysians, 1,100,000 Chinese and 180,000 Indians. The MCA still complained that this left the Chinese in an inferior position in the Malayan Civil Service compared with the Malays. The British authorities agreed in December 1952 that non-Malay Federal citizens would be admitted to the service in the ratio of one to every four Malays appointed, but "this was as large a concession as the British officials could persuade the Malays".[63]

Alliance Demand for Independence

In 1952 Tunku Abdul Rahman, with the support of UMNO, demanded that Malaya be given independence within three years in response to the IMP's demand within seven years.[64] In March 1953 the leaders of UMNO and MCA announced they had reached agreement on the principle of general elections for the federal legislative council. Attempts were made to reconcile differences between Datuk Onn and Tunku Abdul Rahman, but their meeting proved unsuccessful. According to one source, the former insisted that "the

Tunku would have to dissolve the Alliance and join his IMP".[65] Soon after this, the UMNO-MCA Alliance demanded the establishment of an Independent Constitutional Commission to inquire into constitutional reforms, aimed apparently at reviewing the 1948 Agreement. Its members were to be composed of eminent jurists from outside Malaya. In February 1954 Onn launched his Party Negara. After the various political parties had aired their proposals on the general elections, the new High Commissioner, General Templer, announced, with the consent of the sultans, that the new Federal Legislative Council would consist of 52 elected and 46 nominated members. Elections would be held early in 1955. The UMNO-MCA Alliance was dissatisfied with an elected majority of only six, and threatened to boycott the elections. It withdrew the threat after the new High Commissioner MacGillivray assured Tunku Abdul Rahman that he would consult with the majority elected party to appoint some five or seven nominated members.[66]

The Alliance under the Tunku's leadership swept to a landslide victory in Malaya's first-ever general elections on 17 July 1955, winning 51 of the 52 seats contested. An example of how much the Tunku had changed from an exclusionary Malay nationalist to a multi-racial nationalist was how he had persuaded his UMNO party to make compromises and to accept the Alliance concept of inter-racial unity. As only a very small proportion of non-Malays had been registered as voters, this first electorate was predominantly Malay. The registered electorate in 1955 comprised approximately 84 per cent Malays, 11 per cent Chinese and less than five per cent Indians. UMNO members, therefore, insisted that the Alliance field 90 per cent Malay candidates, but the Tunku rejected the suggestion. He threatened to resign and got his way. Consequently, the Alliance fielded 35 UMNO, 15 MCA and two Malayan Indian Congress (MIC) candidates in the 52 constituencies. UMNO lost one candidate to the Pan-Malayan Islamic Party (PMIP). The elections represented a test for "UMNO discipline, and the Alliance concept".[67]

However, in their election manifesto, the Alliance had, in fact, recognized that the communists' armed insurrection was pivotal to winning the independence struggle. Aware of the people's need to bring this "war" to a peaceful end, the Alliance had campaigned on a platform of peace and amnesty for the insurgents.[68] This had alarmed the British authorities who feared that both the nationalists and the communists would do a deal behind their backs. In November 1955, shortly before the talks began, the British Government in London announced that the continuation of the Emergency would not be an obstacle to Malaya's advance towards self-government nor would it be an obstacle to the establishment of a commission to review the constitution, [as demanded by the Alliance] "provided that no concessions are made to the communists during the forthcoming talks which would affect the ability of the Federation Government to keep the internal security position under control".[69]

Baling Talks: Tunku Secures Trump Card from Chin Peng

Clearly, the British officials feared that the Tunku would make concessions to the communists at the peace talks on the issues relating to the recognition of the CPM, the amnesty terms, and the repeal of the Emergency regulations.[70] The Alliance strategy of offering amnesty to the communists had proved "politically correct". It had stirred the British to hasten the pace of decolonization.

The British officials had, however, underestimated the negotiating skills of the Tunku at the talks which eventually took place at Baling in Kedah state, near the Malay-Thai border, on 28 and 29 December 1955. The Tunku was flanked by David Marshall, the Chief Minister of Singapore, and Sir Cheng Lock Tan, the MCA leader, while facing them at the table were the CPM representatives, Chin Peng, Chen Tian and Rashid Mydin. From the start, they were bogged down over the demand for recognition by the CPM, which was flatly rejected by the Tunku and his team. The Tunku, in fact, challenged the arguments of the communists that they alone were fighting for nationalism and freedom from British imperialism. The Tunku argued that the Alliance was also doing the same and that the electorate had recently endorsed its programme. An exchange followed between the Tunku and Chin Peng, during which Chin Peng made a "voluntary" commitment that the communists would lay down their arms if the Alliance could obtain independence and get the British to transfer internal security and defence powers into its hands. The exchange, according to the official minutes of the meeting, went as follows:

Chin Peng then continued: The present Government, although it is a popularly elected government still is not an independent government.

Mr Marshall: Tell him that we recognize that fully.

Chin Peng: Under such circumstances, therefore, when we bring out our suggestions we have got to have regard to this situation. If those popularly elected Governments of the Federation and Singapore have self-determination in matters concerning internal security and national defence, then all problems could be solved easily. As soon as these two Governments have self-determination in internal security and national defence matters, then we can stop the war immediately.

Tunku: Is that a promise? When I come back from England that is the thing that I am bringing back with me.

Chin Peng: That being the case, we can straightaway stop our hostilities and also disband our armed units.[71]

The implications arising from this communist undertaking were extremely far-reaching. The mass media gave Chin Peng's pledge much publicity. The Tunku, indeed, had obtained a trump card.[72] The British authorities who had been trying to end the Emergency, now discovered that the Tunku had won a promise from the communists. If the British wanted to end the Emergency, they had no choice but to expedite independence and grant him the powers on internal security and national defence, as suggested by the communists.

Soon after the Baling talks, the Tunku led an Alliance delegation to London to discuss independence and constitutional advance for Malaya scheduled to start on 18 January 1956. In view of the widespread publicity on the CPM's conditional offer, the Tunku tried to pre-empt the talks by committing the British Government, stating that it had already agreed to grant internal security to his government.[73] There was no denial from London, but clearly on the agenda were control of defence, internal security and finance and the future of the public service. At the talks, the British Government was extremely conciliatory and granted most of the Alliance demands, including the achievement of independence, if possible, by 31 August 1957.[74] Both sides agreed that Britain would gradually start transferring the powers of internal security and external defence to the hands of local ministers. A Malayan Minister of Finance would continue to regulate the country's dollar expenditure in general conformity with the policy followed by the sterling area. A Public Service Commission would be set up from 1 July 1957. A compensation scheme for expatriate British civil service staff would be implemented. It was decided that a British judge, Lord Reid, would head the Independent Constitutional Commission with members coming from Canada, India, and Pakistan.[75] The Alliance demand for a team of experienced foreign jurists to draft the Constitution was clearly meant to make its terms as impartial and respectable as possible.

On the matter of the Emergency, although the CPM did not make good its promise to end its struggle and lay down its arms on the achievement of independence in 1957, the party's continued armed struggle had unavoidable consequences for the country's nation-building efforts in the future. Expenditure for defence and internal security would remain high in the national budget, and the national government would justify the continuation of the draconian colonial Emergency laws which infringed fundamental human rights. Under these laws, the government imposed restrictions on freedom of the media and arrested and detained suspected persons with communist leanings indefinitely without trial. Consequently, under the conditions of the Emergency which did not end till 1960, freedom was not fully nurtured. As the communist threat continued until its armed struggle ended in 1989, the national government retained and used its authoritarian powers whenever it felt the "interests of national security and racial harmony" were threatened, despite the democratic trappings of the country's political system.

Self-Government 1955: The Start of Nation-Building

Thus, in our survey so far, "Malayan nationalism" had come about largely as a result of local compromises among the various communities in response to British efforts to decolonize. They thereby helped to accelerate the pace for Malaya's self-determination and independence, the last a goal which the British Government had repeatedly stressed could not come about without inter-racial unity. When Malaya's independence did come about on 31 August 1957, Tunku Abdul Rahman and the other leaders of the Alliance had already been at the helm of an interim democratically-elected government for about two years. The title of his office was immediately changed from Chief Minister to Prime Minister. Malaya became a full-fledged sovereign state and a member of the United Nations and the Commonwealth.

However, the Alliance Government had already put into place several measures and governmental structures within those crucial two years. Some of the Alliance programmes underwent further changes in the first decade of independence, but a few remained intact and survived well into the 1970s and 1980s. It is necessary to look briefly at a few of these initial policies and measures.

Since the British Government had only initiated nation-building in Malaya in the post-war period, much was left undone. The newly-elected Alliance government had to continue laying the foundations for its future nation-state by adopting a number of measures, the most important of which was the establishment of a system of national schools. The idea of national schools had already been accepted and incorporated into the 1952 Education Ordinance, after the British authorities had considered various studies such as the Barnes Committee on Malay Education and the Fenn-Wu Committee on Chinese education. The Ordinance provided that these national schools would be established with Malay and English as the media of instruction but agreed that the teaching of other vernacular languages would be allowed. However, the Tunku's government felt that the matter needed to be studied further. A multi-racial committee headed by the Minister for Education, Datok Abdul Razak, was appointed with the following terms of reference:

... to examine the present educational policy of the Federation of Malaya and to recommend any alterations or adaptations that are necessary with a view to establishing a national system of education acceptable to the people of the Federation as a whole which will satisfy their needs and promote their cultural, social, economic, and political development as a nation having regard to the intention to make Malay the national language of the country whilst preserving and sustaining the growth of the languages and culture of other communities living in the country.[76]

Although the Razak Education Report was controversial, arousing strong criticisms from leading educationalists of the Chinese community, especially from the United Chinese School Teachers' Association and the All-Malaya Chinese Schools Management Association,[77] the MCA representatives in the Legislative Council endorsed it. They also supported the 1957 Education Ordinance incorporating its provisions when its bill was presented in the Legislative Council. The Ordinance, which incorporated many of the Razak Report's recommendations, outlined the priorities to introduce a single system of national schools for all races. It would bring more Malay children into the secondary schools, and use English and Malay temporarily as the media of instruction, with the view of ultimately elevating Malay as the sole official language and sole medium of instruction. Nevertheless, the Ordinance allowed the vernacular primary schools to continue to teach in the existing media, that is, Standard Primary Malay Schools would be established with Malay as the medium of instruction, while Standard-Type Primary Schools in English, Chinese or Tamil would also be maintained or established. Only for the secondary schools, would there be "one type of National secondary school open to all races by competitive selection and with a common syallabus, a flexible curriculum permitting the study of all Malayan languages and cultures and room for diversity in the media of instruction". Two new secondary school examinations, the Lower Certification of Education and the Federation of Malaya Certificate of Education, were to be available in the two official languages, English and Malay. "It meant that though Chinese secondary schools were permitted", observed a foreign educationalist, "Chinese was elbowed out in respect of these two important examinations that were based on a common content syallabus".[78] The Chinese secondary schools' struggle for Chinese language to be included within the national educational system would pose a problem in nation-building. They did not press this issue, preferring to put it aside for the time being, arguing that the overall interests of the UMNO-MCA Alliance's need to secure complete self-government and national independence were more important. Chinese education and Chinese language were two issues which would continue to plague racial relations and nation-building in Malaya.

Malaya's first Development Plan covered the period 1950–55. It was aimed at providing social services, eradicating poverty and uplifting the predominantly Malay rural areas. Under the Tunku's Alliance Government, Malaya's first Five-Year Plan (1956–60) was introduced to develop the Malayan economy and to improve the standards of living of the people, in particular those in the rural areas. The Alliance had inherited from the British administration a lop-sided economy. The Malays remained largely in the rural sector, engaged in subsistence economy, and were economically backward, while the other major communities, the Chinese and Indians, were involved in the more thriving activities of the business, plantation and mining sectors. The Alliance partners had recognized that it was their major responsibility to uplift the economic livelihood of the Malays, many of whom lived below the poverty line. The Alliance aim was apparently to work out a political equation between Malay political primacy/Malay economic backwardness and Chinese citizenship/Chinese economic dominance.

The Social Contract

The best example of Alliance compromises is to be seen in their representations to the Constitutional Commission on what basis the Federation of Malaya was to be established and what its nationality was to be.[79] Given the precedents set up in the Federation of Malaya Agreement of 1948, the terms could not vary much. For UMNO, the trappings of a Malay state had to be preserved. The Malays had to be given political primacy. On the other hand, for the MCA and the MIC, the terms of citizenship had to become as open and loose as possible to the non-Malays and their rights had to be protected.

The Alliance memorandum to the Reid Constitution had, in fact, agreed to all the features of a Malay state — "special position of the Malays", "Malay as the national language", "Islam as the official religion" and the Malay Rulers as "constitutional monarchs". There were also "Malay land reservations" and "reservation for Malays of a certain proportion of jobs in the civil service". But the controversial questions of citizenship and nationality had been left vague. The MCA had pressed for the principle of *jus soli* for all those born *before, on* or *after* Malaya's independence, but UMNO's demand was that only those born in the country "*on* and *after* the declaration of independence" should become nationals of the country. UMNO's demand was accepted by the Reid Constitution.

A vague "common nationality" was propounded in the UMNO-dominated Alliance memorandum to the Reid Constitutional Commission in September 1956:

The constitution should provide for nationality laws that would build a peaceful and stable independent federation, with a contented and unified people whose loyalty is unquestioned and undivided, so that, in due course, the country can take its proper place in the comity of nations. To achieve this end, it is essential to have a nationality law which provides for a *common nationality*, to the exclusion of all others.[80]

In fact, UMNO had suggested the name of "Malaysia" for the new nation-state, but the MCA had preferred the name "Malaya" to be retained. "Federation of Malaya" was instead accepted. Consequently, the future "Malayan" nationality became problematic. Interestingly, the "common nationality" which had been recommended in the Alliance memorandum to the Reid Constitution remained undefined. But by 1963, six years after independence, Malaya was superseded by the formation of Malaysia. The new name was the one UMNO had originally desired. Thereafter, the evolution of a "Malaysian" nationality became a real possibility.

"Malayan" and "Malaysian" as possible names for its nationality were held out in the comments made by the commission's chairman, Lord Reid, during hearings of the Alliance memorandum. The memorandum had insisted that those persons born in Malacca and Penang after independence would have to become "nationals of Malaysia". If they chose to remain "British subjects" or "citizens of the Commonwealth", to which they were entitled as Malacca and Penang were former British territories, they could no longer remain "nationals of Malaysia". This invited a remark from the commission's chairman, Lord Reid:

> There are many people with dual nationality and it does not cause much trouble. *Of course, anybody who is a Federal citizen is, in the eyes of the international law, a Malayan or a Malaysian.* There is no question as to his nationality in international law. It is possible to have two nationalities both within the Commonwealth, or maybe one within and one outside. There are lots of people like that. It does not seem to cause much trouble.[81]

However, in the end, the adopted Constitution made it explicitly clear that dual nationality was not acceptable.

In an overall assessment, it is clear that Britain left some durable and some not so durable legacies in the early years of Malaya's nation-building. Its most important contribution, according to one British historian T.N. Harper, was in community development. "Britain sought to break down the divisions of a plural society, and create an integrated economic and political entity, bound together by a shared allegiance, a common culture and the obligations of active citizenship," says Harper.[82] Britain also did attempt to introduce a system of parliamentary democracy, constitutional monarchy and independence of the judiciary. Over the years, however, constitutional amendments have further eroded some of the foundations of these institutions. Britain tried but failed in creating a multi-racial "Malayan" national identity and a "Malayan" political consciousness. It gave way to the creation of a "Malay" nation-state.

On 31 August 1957, a multi-ethnic nationalism, based on the UMNO-MCA-MIC historic bargain, achieved through their own efforts without British intervention, had brought about full self-government and national independence. The first decade and a half of independence had shown that the "historic bargain" had worked well on the basis of compromise, consensus and reciprocity. An American scholar's assessment of the working of the "historic bargain" in 1972 seemed to have been positive:

> This political bargain realized great benefits for all parties, in many cases more than the original participants had expected to achieve. The Malays gained political independence, control of government, and a polity which was to be Malay in style and in its system of symbols. In return the Chinese gained more than overseas Chinese in Southeast Asia had dreamed of — equal citizenship, political participation and officeholding, unimpaired economic opportunity, and tolerance for their language, religion and cultural institutions. In the decade and a half since this great bargain was struck the leadership of the major structures of the Alliance has been remarkably stable, notwithstanding costly defections on both sides.[83]

The Indian position may be said to be similar to that of the Chinese described above. But these goals were achieved in the early years of nation-building under Tunku Abdul Rahman's leadership. The bargain has remained the basis of the country's nation-building efforts.

NOTES

1   T.N. Harper, *The End of Empire and the Making of Malaya* (Cambridge: Cambridge University Press, 1999), p. 309.

2   See L.A. Sheridan, "Federation of Malaya Constitution", *University of Malaya Law Review* (Singapore), 1961, [Article 3. (1) on Islam], p. 4; [Article 88 and 89 on Malay reservations], pp. 96–97; [Article 152.1 on national language], p. 140; [Article 153.(1) on special position of the Malays], p. 141.

3   See Article 153.(1) of the Federation of Malaya Constitution, in *ibid.*, p. 141.

4   Article 152.(1) in *ibid.*, p. 140.

5   Article 3.(1), *ibid.*, p. 4.

6   Article 152.(3), (4) and (5), *ibid.*, pp. 140–41.

7   The preamble of the officially adopted 1957 Federation of Malaya Constitution states: "The Federation shall be known by the name of Persekutuan Tanah Melayu (in English the Federation of Malaya)." *Ibid.*, p. 1. However, the preamble of the draft Constitution of the Federation of Malaya which was proposed by the Reid Constitutional Commission reads: "Malaya shall be a Federation of States and its name shall be the Federation of Malaya, hereinafter called the Federation". See Appendix II of *Report of the Federation of Malaya Constitutional Commission* (Kuala Lumpur: Government Press, February 1957), p. 123. It may be worthwhile to compare it with the preamble of the constitution which was proposed and adopted under the *Federation of Malaya Agreement 1948* which stated that it would "establish under the protection of Great Britain a Federation, to be called Federation of Malaya, and in Malay, Persekutuan Tanah Melayu, which will consist of the nine Malay States and the Settlements of Penang and Malacca."

8   See 'Political testament of the Alliance': memorandum by Tunku Abdul Rahman for the Reid Commission. Appendix: 'Fundamental rights', CO889/6, ff219–239, Document 426, in Anthony Stockwell, ed. *Malaya: Part III The Alliance Route to Independence, 1953–1957*, British Documents on the End of Empire, Series B, Vol. 3 (London: HMSO, 1995), p. 307.

9   According to one definition, "citizenship is not merely about formal rights, but about participation in social life and therefore contributes to the integration of society. In its most developed form, it is real membership of a real society, based on loyalty to a civilization commonly shared." See J.M. Barbalet, *Citizenship: Rights, Struggle and Class Inequality* (Milton Keynes: Open University Press, 1988), cited in Michael Hill and Lian Kwen Fee, *The Politics of Nation Building and Citizenship in Singapore* (London: Routledge, 1995), p. 30. Nationality, as David Miller explains, however, means something more than citizenship; it means national identity, a collective personality of the nation or a set of features which the citizens, including those who were immigrants, come to share in a public culture. It is not necessary that such features must be shared or displayed *in equal measure*, but merely constitute a national identity which exercises a pervasive influence on people's behaviour. "A public culture may be seen as a set of understandings about how a group of people is to conduct its life together," says Miller. "This will include political principles such as a belief in democracy or the rule of law, but it reaches more widely than this. It extends to social norms such as honesty in filling your tax return or queuing as a way of deciding who gets on the bus first. It may also embrace certain cultural ideals, for instance religious beliefs or a commitment to preserve the purity of the

national language. Its range will vary from case to case, but it will leave room for different private cultures within the nation." For an interesting discussion of the complex nature of national identity, see David Miller, *On Nationality* (Oxford: Clarendon Press, 1995), pp. 27–31.

10 Harper, *The End of Empire and the Making of Malaya*, p. 350.

11 For a study of the wartime and post-war interracial conflicts in Malaya, see Cheah Boon Kheng, *Red Star Over Malaya: Resistance and Social Conflict During and After the Japanese Occupation, 1941–1946* (Singapore: Singapore University Press, 1983).

12 *Ibid.*, p. 298.

13 *Ibid.*, p. 301.

14 See *Report of the Working Committee appointed by a Conference of the Governor of the Malayan Union, The Rulers of the Malay States and the Representatives of the United Malays National Organisation* (Revised up to the 19th of December, 1946) (Kuala Lumpur: Malayan Union Government Press, 1946), p. 9.

15 See the objections of Dr Burhanuddin Al-Helmy, the Malay Nationalist Party leader, to the concept of "Malayan" and a "Malayan nationality" in his book, *Falsafah Kebangsaan Melayu*, 1954, reproduced in *Dr Burhanuddin Al-Helmy: Politik Melayu dan Islam*, compiled and edited by Kamaruddin Jaafar (Kuala Lumpur: Yayasan Anda, 1980), pp. 108–109.

16 *Ibid.*

17 Michael Ardizzone, *A Nation is Born* (London: Forum Books, 1946), p. 34.

18 K.J. Ratnam, *Communalism and the Political Process in Malaya* (Singapore: University of Malaya Press, 1967), p. 29.

19 See his essay, "Malayan Nationalism", in Wang Gungwu, *Community and Nation: Essays on Southeast Asia and the Chinese* (Singapore: Heinemann, 1981), p. 205.

20 See Cheah Boon Kheng, "Asal-Usul dan Asas Nasionalisme Malaya [The Origins and Basis of 'Malaya' Nationalism]", in *Nasionalisme: Satu Tinjauan Sejarah [Nationalism: A Historical Perspective]*, ed. R. Suntharalingam and Abdul Rahman Haji Ismail (Kuala Lumpur: Fajar Bakti, 1985), pp. 81–103; see also Hanapi Dolah, "Nasionalisme Malaya: Satu Versi Yang Defektif", in *Ilmu Masyarakat* 5 (Jan.–June 1984): 71–76.

21 See *Report of the Working Committee*, 1946, *op.cit.*, p. 7.

22 This was first used by Benedict Anderson in his book, *Imagined Communities: Reflections on the Origin and Spread of Nationalism* (London: Verso, 1983), p. 15. Anderson quotes a line from page 5 of Hugh Seton-Watson's *Nations and States: An Inquiry Into the Origins of Nations and the Politics of Nationalism* (Boulder, Colorado: Westview Press, 1977) as follows: "All that I can find to say is that a

nation exists when a significant number of people in a community consider themselves to form a nation, or behave as if they formed one." Anderson adds, "We may translate 'consider themselves' as 'imagine themselves'."

23 W.R. Roff, *The Origins of Malay Nationalism* (Kuala Lumpur: University of Malaya Press, 1967), pp. 232–33; Angus McIntyre, "The Greater Indonesia Idea of Nationalism in Malaya and Indonesia", *Modern Asian Studies* 7, no. 1 (1973): 75–83; see also Cheah Boon Kheng, "The Japanese Occupation of Malaya, 1941–1945: Ibrahim Yaacob and the Struggle for Indonesia Raya", *Indonesia*, no. 28 (October 1979), pp. 85–120.

24 See this interesting definition of nationalism by Anthony D. Smith, "Nations and Their Past", in *Nations and Nationalism* 3, Pt. 3 (November 1986): 359. There are, of course, numerous definitions of nationalism. Another which is extremely pertinent and may be said to be incorporated within Anthony Smith's definition is that by Hans Kohn: "Nationalism is a state of mind, permeating the large majority of a people and claiming to permeate all its members; it recognizes the nation-state as the ideal form of political organization and the nationality as the source of all creative cultural energy and of economic well-being. The supreme loyalty of man is therefore due to his nationality, as his own life is supposedly rooted in and made possible by its welfare." See Hans Kohn, *The Idea of Nationalism* (Toronto: Collier Books, [first published 1944 and since revised several times], 1969), p. 16. See his reiteration in Hans Kohn, *Nationalism: Its Meaning and History* (New York: Van Nostrand, 1965), p. 10. Throughout this work, when I use the term "nationalism" its meanings will incorporate those ideas which have been defined by both Smith and Kohn.

25 T.H. Silcock and Ungku Abdul Aziz, "Nationalism in Malaya", in *Asian Nationalism and the West*, ed. W.L. Holland (New York: McMillan, 1953), p. 330.

26 Lennox A. Mills, *Malaya: A Political and Economic Appraisal* (Westport, Conn.: 1973), Greenwood Press, p. viii. The "non-communal party" was the multi-racial Independence of Malaya Party led by Dato Onn Jaafar.

27 Wang Gungwu, "Malayan Nationalism", p. 205.

28 Jan M. Pluvier, "Malayan Nationalism: A Myth", *Journal of the Historical Society, University of Malaya*, 1967/68, pp. 26–40.

29 J.P. Ongkili,"Perkembangan Nasionalisme", *Jebat* I (1971/1972), pp. 24–43; J.P. Ongkili, "The British and Malayan Nationalism, 1946–1957", *Journal of Southeast Asian Studies* V, no. 2 (September 1974); and also James P. Ongkili, *Nation-building in Malaysia, 1946–1974* (Kuala Lumpur: Oxford University Press, 1985), p. 89.

30 Hill and Lian, *The Politics of Nation Building*, p. 58.

31 See file "Malayan Press Comment on the White Paper on the Malayan Union", March 1946, in SCA 26/46, CC1/2, Malayan Union, Arkib Negara Malaysia.

32   Mills, *Malaya: A Political and Economic Appraisal*, p. 36.

33   For an excellent account of this Pro-Consular campaign, see James de V. Allen, *The Malayan Union*, Monograph No. 10, Southeast Asian Studies Council (New Haven: Yale University, 1967).

34   Ratnam, *Communalism and the Political Process in Malaya*, p. 75.

35   See Cheah Boon Kheng, "The Erosion of Ideological Hegemony and Royal Power and the Rise of Postwar Malay Nationalism, 1945–46", *Journal of Southeast Asian Studies* XIX, no. 1 (March 1988): 25–26.

36   Here we may quote Hans Kohn: "It is this will which we call nationalism, a state of mind inspiring the large majority of a people and claiming to inspire all its members. It asserts that the nation-state is the ideal and the only legitimate form of political organization and that the nationality is the source of all cultural creative energy and of economic well-being." See Hans Kohn, *Nationalism: Its Meaning and History*, p. 10.

37   Allen, *The Malayan Union*, p. 42.

38   See Benjamin Batson, *The End of Absolute Monarchy in Siam* (Kuala Lumpur: Oxford University Press, 1984), pp. 236–64. See also Cheah Boon Kheng, "The Erosion of Ideological Hegemony and Royal Power and the Rise of Postwar Malay Nationalism", pp. 4–5.

39   Ratnam, *Communalism and the Political Process in Malaya*, p. 29.

40   Hill and Lian, *The Politics of Nation Building*, pp. 58–59.

41   Ratnam, *Communalism and the Political Process in Malaya*, p. 83.

42   *Ibid.*

43   Discussed in Yeo Kim Wah, "The Anti-Federation Movement in Malaya, 1946–1948", *Journal of Southeast Asian Studies* 4, no. 1 (1973): 31–51.

44   Hill and Lian, *The Politics of Nation Building*, p. 46. The cited work by J.Nagata is entitled, "In Defence of Ethnic Boundaries: The Changing Myths and Charters of Malay Identity", in *Ethnic Change*, ed. C. Keyes (Seattle: University of Washington Press, 1981).

45   Cheah Boon Kheng, "Malayan Chinese and the Citizenship Issue, 1945–1948", *Review of Indonesian and Malayan Affairs* 12, no. 2 (December 1978): 1–25.

46   See *Report of the Working Committee, Constitutional Proposals for Malaya* (Kuala Lumpur: Malayan Union Government Press, 1946), p. 6.

47   Tunku Abdul Rahman Putra, *Lest We Forget: Further Candid Reminiscences* (Singapore: Eastern Universities Press, 1983), p. 34.

48   See R.T. McVey, *The Calcutta Conference and the Southeast Asian Uprisings* (Ithaca: Cornell Modern Indonesia Project, 1958).

49   See letter from Sir H. Gurney to J.J. Paskin on a variety of recent developments, in CO537/4741, no. 78, 2 December 1949, and letter from Mr Creech Jones to Sir H. Gurney (Policy Towards the Chinese community), in CO537/4741, no.

76, 5 Dec. 1949, in Stockwell, *op.cit.*, *Malaya: Part II The Communist Insurrection, 1948–1953*, pp. 187–92.

50 A British Colonial Office document, commenting on the committee's work, states: "Mr Macdonald is optimistic at the progress made in the [Communities Liaison] Committee, and feels that it is on the way to solving the fundamental political problems of Malaya. He has found that the men whose names count most in Malaya have been able to agree on matters where two years ago they would have disagreed, even if they had been prepared to sit around the same table for discussion." See CO brief for D.R. Rees-Williams, Parliamentary Under-secretary of state, CO, for his tour of Hong Kong, Singapore and Malaya, Oct.–Nov. 1949, in CO967/84, no. 70, in Stockwell, *ibid.*, p. 157.

51 See Ramlah Adam, *Dato Onn Jaafar: Pengasas Kemerdekaan* (Kuala Lumpur: Dewan Bahasa dan Pustaka, 1992), p. 182.

52 *Ibid.*, p. 204.

53 See *ibid.*, pp. 192–96, for details on the second UMNO crisis over Onn's leadership.

54 In a letter to Datuk Onn, MacDonald said: "The point is that I think there would be immense advantage if you retained your Presidency of UMNO at the same time as you form and lead the new party [IMP]. I know that in some ways this would be troublesome and add to your already tremendous burdens of work, but I believe it may be a real mistake if you abandon the leadership and guidance of UMNO." Cited in Pamela Ong Siew Imm, *One Man's Will: A Portrait of Dato' Sir Onn bin Jaafar*, published by author (Penang, 1998), p. 204.

55 MacDonald's admiration for Onn is clearly stated in a letter to the British Minister of Colonial Affairs, Creech-Jones as follows: "Without question he is the outstanding Malay leader, with qualities of courage, constructive thought and action, and statesmanship which command attention. At the same time, he is a person of considerable attraction and charm, and I am only one of many Europeans who feel affection as well as admiration for him." Cited in *ibid.*, p. 166.

56 See the three volumes of the C.O. 537 and other secret and confidential records compiled and edited by Anthony Stockwell, *ibid.*

57 Harper, *The End of Empire and the Making of Malaya*, p. 322.

58 The Tunku recalls these years in two chapters, "The Day I Was Vindicated", pp. 88–93, and "The Alliance That Led to Independence", pp. 94–100, in his book of memoirs, *Lest We Forget, op.cit.*

59 According to T.H. Tan, one of the founding members of the Alliance, the initiative for co-operation was undertaken by Ong Yoke Lin and Datuk Yahaya bin Abdul Razak, both of Kuala Lumpur, who were former school friends. This

led to a formal meeting between UMNO and the MCA, under the chairmanship of Col. (Later Tun) Henry H.S. Lee. The idea was later endorsed by both the Tunku and Tan Cheng Lock, the MCA president. See T.H. Tan, *The Prince and I* (Singapore: Mini Media, 1979), pp. 25–26.

60   Ratnam, *Communalism and the Political Process in Malaya*, p. 86.

61   Lennox Mills, *Malaya: A Political and Economic Appraisal*, pp. 81–82.

62   *Ibid.*, p. 83.

63   *Ibid.*, p. 84.

64   On the IMP's demand, the British High Commissioner, Sir Henry Gurney, in a note to the Colonial Office in London, dated 22 June 1951, said: "Onn told me that Press reports of his first statement referring to independence in 7 years were incorrect, but he had not contradicted them because that might have made the situation worse." Cited in Stockwell, *op.cit.*, p. 295.

65   T.H. Tan, *The Prince and I*, p. 28.

66   *Ibid.*, pp. 97–98.

67   Diane K. Mauzy, *Barisan Nasional: Coalition Government in Malaysia* (Kuala Lumpur: Maricans, 1983), p. 26.

68   According to Chin Peng, former secretary-general of the CPM, the party's cadres had been urged to support and campaign for the Alliance candidates in the general elections. "We wanted the party to win because its programme of amnesty was most favourable to us," he said in an interview with this author in February 1999 after a workshop on the writing of his memoirs at the Australian National University in Canberra.

69   See "Federation of Malaya: minute no PM (55) by Mr Lennox-Boyd to Sir A Eden on the forthcoming talks between Tunku Abdul Rahman and Chin Peng", 31 Oct. 1955, FO371/116941, no 77, in Document No 381 in Stockwell, *ibid.*, Vol. 3, pp. 192–93.

70   It was debated among British officials in London and Malaya whether to put all their fears in writing to the Tunku, but finally the idea was rejected for fear it would create an "atmosphere of distrust" and "impel him to go up to and beyond the limits set simply in order to avoid being called a British stooge." See file 'Meeting between Tunku Abdul Rahman and Chin Peng: inward telegram no. 691 from Sir D MacGillivray to Mr Lennox Boyd,' dated 8 Nov. 1955, in FO 371/116941, no 80, in Document 382, in Stockwell, *ibid.*, pp. 193–95. See also MacGillivray's decision not to put these points in writing to the Tunku before the meeting took place, in CO1030/27, no 10, "Meeting between Tunku Abdul Rahman and Chin Peng: letter from Sir D MacGillivray to Sir J Martin," 1 Dec. 1955, in Document 385, Stockwell, *ibid.*, pp. 199–201.

71   "Report of the chief minister of the Federation of Malaya on the Baling Talks":

draft summary by Tunku Abdul Rahman on the verbatim record, 29 Dec. 1955, in CO1030/30, ff3–16, in Stockwell, *op.cit., Malaya: Part III The Alliance Route to Independence, 1953–1957*, p. 224.

72 When asked whether he had voluntarily made the concession or been trapped into doing it, Chin Peng said: "No, we were not trapped. We really desired the Tunku to gain independence because we wanted to end colonial rule quickly. We felt we could strengthen his bargaining position with London. The other matters could be taken up later with the Tunku." Interview with Chin Peng, Jan. 1999.

73 A report by the British High Commissioner, Sir Donald MacGillivray, to the Colonial Office, dated 9 Jan. 1956, said: "During the 24 hours before leaving Kuala Lumpur, Abdul Rahman twice stated publicly that Her Majesty's Government had already agreed in principle that the Elected Ministers should be responsible for internal security and that the Alliance was going to London merely to work out the details. He must be aware that this advance was not being achieved on account of Chin Peng's conditional offer but had been obtained by the Alliance before the Chin Peng meeting took place. He would not wish it to appear that he was beholden to the Communists for this achievement or to allow them to get a measure of credit for it." See Stockwell, *op.cit.*, Part III, "The Alliance Route to Independence, 1953–1957", p. 242.

74 In fact, in a paper drawn up for the British negotiating team, the view was put across that Britain needed to meet Alliance demands for self-government and independence as much as possible: "…I see no effective counter to the answering argument that a determined Malayan Government with full responsibility for their own internal affairs could deal more successfully with the Communists than a 'Colonial' regime running a country anxious to be rid of it….The indications are that, if we accept the Alliance view on this, we shall be able to secure satisfactory agreements on defence and the other issues of particular concern to us…." See the Minister for Colonial Affairs, Lennox Boyd, to the British Cabinet Colonial Policy Committee.

75 See "Federation of Malaya": Cabinet Memorandum by Mr Lennox Boyd on the constitutional conference. Annex C: "Notes on the main conclusions and recommendations of the conference", CAB 129/79, CP (56)47, 21 February 1956, in Stockwell, *Part III: The Alliance Route to Independence, 1953–1957*, pp. 260–65.

76 *Report of the Education Committee, 1956* (Kuala Lumpur: Government Printing Office, 1956). Preamble, p. 1.

77 For a good account of the Chinese educationalists' struggle, see Tan Liok Ee, *The Politics of Chinese Education, 1945–1957* (Kuala Lumpur: Oxford University Press, 1997).

78 J.E. Jayasuriya, *Dynamics of Nation-Building in Malaysia* (Colombo: Associated Educational Publishers, 1983), p. 70.

79 See "Political Testament of the Alliance": memorandum by Tunku Abdul Rahman for the Reid Commission. *Appendix*: "Fundamental rights", 25 Sept. 1956, in CO889/ff.219–239, in *ibid.*, pp. 307–17.

80 *Ibid.*, p. 312.

81 See "Constitutional Commission and the Alliance Submission: transcript," 27 Sept. 1956, in CO889/6, ff281–290, in Stockwell, *ibid.*, p. 319. Emphasis added.

82 Harper, *The End of Empire and the Making of Malaya*, p. 358.

83 Milton J. Esman, *Administration and Development in Malaysia* (Ithaca: Cornell University Press, 1972), pp. 25–26.

CHAPTER TWO

1957–2001
The "Bargain" and
Contesting Nationalisms

*More potent than state nationalism in Sabah and Sarawak was the growth
of communalism, in the sense that communal sentiments were becoming
more prominent and communal groups becoming larger and more inclusive.*
Milne and Ratnam, *Malaysia:
New States in a New Nation*, p. 61

*Sabah and Sarawak are multiethnic societies but due to the different ethnic
patterns prevailing there, their electoral politics have unfolded quite
differently from that in the Peninsula ...... With the demise, at least
temporarily, of the non-Muslim Bumiputera ethno-nationalist movements
in the early 1990s, reconfiguration of the political process seems underway,
perhaps towards a political system more clearly dominated by the Muslim
Bumiputera, as in the case of the Peninsula.*
Francis Loh Kok Wah, "Understanding Politics in Sabah and
Sarawak: An Overview", *Kajian Malaysia* XV (1997): 12

MALAY POLITICAL primacy has always been a matter of perception.
During the 1957–63 period, it seemed like an illusion. As peninsular
Malaya's population was slightly still predominantly non-Malay, the UMNO-
led Alliance leaders attempted to project the image of Malaya as one
belonging to all citizens. They had put little emphasis on the creation of an
integrated new society. They could not decide what to call it. Every effort

was made to avoid endangering communal harmony and straining constitutional democracy. These were the early fragile years of a newly-independent state.

Malay political supremacy was, therefore, not openly stated or touted. As Diane Mauzy has observed, even UMNO's dominance within the Alliance was not overtly stressed: "The MCA and MIC combined did not have the electoral weight, the unity, the support, or the historical precedents to be exact political equals with UMNO. This fact was obscured, however, because for years the dominance of UMNO was masked, though at times not altogether convincingly, under the façade of an equal partnership. UMNO's supremacy was understood by its partners, but the MCA and the UMNO top élite did not want any obvious public demonstration of this fact. The lower echelon officials, however, were often not so sensitive to this point."[1]

Malay poverty, Malay special rights, Malay quotas in the civil service, and Malay as one of the two official languages (the other being English), did give the impression that the Malays were being treated as a "special" people who needed a lot of government assistance. Economically weak, the Malays lagged behind the other races in education, commerce and finance, and seemed unable to compete with the other races. Although Malay Sultans were the sovereign rulers of nine Malay states, they did not have executive power; they appeared merely as symbolic heads of state. Malaya's Prime Minister was a Malay. Malays outnumbered non-Malays in the Cabinet, in the armed forces and in the police. But there were Chinese Cabinet Ministers and an Indian Cabinet Minister, and most of the top civil service posts were still held by non-Malays. The image of the country did not appear, therefore, as one of Malay political supremacy, but of power-sharing among the races.

Most Malays were acutely conscious of this illusion constructed by the Government. For this reason, Malay nationalists had urged the UMNO-led Alliance Government to adopt Malay as the National Language immediately and start making Malay political dominance a reality. Until the National Language Act was introduced in 1967, this issue alone gave the Malay nationalist movement the excuse to begin demanding that the Government demonstrate that Malaya was a "Malay country". Leading this agitation were the "language nationalists", especially the Malay schoolteachers and academics, Malay writers and Malay journalists as well as the PMIP, which adopted a very high nationalistic profile in 1962 by its attempts to put on record in the Constitution that Malaya belongs to the Malays. The PMIP, which later became known as PAS, was at this time led by an ethno-centric Malay leadership, which advocated a Muslim-Malay nation-state. UMNO itself had been committed to the slogan "Malaya for the Malays", but for the sake of independence had agreed to a mixed government by different ethnic groups rather than by the Malays alone. It was not long before the Prime Minister Tunku Abdul Rahman had felt the need to acknowledge Malay ethno-centric sentiments by describing them as the original inhabitants of Malaya or *bumiputra* (literally "sons of the soil"), over non-Malay opposition.

Although the Constitution safeguarded Malay rights, the Malay nationalists were still unsure what this meant. Their "Make Malay the National Language" campaigns began to cast a powerful shadow over society and politics. As Malaya was a racially-divided country, race and politics were a heady mix. The Malay nationalist movement's demands made it clear to the non-Malays that Malay political supremacy was not yet a political reality, but might soon very well be. Malay nationalist demands were countered by non-Malay demands for immediate equality of civic rights.

The "historic bargain" was initially regarded only as a compromise to accommodate the interests of the ethnic groups in government policies, but after the 13 May 1969 riots it was elevated to a binding and cast-iron "social contract" which became sacrosanct to control or prevent communal differences. During this interval there were frequent attempts by members of the UMNO-MCA-MIC Alliance or those of the opposition parties to change the terms of the bargain and extend its parameters. This was a period of the "politics of accommodation". The Tunku was a moderating influence on the Malay nationalists. He would restrain them or urge them to agree to the concessions that he had made to the non-Malays under the pretext that the Malays already possessed political primacy. British scholar J.M. Gullick, writing in 1967, praised the Tunku's "gift for compromise and conciliation" and said his influence was largely a matter of personality.[2] But before long, the Tunku could no longer play this role, himself becoming a target of communal politics.

Rise of Communalism

Based on the experiences of the Alliance and opposition parties, studies revealed that communal/religious parties were more successful than non-communal parties in winning popular support in Malaya during this period. In the case of the Alliance, political scientist K.J. Ratnam's study of communalism, published in 1965, showed that the Alliance parties could not sustain the Alliance if they continued to remain communal themselves. Yet, when they acted as an inter-communal partnership, by making mutual concessions and adopting common policies, their popular support declined. Because they did not act constantly as communal organizations, their supporters felt that they had failed to represent their respective communal interests effectively. This contributed "very substantially" in a shift of increased public support to communal parties during the 1959 elections.[3]

Another study, done by political scientist R.K. Vasil, published in 1971, showed that Malays were not keen to join non-communal parties. As a result, non-communal parties, especially those based on the socialist ideology, did not get enough popular Malay support. These parties turned into essentially non-Malay parties, "in terms of leadership and rank and file, though not necessarily, initially, in terms of policy and programme, and thus made them even more unattractive to the Malays", who felt they were not specially committed to safeguard the interests of their Malay community. Over the years, the leaders of these non-communal parties succumbed to the pressures of their own members. They were unable to stop their parties from championing mainly the cause of the non-Malays.[4] The left-wing parties had on occasion been vehement critics of Malay special rights entrenched in the constitution. This may perhaps explain their success in securing 13 parliamentary seats in and around the predominantly non-Malay and urban centres of Penang, Ipoh and Kuala Lumpur in the 1959 general elections. On the other hand, the Alliance still managed to poll over half the total votes cast and won 73 out of the total of 104 seats. The Malay nationalists in the PMIP/Party Negara won 14 seats all in the east coast states of Kelantan and Terengganu.

Parliamentary democracy had worked justly and with some success, but the Federation faced grave problems in this period. In 1959 the unresolved problem of the further assimilation of the Chinese schools to the rest of the educational system had caused friction within the Alliance coalition, between the UMNO and the MCA, and also, outside the Alliance, between the MCA and the Chinese school management committees and the Chinese school teachers. Due to the forthcoming 1959 general elections, it was agreed by the Alliance coalition that the policy on Chinese schools would be reviewed after the polls. Another problem that threatened to split the Alliance was the internal conflict over the allocation of constituencies between the parties for the 1959 elections. The issue was resolved only after the "militants" in the MCA who had asked for more MCA candidates were expelled and the MCA's "moderates" who had taken over the party's leadership had accepted the formula devised by the Tunku. The Alliance victory in the polls was largely due to its success in ensuring communal harmony and achieving economic prosperity after independence.

The Bargain's First Serious Challenge, 1963–65

It was during Singapore's membership of Malaysia, from September 1963 until its departure in August 1965, that the first serious challenge to the Alliance's "historic bargain" took place. Many points of disagreement had developed between the Singapore Government and the Federal Government. The most serious had centred largely around party policy and leadership differences between the Alliance and the ruling People's Action Party (PAP) of Singapore. Other contentious issues related to interpretations of the Malaysia Agreement with regard to finance, revenue sharing and a common market. Both the Alliance and the PAP also adopted different approaches to communalism. The former did not believe in an open discussion of communal issues, while the other considered that communal issues could be discussed rationally.

Relations began to deteriorate further when the PAP leader, Lee Kuan Yew, criticized the Tunku and his UMNO colleagues for not giving up their policy of total Malay dominance in Malaysia for a more balanced position between the races.[5] Although he was careful not to attack the Malays' special rights, or Malay as the official language, he did question the basis of Malay rule. His calls for an equality of status between Malays and non-Malays, or what he termed "Malaysian Malaysia" did not go down well with UMNO's leaders and even with MCA leaders like Tun Tan Siew Sin, who felt he was "rocking the boat". The "historic bargain" had been based on the assumption of Malay supremacy in the government and administration of the country as a counter-weight to Chinese economic and commercial power. But the PAP refused to accept this.

Lee attacked the "ultras" (extremists in UMNO) and the Malay newspaper *Utusan Melayu* for attempting to foster Malay dominance over Malaysia. He argued for a re-alignment of forces between those who wanted a "Malaysian nation" and those "who preferred a communally segregated nation dominated by one of the constituent parts".[6] The PAP next joined with two parties in peninsular Malaysia, the United Democratic Party led by Dr Lim Chong Eu and the People's Progressive Party of Ipoh under the Seenivasagam brothers, and two in Sarawak, the Sarawak United People's Party (SUPP) and MACHINDA, to form the Malaysian Solidarity Convention, to campaign for "Malaysian Malaysia" in 1964. In the same year, tensions rose over racial issues and race riots occurred in Singapore in July and September. The causes were attributed to alleged Malay dissatisfaction with PAP rule and to the heat generated by the Alliance-PAP conflicts. Feelings had been heightened by the Alliance's earlier participation in Singapore's general elections in September 1963, and, in turn, by the PAP's later participation in Malaya's general elections in 1964.

Later, Alliance leaders like Malaysian Deputy Prime Minister Tun Razak replied to Lee's arguments by stating that although they, too, subscribed to a concept of a "Malaysian Malaysia", their approach was different from that of the PAP leaders. The Malay "ultras" called on the Alliance leaders to arrest and detain Lee for making allegedly seditious remarks against Malay-dominated rule in Malaysia. These events led the Tunku to conclude that

Singapore's presence in Malaysia had become untenable and the political crisis had reached a point beyond his control. He took the decision, which was approved by his Cabinet and the Malaysian Parliament, to expel Singapore from Malaysia on 9 August 1965. The PAP's struggle for "Malaysian Malaysia" is still continued in Malaysia by the DAP, generally regarded as its off-shoot, although the latter has distanced itself from the PAP and its policies in Singapore.

Nation-Building in Sarawak and Sabah, 1963–2000

Since independence in 1957, the informal UMNO-MCA-MIC "historic bargain" had been the basis for establishing national integration and racial harmony in peninsular Malaya. But with the formation of Malaysia in 1963 the application of this "bargain" to Sarawak, Sabah and Singapore had become rather problematic. These states had joined the federation on their own special terms, and not on the basis of Malaya's "historic bargain". Those terms not only tended to protect their state rights and their own specific *bumiputra* status, but also engendered conflict between building loyalties at state level and at national level. Sarawak and Sabah versions of *bumiputra*-ism fostered their own state nationalisms and contested Malay *bumiputra*-ism from peninsular Malaysia. While UMNO attempted to influence and unify the indigenous *bumiputra* in Sarawak and Sabah within the ambit of its policy of Malay political primacy, its efforts were being resisted. In fact, after Malaysia was formed, the various ethnic communities became more conscious of their need to reinforce communal unity and saw themselves more and more as communal groups.

Whenever Sarawak or Sabah raised criticisms towards federal government policy affecting their respective ethnic communities or state rights, the contribution to Malaysian nation building might have been negative, said Milne and Ratnam, both political scientists, adding,[7] "Viewed from Kuala Lumpur, the conversion of Kenyahs and Punans in Sarawak to Islam could be seen as promoting nation-building. However, in Sarawak such conversions could be regarded as splitting ethnic groups which had already acquired a group identity." Singapore's challenge to ethnic Malay rule, too, had aroused Singapore nationalism and created divisiveness rather than national unity.

Because of the initial reluctance of Sarawak and Sabah to join Malaysia, and also due to strong opposition by the left-wing labour and political movement in Singapore to the idea, concessions had to be made on the part of Malaya to these three territories. Malaya had found the Malaysia proposal (originally proposed by Britain, then adopted by Malaya's Tunku Abdul Rahman) attractive because the Borneo territories, with a predominantly non-Chinese population, would in some sense help to balance, or offset, a union between Malaya and predominantly-Chinese Singapore. By joining an enlarged federation of Malaysia, the Borneo territories would achieve independence from colonial rule and be "partners of equal status" with Malaya. But Malaya had no intention to replace one form of colonialism with another, Malaya's Prime Minister Tunku Abdul Rahman assured Malaya's Parliament on 28 April 1962.

The Borneo States were, therefore, given a wide variety of privileges and benefits, while Singapore was given safeguards in the areas of education and labour. Initially, none of the leaders of these three territories objected to the political dominance of Malaya's ruling national leadership of UMNO-MCA-MIC. Nor did they object to the terms of the "historic bargain", or to its constitutional contract, as embodied in Malaya's Constitution. They had separately negotiated for, and finally agreed to, the additional safeguards respectively for Sarawak, Sabah and Singapore. "It was decided," observed political scientists Milne and Mauzy, "that Malaysia should be brought about by amendment to the existing Constitution of Malaya rather than by the adoption of a new Constitution."[8] When Malaya had reached agreement with the leaders of the other three states, and with the British, its government amended the Constitution accordingly by passing the Malaysia Act (1963). Malaya's Parliament also passed an Immigration Act which restricted entry to North Borneo (Sabah) and Sarawak, as demanded by these two states. Although such restrictions did not foster national integration, the founding fathers of Malaysia agreed it was a temporary measure to safeguard Sabah and Sarawak's interests. After Malaysia was formed, Malaya's relationships with Sarawak & Sabah appeared more harmonious than those with Singapore, largely because Singapore's ruling People's Action Party (PAP) leaders continued to be excluded from the UMNO-MCA-MIC Federal Government. It was this factor that caused the PAP leaders to voice dissatisfaction with the "historic bargain", and later to challenge its terms.

Singapore's departure was nearly followed by Sarawak and Sabah. But secession was nipped in the bud by tough action on the part of the Federal Government's leaders. With Singapore out of Malaysia, attempts have been made to extend the "bargain" to both Sarawak and Sabah, but there have been occasional objections and resistance. According to Milne and Mauzy, it had been made plain by Federal Government leaders that, socially as well as politically, the policy of integration assumed a "native", that is, a Malay, base. "It has been well said", they added, "that Malayan [now Malaysian] nationalism" consists of two parts, 'a nucleus of Malay nationalism enclosed by the idea of a Malay-Chinese-Indian partnership'. Since the formation of Malaysia, this outer ring would include contributions from Sarawak and Sabah."[9] But the various indigenous communities in Sarawak and Sabah have not necessarily accepted such a Malay base.

Although Singapore had questioned Malay dominance, it had accepted two aspects of the constitutional contract — Malay special rights and the Malay language as the national language of Malaya. In fact, most of the island's political leaders had previously inculcated a sense of nationhood based on the merger of Singapore and the Federation of Malaya. Such a union, they believed, would bring about a united nation, a United Malaya, comprising Malays, Chinese and Indians and other races with kinship and cultural ties in both territories. This merger goal appeared in the manifesto of most political parties in Singapore until 1963. In 1959 the PAP Government of Singapore adopted Malay as an official language and even had its state anthem in Malay, *Majulah Singapura* (Long Live Singapore). But Malay nationalists in Malaya had refused to accept a merger with Singapore because the total Chinese population in Malaya would then outnumber the Malays in the country. It was only with the inclusion of the Borneo territories whose "indigenous natives" were regarded as "brothers" by Malays in

Malaya, and the communist threat in Singapore that Malaya's Prime Minister, Tunku Abdul Rahman, accepted Singapore in Malaysia. This is more fully discussed in Chapter III, which deals with the Tunku's period of administration.

Sarawak and Sabah had obtained special guarantees in the Malaysia Agreement with regard to the following items: language; education; qualification to be Head of State; ethnic composition of the civil service; citizenship; religion; native privileges; immigration; and representation in the Federal Parliament. Sabah especially presented a list which has become known as the "Twenty Points", which was accepted by Malaya and included special rights for the "natives" including the "Sino-Kadazans", "Borneonization" of the public services and "appropriate representation" to offset its smaller population in Parliament.[10] Non-implementation of some of these "Twenty-Points" by the Federal Government would be a bone of contention between the Sabah state government and the Federal Government. The present Constitution of Malaysia contains lists of state powers and concurrent powers which belong only to the two Borneo states. Sabah was given a special grant, while both states were given additional sources of revenue. Special safeguards included immigration controls to prevent citizens from peninsular Malaysia moving to live in Sarawak and Sabah or to take up jobs in these two territories. The Malaysia Act allowed both territories to use the English language as an official language until 1973, although in Malaya the Malay language had become the national language in 1967 and been enforced since 1970. Sarawak was given 16 seats in the Malaysian Parliament and Sabah 24, while Singapore was only offered 15. The present total parliamentary representation for Sarawak and Sabah has risen to 44 following the re-delineation of electoral boundaries in the two states and the increase of the number of seats in Parliament.

From the formation of Malaysia until 1974, the Alliance parties had ruled these two states. Later, the parties were replaced by components of the Barisan Nasional coalition (which replaced the tripartite Alliance Party in 1974). Their ability to capture all or almost all the 44 seats in the two states in national elections has enabled the UMNO-led BN to retain a two-thirds majority of seats in Parliament and form the Federal Government. This two-thirds majority enables them to change the Constitution, whenever necessary. For UMNO leaders, the inclusion of Sarawak and Sabah has been fortuitous, for it has enabled them to remain in power, prolong the terms of the "historic bargain" and promote Malay political primacy.

On the other hand, Opposition parties in peninsular Malaysia have failed to make headway in the two Borneo territories. UMNO has now established itself firmly in Sabah, but not yet made any inroads into Sarawak, due to the opposition of the BN component parties there. The DAP had been able to capture one or two parliamentary or state seats in Sarawak, but has made no headway in Sabah. It is largely due to UMNO's political skill and experience in establishing alliances with BN component parties in the two states that has allowed it to obtain their crucial combined 44 parliamentary seats to rule Malaysia.

The UMNO-led federal government has used various means such as ministerial contacts, federal-state party relations, civil service contacts, development projects, language and education policies, and financial and economic arrangements to strengthen federalism and national integration in the two territories.[11] The occasional appointment of state representatives to the Federal Government posts of Minister of Sarawak Affairs and Minister of Sabah Affairs in the early years of Malaysia[12] had also involved them directly in decision-making at the Federal Cabinet level. However, difficulties between the states and the centre have taken place. In the Sabah crisis of 1964 and the Sarawak crises of 1965 and 1966 the combined governmental-party influence of the federal Alliance government had prevailed. Recalcitrant Chief Ministers of Sarawak and Sabah were removed. Although the crises were resolved, they fomented state nationalisms.

State Nationalism vs. Malaysian Nationalism

Sarawak nationalism and Sabah nationalism emerged in the respective state's struggles with the Federal Government over state rights. Their political and constitutional disputes have sometimes been seen in terms of "rival nationalisms", i.e., ethnic state nationalism versus Malaysian nationalism.

Ethnic state nationalism in Sarawak was seen in the rise of Iban nationalism, and in Sabah, Kadazandusun nationalism.[13] In 1965 Sabah nationalism erupted when its Kadazandusun Chief Minister, Datuk Donald Stephens, was removed for raising the question of a re-examination of the "Twenty-Points" between Sabah and the Federal Government in the light of Singapore's departure from the federation. Sarawak nationalism was aroused during the 1966 constitutional crisis when the Iban Chief Minister Datuk Stephen Kalong Ningkan was removed by the State Governor, under Federal Government pressure, for campaigning for state rights following the exit of Singapore.

Unlike Sabah nationalism, a certain degree of national consciousness had already existed in Sarawak before the formation of Malaysia in 1963. Ethnic awareness of the Ibans during Brooke rule before 1941 was already formed, and Sarawak Malays owed strong loyalty to the Brookes. In 1949 Malay nationalists who opposed the cession of Sarawak by the last Brooke ruler to the British Government assassinated the British Governor, Duncan Stewart.[14] The first two Chief Ministers of Sarawak after the formation of Malaysia were Ibans, Datuk Kalong Ningkan (1963–66) and Penghulu Tawi Sli (1966–70). "Casting himself in the role of the Sarawak nationalist fighting the Malay hegemony of Kuala Lumpur, Ningkan won considerable sympathy and support particularly from the Iban and Chinese communities," says one source.[15]

Although the Ibans constitute the majority ethnic group in Sarawak, they are politically disunited, weak and present the image of being a disadvantaged minority. Due to divisions within the non-Muslim Iban community and to political alliances between Malays and Muslim *bumiputra* (Melanaus) and Chinese parties, the office of Chief Minister has since fallen to Sarawak Melanaus, first to Datuk Abdul Rahman Yaakub and, now to his nephew Datuk Mahmud Taib. In the "check and balance" political system in Sarawak which now forms the basis of power-sharing, the State Government has come under the dominance of the Malay/Melanau party, the Pesaka Bumiputera Bersatu (PBB). This suits the UMNO-led Federal Government fine, as it ensures Malay political primacy in Sarawak.

However, the Chinese party, the Sarawak United People's Party (SUPP), is the power broker whose support is needed by the other two groups — the Malays/Melanaus and the Ibans, represented by the Sarawak National Party and the Parti Bangsa Dayak Sarawak. Initially the SUPP preferred to ally itself with the former.[16] These parties are now component parties of the BN whose national leaders in Kuala Lumpur are quite happy with the present arrangements, under which Iban nationalism has been checked. The state government's economic and development policies appear to be "integrationist" and in line with federal government's nation-building goals. However, in mid-August 2001, as the Sarawak state elections approached, there were signs that the Melanau Taib Mahmud-led coalition of parties might split, as Malay leaders within his government had broken away to form a group known as "Parti Bebas" to challenge Melanau primacy and displace him from the Chief Ministership. If they had succeeded in the elections in returning a large Malay electoral base and been accepted within the BN coalition, they would have taken over the state BN leadership from the Melanaus and led the BN coalition government with the support of the SUPP and the Iban parties. They could then form UMNO and emplace UMNO into a dominant position in Sarawak in the same way that Tun Mustapha's former USNO had done in Sabah.

The Malay group's leader, Datuk Abang Abu Bakar Mustapha, a former Federal Defence Minister, resigned from the PBB in January 2001 after tabling a motion in the PBB's general assembly asking for UMNO's entry.[17] In 1998 the UMNO president and Malaysian Prime Minister, Dr Mahathir, when opening the PBB Assembly, had said it was UMNO's intention to spread its wings to Sarawak, but it was up to the people of Sarawak to decide. The PBB's Melanau leaders were not enthusiastic to the idea. When Sarawak went to the polls in September, Federal UMNO leaders quickly denied that UMNO would become involved in Sarawak politics by standing behind Datuk Abang Abu Bakar's group. Although Datuk Abang's group contested in a large number of the 45 state constituencies, UMNO's failure to endorse his group saw it suffer total defeat. This indicated that UMNO preferred the coalition to be led by the

Malay/Melanau leadership of Datuk Mahmud Taib and did not wish to rock the BN "scales" in Sarawak.

In Sabah, Kadazandusun nationalism had appeared to be a post-Malaysia phenomenon. Its rise and fall in the 1960s was related to the rise and fall of the Kadazandusun leader, Donald Stephens. Thereafter, it was said to have suffered a demise,[18] but it began to revive itself in the 1980s. The period of Tun Mustapha's regime (1967–76) saw the processes of Malayization and Islamization, which from Kuala Lumpur's view appeared to be a check on Kadazandusun nationalism and was therefore "integrationist". Subsequently, however, Mustapha began to assert state rights and arouse Sabah nationalism in order to enhance his political authority in the state, and was in turn removed by the Federal Government.

The successor Berjaya government under Datuk Harris Salleh (1967–84) continued the Malayization and Islamization policies. The Malay language was promoted in government-aided schools in Sabah, while the Kadazandusun language was no longer taught anywhere at all. The state sponsored Koran-reading competitions and organized various *dakwah* (missionary) activities. All these the Berjaya government considered to be in line with the promotion of "national culture", the core of which was to be derived from Malay-Muslim elements. "The Federal Government believed this would help to promote national unity," says one observer.[19]

However, in the 1985 state elections, the Parti Bersatu Sabah (PBS), formed by a Berjaya breakway group of Kadazandusun and Chinese members, which was led by Datuk Pairin Kitingan, swept to power. In 1986 PBS joined Barisan Nasional, but left the BN in 1990 and joined the opposition at the federal level. Its period of office saw a revival of Kadazandusun nationalism and a reversal of policies adopted by the Mustapha and Harris Salleh governments. Kadazandusun music and songs were played again over Radio Sabah, and the Kadazandusun language was once more taught in state schools. However, as PBS remained with the opposition, its conflict with the Federal Government caused the latter to cut back aid to weaken the PBS government's ability to provide for economic development. From 1991 to 1994, Sabah received some of the lowest levels of development aid. The federal Anti-Corruption Agency arrested and charged Pairin for misusing his powers over a government contract. He was convicted, but the court's imposition of a fine allowed him to retain his office and his state assembly seat. His brother Jeffrey was next detained under the ISA on a charge of plotting secession. In the 1994 election, although PBS under Pairin's leadership was returned to office, its majority in the state assembly was gradually eroded by cross-overs of PBS assembly members to the BN component parties. Eventually the BN parties had the majority of seats to form the state government and to oust Parin from office. Tun Mustapha's party, United Sabah National Organization (USNO), was eventually dissolved and replaced by UMNO. Even Sabah's Parti Angkatan Keadilan Rakyat (Akar), comprising Kadazans and Sino-Kadazans, has been dissolved, and its members absorbed into UMNO.[20]

The Barisan Nasional headquarters in Kuala Lumpur has since devised a system to rotate the Chief Minister's post every two years among its component parties representing the Muslim *bumiputra*, non-Muslim (Kadazandusun) and Chinese. The system was introduced in 1994 after the BN took over the state from the Parti Bersatu Sabah.[21] The present Chief Minister, Datuk Chong Kah Kiat, is from the Liberal Democratic Party.[22] The rotation system, the idea of the Malaysian Prime Minister Datuk Seri Dr Mahathir Mohamed, has given rise to dissatisfaction among some component parties, especially those representing the Kadazandusun who feel they have to wait a longer period for their turn, while UMNO's Malay Muslim leaders in Sabah feel the Chief Minister's post should come from their party and should remain in its hands to reflect Malay dominance. The power-sharing system had been created to ensure co-operation among the different communities in Sabah, including the Kadazandusuns, and to prevent the return of PBS and Kadazandusan nationalism to power. However, bearing in mind that the use of *bumiputra* as an ethnic symbol by the dominant party UMNO to extend Malay political primacy and forge an alliance with the other indigenous communities in Sabah, UMNO has not yet established its predominance in the State Government. This is largely because the divergent strands of *bumiputra*-ism seem to represent a challenge to *Malayness* and Malay rule. The role of the Chinese parties as power brokers complicates the issue further.

With hindsight, it is possible to state that Sabah ethnic or state nationalism was not in conflict with Malaysian nationalism during Indonesia's "Confrontation" of Malaysia and Malaysia's resistance to the Filipino claim for Sabah from 1963 to 1966. Sabah remained loyal and supportive of Malaysia. In Sarawak, "both state nationalism and Malaysian nationalism were opposed to the Indonesians when Confrontation existed, and both types of nationalism were also behind government measures against Communist terrorists", observed Milne and Mauzy (1978, p. 65). Thus, it seems that in facing external threats, both Sabah and Sarawak have remained loyal to Malaysia and worked to reinforce national unity. Even as independent states, Sarawak and Sabah are likely to face serious threats from their stronger neighbours.

Nevertheless, from the viewpoint of nation-building in Malaysia, the twin threats of ethnic nationalism and secession will always remain in Sarawak and Sabah if Kuala Lumpur mishandles its relations with them. Since 1965 after the exit of Singapore, national leaders in Kuala Lumpur visit the two states almost weekly to keep in touch with state leaders and oversee development projects. Since the administration of Malaysia's fourth Prime Minister Datuk Seri Dr Mahathir Mohamed, Sabah time has officially become Malaysia's Standard Time. The Federal Government has even held the official National Day celebrations and parade in Kuching and in Kota Kinabalu on separate occasions to foster national unity with the people of the two states.

It was during the administration of the second Malaysian Prime Minister Tun Razak, that Sabah under the Chief Minister Tun Mustapha posed the threat of secession once again, and Tun Mustapha was removed from office. The secession problem continued during the administration of Tun Hussein Onn, Tun Razak's successor. Tun Mustapha's supporters attempted to create trouble after the Berjaya government had been installed. Kota Kinabalu, the state capital, was continuously rocked by bomb explosions, believed to have been set off by Tun Mustapha's immigrant Filipino supporters. Federal troops had to be used to maintain security in the city, and military reinforcements sent from Kuala Lumpur.

Military force from the Federal Government will be used as a last resort to crush any secession bid in Sabah or Sarawak, after political and constitutional means have been exhausted. In 1965, when Sabah under Kadazandusun leader Datuk Donald Stephens had threatened secession, Malaysia's first Prime Minister Tunku Abdul Rahman had declared that: "Any who intends to secede by force or by any other action will be regarded as rebels and traitors and will be dealt with as such."[23] Sarawak and Sabah would remain in Malaysia for ever, he said. Initially, in the 1970s, Tun Mustapha helped to accelerate "integration" by pushing the Malay language to replace English and follow the federal example in the sphere of education. He remained devoted to the idea of achieving national unity. However, when he attempted to remain undisputed leader of Sabah and arouse state nationalism, the Federal Government intervened to check his powers. When he threatened secession, he was removed from office.

Nation-building in Malaysia is likely to encounter this pattern of politics time and again in Sarawak and Sabah. It would appear that any strong leader in Sarawak or Sabah could easily arouse state nationalism at the expense of Malaysian nationalism. But such nationalisms will in turn be checked by the Federal Government. No such problem of state nationalism has been encountered in peninsular Malaysia probably because the Borneo states are new states and more ethnically distinct from the rest of Malaysia, while the peninsular states had experienced federation earlier, some as far back as in 1896, while the others in 1948.[24]

The Bargain and Mahathir's "Vision 2020", 1990–2001

It was during Datuk Seri Dr Mahathir Mohamed's administration that the "social contract" became a controversial issue once again in peninsular Malaysia. In 1991 he declared that he had a Vision of creating a *Bangsa Malaysia* (Malaysian nation) by the year 2020. This would be a country with a "fully developed" status, with the winning formula of an accelerated industrialization programme. It would be a just and egalitarian nation, "a full and fair partnership", possessing "a sense of a common and shared destiny", irrespective of race. Although there was no reference to the "social contract", many observers interpreted it to mean that by the time Vision 2020 materialized, the contract might no longer be needed. The Malays would have economically progressed and developed the ability to compete on equal terms with the other races. Malay special rights might be given up, and Malaysia would move towards Mahathir's version of a kind of Malaysian Malaysia which Lee Kuan Yew could only have dreamed of. However, Malays were generally lukewarm to Mahathir's *Bangsa Malaysia* idea, while non-Malays were very enthusiastic. To the Malays *Bangsa Malaysia* apparently meant giving up their special status and special rights and sharing equality with non-Malays, which was something they did not seem to cherish.

So for 10 years there was talk and rhetoric about *Bangsa Malaysia* but mostly on the non-Malay side. Then non-Malay doubts began to set in about achieving *Bangsa Malaysia*. In September 1999 just prior to the general elections a group, the Chinese Associations Election Appeals Committee or known as SUQIU by its acronym in Chinese, urged the Mahathir Government to accord non-Malays equality of status with Malays and end Malay special rights, including education quotas, to make his Vision 2020 a reality. Their recommendations were made in an 83-point memorandum under 17 headings. The SUQIU represented 2,095 Chinese organizations, among them the United Chinese School Committees Association of Malaysia (Dong Zong), the United Chinese School Teachers Association of Malaysia (Jiao Zong) and the Nanyang University Alumni Association of Malaysia. The main thrust of their recommendations was that the government should restructure society towards *Bangsa Malaysia* by reviewing existing policies and laws, like the Internal Security Act and other regulations, that it deemed unnecessary in the creation of a modern, democratic society. Its ideas, the SUQIU argued, represented the natural evolution of a Malaysian Nation, or *Bangsa Malaysia*.

As the UMNO-led BN Coalition had just suffered a split over the sacking of Mahathir's Deputy Prime Minister Datuk Seri Anwar Ibrahim, the BN had begun to lose Malay support and was facing the possibility of serious electoral losses in the forthcoming 1999 elections. Aware of the BN's need for non-Malay support to win the elections, the SUQIU had submitted the demands apparently in the hope that the government would appear conciliatory since it needed such non-Malay support. Dr Mahathir did not reject the demands outright. He, in fact, agreed to most of them in principle, but said they merited further study.

In the elections, the BN was returned to power by a largely non-Malay electorate, while 70 per cent of the Malay voters had swung to the opposition Malay parties like Parti Islam (PAS) and the Parti Keadilan, the breakaway group of UMNO, largely due to the Anwar Ibrahim issue and dissatisfaction with Mahathir's leadership. After about eight months without any positive response from the Mahathir Government on the *Bangsa Malaysia* idea, a Chinese businessman Datuk David Chua was reported in the Malay-language newspaper, *Utusan Melayu*, on 14 August 2000, under banner headlines as calling for the abolition of Malay special rights and privileges. He said that in order to carry out a restructuring of society the government needed to do this, so that Malays could become competitive. Chua, who was deputy secretary-general of the Association of Chinese Chambers of Commerce and Industry Malaysia, was also a member of the Second National Economic Consultative Council (NECC II), at whose deliberations he had raised such views. *Utusan Malaysia* had interviewed Chua after the *Far Eastern Economic Review* had leaked his views at the NEEC II meeting. In a statement the following day, Chua denied he had asked for Malay special rights to be abolished. He clarified that he had asked instead for "special assistance and affirmative action policies" to be phased out gradually. The same day the Deputy Prime Minister Datuk Seri Abdullah Ahmad Badawi, in a commentary on Chua's statement, said Malay special rights would remain as they had been "agreed upon by the Government which is represented by the various races".[25] Other UMNO leaders criticized recent statements raising the issue of Malay privileges, with one Cabinet Minister and UMNO vice-president, Tan Sri Muhyiddin Yassin, stating that Malay privileges were a "social contract" which had been agreed to by the other BN leaders to develop the Malay community after Independence.

On 16 August 2000 the SUQIU at a press conference on the anniversary of its 83 demands called on the government and on Members of Parliament to give further thought to its demands. It reiterated its call for an end to the different status between *bumiputra* and non-*bumiputra* in all fields, the abolition of the Internal Security Act and the cancellation of the Vision Schools project, under which Malay, Chinese and Tamil schools would be integrated at one site and share school facilities. Present at the press conference was a PAS representative, Subky Latif, who had been invited by SUQIU. SUQIU's executive secretary, Ser Choon Ing, explained that SUQIU did not challenge Malay political primacy, but only demanded equality of status for Malays and non-Malays. On 17 August the Prime Minister Datuk Seri Dr Mahathir assured the Malays that their rights and privileges would be protected, "until they themselves do not want the government's help any more". He said the Government on its own would "not even take one step backward" in this matter. He was addressing a crowd of about 500 from 11 Malay organizations, representing the business community, Malay women and students. The Prime Minister said he did not want any racial misunderstanding and animosity in the country, and for that matter, all races "need to be careful when making statements". They had the right to make statements, but this should be done behind closed doors, so that it would not trigger racial hatred. Of late, he said, there was disunity among the Malays which meant "we are weak", and "when we are weak, there are calls to drop the Malay rights".

On 23 August 2000 it was reported that David Chua had met Dr Mahathir and explained his position that he did not call for the abolition of Malay special rights. The Prime Minister advised him not "to raise the sensitive matter again". On 30 August in his National Day eve message, the Prime Minister attacked SUQIU's demands as "extreme" and compared them to the "communists" and the Islamic terrorist Al-Maunah group which had recently raided two Army camps in Perak to seize arms.

For the next four months, debates raged in the newspapers over SUQIU's 83 demands. Numerous Malay organizations called on SUQIU to withdraw its demands. On 13 November at a by-election in Lunas, Kedah state, the Barisan Nasional lost to the opposition Parti Keadilan. Several days later the BN accused SUQIU of campaigning in the by-election and influencing the Chinese electors to vote against it. The BN by-election defeat, according to the opposition DAP and an UMNO Government backbencher, Shahrir Ahmad, was due to the Chinese community's "anger" at the Prime Minister's remarks in calling SUQIU "no different from the communists".

The debates reached their climax in December when the Prime Minister declared he could not prevent Malays and Malay organizations from expressing their feelings and hostility towards SUQIU. This apparently was a reference to the Federation of Peninsular Malaysia Malay Students (GPMS)'s move to hold a mammoth rally in Kuala Terengganu on 6 January 2001 to protest SUQIU'S demands. On 11 December 2000 at a meeting in Parliament, in reply to a DAP member's question, Dr Mahathir said the Government could not entertain demands by SUQIU as they were "tantamount to abolishing Malay rights, a move which will result in chaos and will paralyse the country's progress". He reiterated his earlier statement that SUQIU was not much different from the communists "who wanted to abolish the special status of Malays". The Prime Minister said while his criticism was only directed at SUQIU, "especially certain leaders of the group, they and in particular Chinese newspapers, made his remarks appear as if they were targeted at the entire Chinese community". He added, "If the Chinese in general are offended by my remarks which had been deliberately distorted by SUQIU and some Chinese newspapers, I apologize to them." He went on to say that any potential chaos arising from SUQIU's demands was defused because he personally forbade UMNO Youth and other Malay groups from resorting to violent protests. Despite the restraint, SUQIU's "disregard for the ban on raising sensitive issues and disrespect for the Government's social contract and national policies are akin to the attitude of communists". Dr Mahathir said that SUQIU had to be reprimanded for challenging the "social contract and attempting to grab all for one community through so-called equal rights and meritocracy which the Malays rejected half a century ago". When asked by the opposition DAP Member of Parliament Kerk Kim Hock why SUQIU's demands had been agreed to "in principle" by the Cabinet and by the MCA, Gerakan and the SUPP on 23 September 1999, Dr Mahathir said, "If we had rejected the demands, we would have lost the elections. We were forced not to take a strong stand, if we did, we would have been defeated. We had to look after our interests just like the DAP... which collaborated with the PAS..."[26]

On 17 December 2000 in his speech to declare open the Sixth World Federation of Foochow Associations Convention in Kuala Lumpur, the Deputy Prime Minister Datuk Seri Abdullah Badawi, urged all the communities to respect the "social contract". "We believe that no one community will be sidelined. We believe that every Malaysian has a responsible role to play in nation-building and we believe that it is this unity in diversity that will define a *Bangsa Malaysia* or Malaysian Nation in the years to come," he said.

Several meetings were held between SUQIU and several Malay organizations to discuss its demands. A meeting between SUQIU and UMNO Youth on 5 January 2001 ended with a joint statement, in which SUQIU agreed to "put aside" seven of its 83-point election appeals in view of the "prevailing ethnic tension". It was later explained that the meeting had nearly collapsed over the wording of the statement, as SUQIU had insisted on the words "set aside" instead of the word "withdraw" to indicate its position.

Both parties agreed that the action was taken "in view of the special rights, position, and privileges of the Malays and the natives of any of the state of Sabah and Sarawak as enshrined in Article 153 and other such relevant Articles of the Federal Constitution not be questioned". Both parties also "expressed regret over the unintended reaction within the Malay and Chinese communities which had arisen from the Seven Points and subsequent incidents". The seven points (demands) put aside were:

- any affirmative action initiated by the government should benefit and protect the weaker groups of society, regardless of their religious, social and racial background;
- efforts be made to abolish the differences between the *bumiputra* and non-*bumiputra* communities in all fields;
- fair and equitable distribution of agricultural land to farmers without racial distinction;

- to abolish the race-based quota system and to replace it with one that is based on merit;
- to do away with the quota system for entry into universities;
- fair treatment be accorded to all religious organizations in terms of development of religion. Government assistance should also be extended to all such organizations which include sufficient coverage from the official media; and
- to establish a loan scheme or financial assistance for needy students regardless of race.[27]

The agreement was hailed by the country's newspapers as welcome news in defusing the racial tensions in the country. Several politicians from the BN component parties such as the MCA, the Gerakan and the MIC were quoted as supporting the settlement. In the following days, UMNO leaders urged SUQIU and non-Malay groups not to raise the demands again in the future. The strong Malay opposition to SUQIU's demands appears to serve as a warning that racial tensions might flare up again if the "social contract" was ever challenged once more. However, the strong reactions to SUQIU's demands have been confined mainly to peninsular Malaysia. It remains to be seen whether the "social contract" will continue to stand the test of time in the new millennium.

Besides the issue of *bumiputra* rights, the other issue that has attracted much attention has been the controversy between the DAP and PAS over the latter's aim to establish Malaysia as an Islamic state. Both parties were members of a coalition, called Barisan Alternatif, which had contested against Dr Mahathir's BN coalition in the 1999 general elections. In the elections PAS performed better than the DAP, which suffered electoral losses attributed to its endorsement of the PAS programme to set up an Islamic state. The DAP continued to urge PAS to drop its "Islamic state" goal, but PAS had refused to do so. As events unfolded in Malaysia and internationally, indicating the rise of radical Islamic militancy, the DAP announced on 22 September that it would pull out of the BN coalition. PAS remained undeterred, believing that the BN coalition had been merely an "electoral coalition" and that it might be possible for both PAS and the DAP to come together again in future elections.

Conclusion

From the foregoing discussion, it is clear that the 1957 historic bargain is more applicable to peninsular Malaysia than to Sarawak and Sabah, where the ethnic communities are more varied than in the former. The contesting communalisms and nationalisms present different problems and challenges. The UMNO-led Federal Government in Kuala Lumpur shows that it has been more adept than the opposition parties in meeting these problems and challenges in Sarawak and Sabah.

Malay political primacy is likely to continue in Malaysia for a long time. Malay political primacy is also ingeniously presented as *bumiputra* political primacy. Given this combined "unity" of both Malays and other indigenous groups in peninsular Malaysia and in Sarawak and Sabah, it is unlikely that Malay if not *bumiputra* political primacy could ever be dislodged.

From Dr Mahathir's handling of the SUQIU issue, it is clear that his "Vision" of Malaysia in the year 2020 will not see the elimination of *bumiputra* rights. His *Bangsa Malaysia* (Malaysian Nation) will not see a revision of the 1957 "historic bargain". It will see a continuation of Malay political primacy. It is no different from that of Tunku Abdul Rahman's vision of first Malaya and then Malaysia nor of that of Tun Razak and Tun Hussein Onn. The non-Malay, or non-*bumiputra* population will have to accept this vision as a reality for a long time to come.

The following studies of Malaysia's four Prime Ministers as nation-builders will show how they had grappled with the complex problem of creating a Malaysian nation-state in which Malay political primacy was entrenched and perpetuated.

NOTES

1   Diane K. Mauzy, *Barisan Nasional: Coalition Government in Malaysia* (Kuala Lumpur: Maricans, 1983), p. 24.
2   J.M. Gullick, *Malaya* (London: Ernest Benn, 1967), p. 122.
3   K.J. Ratnam, *Communalism and the Political Process in Malaya* (Kuala Lumpur: Oxford University Press, 1965), p. 215.
4   See R.K. Vasil, *Politics in a Plural Society* (Kuala Lumpur: Oxford University Press, 1971), p. 292.

5   Lee Kuan Yew, *The Singapore Story* (Singapore: Times Editions, 1998), p. 572.
6   Albert Lau, *A Moment of Anguish: Singapore in Malaysia and the Politics of Disengagement* (Singapore: Times Academic Press, 1998), p. 233.
7   R.S. Milne and K.J. Ratnam, *Malaysia — New States in a New Nation: Political Development of Sarawak and Sabah in Malaysia* (London: Frank Cass, 1974), p. 61.
8   R.S. Milne and Diane K. Mauzy, *Politics and Government in Malaysia* (Singapore: Federal Publications, 1978), p. 60.
9   Milne and Mauzy, *Politics and Government in Malaysia*, p. 366. The quotation is taken from Wang Gungwu's essay, "Malayan Nationalism", *Royal Central Asiatic Society Journal*, Parts 3 and 4 (July–October 1972), p. 366.
10   Francis Loh Kok Wah, "Modernization, Cultural Revival and Counter-Hegemony: The Kadazans of Sabah in the 1980s", in *Fragmented Vision*, ed. Joel S. Kahn and Francis Loh Kok Wah (Sydney: AAS-Allen & Unwin, 1992), p. 227.
11   Milne and Ratnam, *Malaysia — New States in a New Nation*, p. 28.
12   The previous incumbents of these posts were Temenggong Jugah of Sarawak and Datuk Donald Stephens and Tun Mustapha of Sabah respectively. Singapore was denied an equivalent post of the Minister for Singapore Affairs during its membership of Malaysia.
13   Milne and Ratnam, *ibid.*, pp. 60–61. The Kadazandusun used to be known as "Kadazan" but recently has adopted "Kadazandusun" as its ethnic name.
14   For an account of this incident, see R.W. Reece, *The Name of Brooke: The End of White Rajah Rule in Sarawak* (Kuala Lumpur: Oxford University Press, 1982).
15   Peter Searle, *Politics in Sarawak, 1970–1976: The Iban Perspective* (Singapore: Oxford University Press, 1983), p. 39.
16   See Jayum A. Jawan, *Iban Politics and Economic Development: Their Patterns and Change* (Kuala Lumpur, Bangi: Penerbit Universiti Kebangsaan Malaysia, 1994), pp. 131–57.
17   See background details in *New Straits Times* report, 8 August 2001, p. 4. In the 1996 elections, the Sarawak BN won 58 seats; the DAP, two; and Independents, two.
18   Margaret Roff, "The Rise and Demise of Kadazan Nationalism", *Journal of Southeast Asian History* 10, no. 2 (1969), pp. 326–43.
19   Francis Loh Kok Wah, "Modernisation, Cultural Revival and Counter-Hegemony: The Kadazans of Sabah in the 1980s", in *Fragmented Vision*, ed. Joel Kahn and Francis Loh Kok Wah (Sydney: AAAS-Allen and Unwin, 1992), p. 233.
20   *New Straits Times*, 22 May 2001, p. 2.
21   See reports in *The Star*, 18 March, 2001, p. 2, and *New Straits Times*, 15 March, 2001, p. 2, and 19 March 2001, p. 21, on the controversy relating to the rotation system of the Chief Minister's post in Sabah.

22 This is the third time that Sabah has had a Chinese Chief Minister. The previous Chief Ministers were Datuk Peter Lo and Datuk Yong Teck Lee.

23 Milne and Ratnam, *ibid.*, p. 65.

24 Lim Hong Hai compares Sabah and Sarawak with the peninsular states of Penang and Kelantan in his interesting article, "Sabah and Sarawak in Malaysia: The Real Bargain, or what have they gotten themselves into?" *Sabah and Sarawak: The Politics of Development and Federalism, Kajian Malaysia* XI, nos. 1 and 2 (Jan/December 1997): 15–56.

25 *New Straits Times*, 15 August 2000, p. 1.

26 See the full text of the question and answer session in Parliament in *Utusan Malaysia*, 12 December 2000.

27 See report, "Suqiu sets aside seven points", *New Straits Times*, 6 January, 2001, pp. 1–2; see also report in *Utusan Malaysia*, "Suqiu gugur 7 tuntutan," pp. 1, 4. Although the latter carried the word "*gugur*" (dropped) in its headline, its report used the words "*bersetuju menarik balik*" (agreed to withdraw) and also carried a column identifying the seven points which it declared as "*yang ditarik balik*" (withdrawn).

CHAPTER THREE

1957–70
"Pluralism" in Nation-Building
during the Tunku's Administration

He [the Tunku] had a simple philosophy: the role of the Malays was to control the machinery of the state, to give out licences and collect the revenue, and most important of all, to ensure that they were not displaced. Unlike the Chinese and Indians who had China and India to return to, they had nowhere else to go. In his soft-spoken, gracious way, he was absolutely open about his determination to maintain the ascendancy of the Malays and ensure that they and their sultans would remain the overlords of the country.

Lee Kuan Yew, *The Singapore Story:*
Memoirs of Lee Kuan Yew, p. 442

TUNKU ABDUL Rahman was not only Malaya's first Prime Minister, but also the leader who led the country to independence; hence, his title *Bapa Kemerdekaan* (Father of Independence).[1] He is also known as *Bapa Malaysia* (Father of Malaysia), or father of the nation, a title given for bringing about the present wider federation of Malaya, Sarawak and Sabah. These are major nation-building achievements. He was also independent Malaysia's first world statesman. He received numerous tributes and awards from foreign countries for his services towards international peace and co-operation. He was best known in the Commonwealth for his strong stand against apartheid, and for his pioneering role in the formation of the Association of Southeast Asian Nations (ASEAN). On retirement as

Malaysia's Prime Minister he held the post of Secretary-General of the Islamic Secretariat in Saudi Arabia.

Domestically, he is best known for his pioneering policy of entrenching Malay political primacy and for his bold "juggling" policies in the cause of racial harmony, pluralism and multi-racialism in the initial years of Malaya's independence and even after the formation of Malaysia. Although he upheld the principle of Malay political primacy, he worked out compromises and attempted to accommodate the demands of the other races in the country. His strategies met with criticisms and setbacks, including the outbreak of inter-racial riots on 13 May 1969. However, succeeding Prime Ministers continued to adopt them, so that Malaysia has been able to enjoy long periods of political stability and racial harmony.

The Tunku's "Pluralism"

The term "nation-building" encompasses both economic progress and social/political integration of a nation, i.e., prosperity and national unity. "A political community is a man-made artifact fraught with destructive tendencies, making its continued cohesion a major task of government," says Cynthia H. Enloe, one of the earliest political scientists to study multi-ethnic politics in Malaysia. "The founding and preservation of a national community calls for the integration of its component parts. The integrative process may be unconscious, without plan, or may be sought after with deliberateness and sophisticated manipulation. Integration must occur at several levels if the polity is to achieve minimal stability and autonomy."[2]

A newly-independent nation, that has been marked by ethnic pluralism, like Malaya and later its successor Malaysia, has been fashioned not only by the integration strategies of the government, but also by the "distinctive roles of, and the potential friction between, the major ethnic groups in the nation".[3] In this chapter the focus is on "nation-building" strategies relating to economic development, education, language, and culture.

The main features of a "Malay nation-state" were framed up, legally and constitutionally, just before the independence of Malaya. However, in the next 12 years, the Tunku's administration would move away from this framework. He delayed the *full* implementation of the "Malay nation-state" project. He began building a more "pluralistic" and "multi-cultural Malaya" in order to fulfil his immediate priority — national unity. He paid less attention to national identity or nationality. He used citizenship instead as the basis of nation-building. Citizenship, or membership of a nation, necessarily entails the rights and duties of citizens in response to policies initiated by the government.

In a nation-state "all citizens as individuals possess equal rights before the sovereign, national authority", but citizenship may be "exclusively or inclusively" defined, says Reinhard Bendix.[4] In nineteenth century Western European nation-building, the lower classes were denied entry into the arena of national politics, but as citizenship became national, the rights of citizenship emerged with the establishment of equal rights under the law. In Malaya and later in Malaysia, the non-Malays did not enjoy equal rights with Malays because national citizenship was "exclusively" defined, with the Malays given more rights.

The Tunku's strategy of national integration, however, was "inclusivist" by co-opting citizens, regardless of race, into government and administration by allowing them to participate and exercise their "civil, political, and social" rights in the public sphere. His era was, therefore, marked by openness and heated debates on the "inclusive" and "exclusive" rights of national citizenship. This was understandable given the problematic nature of a "Malayan" nationality. Only after the formation of Malaysia in 1963 did he attempt to define and develop a "Malaysian" nationality. To him, it seemed logical that a strong citizenship should be laid and strengthened before developing a nationality. The nation-state that he strove to establish during this early period was based on pluralism, particularly "multi-lingualism" and "multi-culturalism". This was in direct opposition to the "exclusivist" agenda of a "Malay nation-state" advocated by the Malay nationalists. For instance, the policy to continue "multi-lingual" primary schools within Malaya's, and later Malaysia's, national education system was initiated under the Tunku's administration. This policy has been retained by succeeding administrations till today.

Why the Tunku "Softened" Malay Nationalism

In promoting pluralism after Malaya's independence, the Tunku's administration decided to "dilute" or "soften" Malay nationalism. It played down "Malayness", the Malay language, Islam and royalty — the four pillars of Malay nationalism. The main agenda of Malaya's first year of national independence was to achieve multi-racial harmony and co-operation. While the Tunku's administration promised to attempt to work towards the eradication of Malay inequality and achieve the goal of "*economic equality*" between Malays and non-Malays, it did not promise multi-racial "*political equality*" — because this would undermine Malay political primacy that was ensured by Malay special rights within Malaya's Constitution. It is clear that, so long as Malay economic backwardness remained unresolved, there was no likelihood of the government ever moving towards multi-racial "*political equality*".

In spite of this scenario, many "non-Malays", especially Chinese politicians in the MCA, were optimistic that if they kept battering at the barriers erected against multi-racial "*political equality*", the barriers might eventually come down. To many Chinese, the government's acceptance of English and not Chinese as an official language, and the Malays "special position", meant that they had the status of second-class citizens and their economic future was uncertain. By not denying their right to make such demands, the Tunku went along as part of a political game to keep inter-racial peace and harmony. He thereby held out hopes that at some future date such political equality might materialize.

In fact, the evolution of his policies shows that he was an extremely astute politician who understood the complexities of multi-ethnic politics. The nature of the Alliance Party required compromises and concessions by the three component parties. If he granted concessions to the Malays, he would offset it later with concessions to the non-Malays. But given the realities of multi-ethnic politics, each concession by the government to one race was seen as a disadvantage to, or a deprivation for, the other races. Each time this happened, political opponents were able to take advantage of such grievances to secure support from the aggrieved community.

Consequently, in the eyes of the exclusivist Malay nationalists, within and without the UMNO party, his concessions to the non-Malays seemed to be a betrayal of Malay interests. The exclusivists wanted him to fulfil every Malay demand in line with the concept of a Malay "nation-state", i.e., "Malaya for the Malays" which he had originally advocated when he fought Dato Onn to wrest the leadership of UMNO. Outside UMNO, opposition came from the religious right-wing party, the Pan-Malayan Islamic Party (PMIP), also known as Parti Islam or PAS. PAS advocated the creation of Malaya as a Muslim-Malay state. It regarded UMNO's compromises and concessions to the MCA and the Chinese as conciliatory and excessive.

Although the Constitution reflected political primacy, the Malay nationalists felt that it had not materialized yet in reality. The Tunku's government was not going far enough, especially as the government had refused to implement the National Language policy immediately in all government departments, schools, universities and the law courts. This "victory" of political primacy, observed one critic, was "all style and appearance". "The very name of the country [both Malaya and Malaysia] emphasizes this fact and the Malay orientation is clearly reflected in the country's constitution and the 'Malay' character of the nation. This is no doubt Tengku's [sic] legacy even if this was all style and appearance and had no substance during his administration."[5]

The Malay nationalists desired to feel and enjoy the economic, political and social advantages that came with Malay privileges and Malay rights. They wanted special transport licences, import and export licences, job quotas and business opportunities to reflect "the special position of the Malays". This was their understanding of the meaning of "Malaya for the Malays", the Malay "nation-state" in the Federation of Malaya, or *Persekutuan Tanah Melayu* (literally, Federation of Malay Lands, or Federation of Malay States).

Demographically, however, Malaya, in 1957, did not reflect a "Malay nation-state". The population, according to the *1957 Census Report*, was 6,278,763, of which just under 50 per cent were Malays (3,126,706). About

37 per cent were Chinese (2,332,936), 12 per cent Indians (695,985), and about 0.2 per cent, 'Others' (123,136).[6] Based on these statistics, Malaya was a "plural" society. It was this preponderance of non-Malays that eventually led the Tunku to form Malaysia. He decided to merge Malaya with the territories of Sarawak, Sabah and Singapore, so that Malays and other "natives" or "indigenous races", combined together, would outnumber the non-Malays. This majority of the "natives" or *bumiputra* (sons of the soil) was guaranteed further when predominantly-Chinese Singapore left the federation in 1965.

However, the Tunku was not an unreasonable man. During negotiations on the "historic bargain" between the leaders of UMNO and the MCA and the Chinese educational groups in 1955, the latter had agreed to defer contentious issues such as language and education until after independence. This meant that the Chinese leaders were prepared to compromise. This arrangement allowed the Tunku's party, UMNO, to entrench Malay political primacy in Malaya's Constitution. The Tunku apparently read the move as a concession. In fact, at one stage of their negotiations, UMNO leaders found the Chinese stand on Chinese as an official language and the retention of Chinese schools as intransigent and a thorn in their side. Negotiations had reached an impasse. Various Chinese groups had threatened to boycott the MCA for allegedly "selling out" Chinese interests to UMNO, but eventually they were persuaded to relent as the Tunku promised that he would re-consider the issues after independence.[7] The Tunku was obliged to keep his word. Later, he relented and made some concessions on Chinese education. But he flatly refused to make Mandarin an official language.

The Emergency was still on at the time of independence. It did not end until 1960. Politically, the armed communists were sidelined, but militarily they still posed a threat. The Chinese-led communist movement could still exploit communalism and cause inter-ethnic conflicts, particularly between Malays and Chinese. The communists' armed revolt was a constant reminder that dissatisfied non-Malays, particularly the Chinese, could run to the jungles to swell the ranks of the communist rebels and fight for social justice if the Alliance Government was seen to act unjustly towards Chinese and non-Malay rights. When the government terminated the Emergency in

1960,[8] the communist insurgents were still not vanquished. They continued to remain a destabilizing force for the next three decades, and played an important role in the "check and balance" of Malaya's multi-ethnic politics, like the armed rebellion of the Tamil Liberation Tigers in Sri Lanka's inter-communal politics today.

These factors apparently persuaded the Tunku to carry on juggling compromises between Malay demands and non-Malay demands. His fine balancing act has earned the Tunku the sobriquet, "high priest of inter-racial harmony" from one Malay critic.[9] This is best seen, for instance, in his language policy. By delaying the implementation of Malay as the national language even past the deadline in 1967, he not only defied the Malay nationalists, but aroused their suspicions about his agenda. The "ultras" worked to bring about his downfall. In their eyes, he had again given the non-Malays more time to delay learning and accepting the Malay language. He was also seen as allaying their fears that they would not lose out in any advantages they might have attained from English education, as more non-Malays than Malays had been educated in English schools in the colonial period. The Malay nationalists' hostility towards the English language and English education stemmed from this period. Later on, when they achieved their goal of making Malay the national language under Tun Razak's administration, the teaching and standard of English suffered a serious decline for three decades until the administration of Dr Mahathir reversed the policy and strove to upgrade the level of English again in the national education system.

The Malay exclusivists' case against the Tunku has been well articulated by his erstwhile critic, Dato' Abdullah Ahmad, a former Deputy Minister in the second Prime Minister Tun Abdul Razak's administration:[10] "The Tengku [sic] when he first started [like Tun Razak and his successors] ... reasserted Malay nationalism to rally the Malays to his side against Dato' Onn. A lot of people blamed his advisers and sycophants for his lack of interest in enhancing the Malays after he was entrenched. This was said because he felt (and it was true) there were already enough laws which were pro-Malay. But it did not seem to occur to him that those laws had to be vigorously implemented to be meaningful. These laws were selectively implemented, which did not satisfy the Malays.... The general effect of his apparent lack of interest in the implementation of the Malay privileges was to reinforce Malay suspicion that he was partial to the Chinese. On the other hand, the Chinese, although they were unhappy with the apparent pro-Malay policies, never once seemed to attack the Tengku. He was personally above criticism but they attacked the government in no uncertain terms. This exasperated the Malays."

The Tunku also encountered "ultras" on the Chinese side. The Tunku and the MCA had branded them as "Chinese chauvinists", especially the Chinese education groups who had demanded Chinese as an official language and the retention of the Chinese school system. They had played a prominent part in the pre-independence negotiations between UMNO and the MCA in the formulation of the national educational policy. An indication of how seriously the Tunku's administration viewed this group was the action it took in 1961 to deprive the president of the United Chinese School Teachers' Association (UCSTA), Lim Lian Geok, of his citizenship.[11] In what is generally regarded as a benchmark case, the Government accused him of indulging in "deliberate misrepresentation and inversion of government education policy calculated to excite disaffection towards the Yang di Pertuan Agong" and of making "emotional appeals of an extreme communal nature calculated to provoke feelings of ill-will and hostility between different races in the Federation in a manner likely to cause violence".[12] On 19 August, 1963 the Registrar of Teachers in Selangor revoked Lim's registration as a teacher. As a citizen of Chinese descent, Lim was made an example of a dissident who had exceeded his limitations. Such citizens were reminded that while the Malays had a "special position" of privileges to enable them to improve and attain economic and social parity with the non-Malays, the non-Malays had only been progressively granted concessions to "Federal" citizenship, and hence to political life. But these concessions could not be abused, and could be revoked at any time. The government's action against Lim Lian Geok "turned the tide" and resulted in more Chinese schools opting for conversion to the government's national-type schools.[13]

Economic Development of the Nation, 1957–70

The national economic development policies of the Alliance Government had two major objectives: (a) to bring about economic prosperity, so that all the citizens could enjoy the benefits derived from it, and (b) to overcome the economic backwardness of the Malays, a moral duty to which every political party in the multi-ethnic Alliance Party had subscribed itself to. The constitutional contract obliged the government to improve the Malay share in the economy. They were committed to it, but decided that gains obtained by one group would not be at the expense of others. The priority of inter-communal redistribution, the uppermost objective of economic policy, was linked to the strategy of economic development, but, according to one observer in 1975, Karl Von Vorys,[14] the real test of economic policy remained its ability to reduce inter-communal income disparity between Malays and "non-Malays".

One problem was that allocations for this purpose from the National Budget in the 1955–60 period were somewhat limited, as other priorities competed for attention. In view of the state of Emergency, defence and internal security, for instance, consumed almost half of the total public expenditure. But the economy was carefully managed, the government opting for a balanced budget, so that little money could be spared for development until 1960. Fortunately, Malaya's economy did very well. "Malaya's finances were fundamentally sound and when compared to other countries in Asia, they were outright enviable", said Von Vorys. "Projections for 1955 called for a deficit of M$149 million, but in fact there proved to be a surplus of M$65 million. In 1956 the total national debt amounted to M$627 million (or 13 per cent of the GNP), and the Treasury could claim about M$365 million in available Surplus Balances".[15]

Despite Malaya's *First Five-Year Plan* (1956–60) being regarded as the "epitome of caution",[16] enough planning went into rural development to lay the infrastructure for its future take-off under the second five-year plan. One of the crucial measures taken was to deal with the urgent Malay problem of scarcity of agricultural land. Accordingly, a new government agency, the Federal Land Development Authority, at first known as FLDA and later FELDA, was created to assist the states in reclaiming large areas from the jungles and developing them as new Malay farming settlements. Specifically, during the *Second Five-Year Plan* (1961–65), some 145,000 acres were opened up as a result of FLDA operations, providing for a settlement of 12,000 families. The *First Malaysia Plan 1966–1970* was to carry the momentum further.[17] Under this scheme, FLDA planned to settle or resettle landless farmers, or those who were affected by fragmentation, or those who had insufficient land to meet their needs and who were consequently underemployed. The key architect behind the scheme was the Deputy Prime Minister, Dato' (later Tun) Abdul Razak, who before long had been allowed to create a Ministry of Rural Development, a portfolio which he held. As more funds were poured into this scheme, the FLDA operations became extremely successful in providing land to Malays.

But Malay critics felt that this scheme alone was insufficient to help rural Malays. They urged the Tunku's administration to carry out large-scale agrarian reforms to solve rural poverty. Rural Malays in non-FLDA schemes, according to the Malay economist Ungku Abdul Aziz, were in the clutches of private middlemen who were said to be mostly Indian or Chinese traders. Aziz said these traders lent the Malay farmers credit, became the buyers and sellers of their products, and controlled prices. He urged the government to cut out the private middlemen by performing their functions at cost, and pour in public investment in the rural economy. The farmer's incomes would thereby rise rapidly.[18] The government did not adopt his scheme, but one measure it adopted was to establish agricultural co-operatives to provide financial loans,[19] fertilizers, and marketing services to farmers. The Tunku's socialist-minded Minister for Agriculture, Aziz bin Ishak,[20] later had "Co-operatives" added to his portfolio. He then decided to go one step further to transform private (mostly Chinese) rice mills into co-operatives. He also pressed state governments to restrict milling licences to co-operatives. But the Tunku intervened and personally revoked a number of the Minister's initiatives which he regarded as violations of the Constitution. Not long after in 1962 Aziz bin Ishak was dismissed from the Cabinet. This came after his cheap urea fertilizer scheme for Malay farmers caused alarm to big Western firms like ICI and was criticized by the Tunku's

Chinese Minister for Finance, Tan Siew Sin.[21] Hence, by the late 1960s, the social and economic disparities between the rural and urban sectors of the economy had remained substantially unresolved.

Unequal Job Opportunities, 1957–70

Immediately after independence, the Alliance Government implemented its promise to replace expatriate (mostly British) officers in the civil service with suitably qualified citizens, at the same time maintaining a high standard of efficiency. By the 1960s most of the posts had been "Malayanized". They were filled initially by "non-Malays". The main problem to national unity was, therefore, the Malay sense of frustration at their disadvantaged position, *vis-à-vis* the "non-Malays" in terms of unequal employment opportunities in the government services. As a 1970 detailed comparative statistical study[22] has shown, the Chinese, for instance, occupied a superior position in administrative, managerial, professional and technical positions in the country's government services.[23] Overall, in 1968, the professional services were dominated by non-Malays, 90 per cent in medicine, 84 per cent in public works (engineering), 67 per cent in agriculture, and 68 per cent in education — just to name a few.[24] Even in other departments like Labour, Income Tax and Immigration, Chinese and Indians were over-represented. In the private labour force, the Chinese dominated in construction, commerce, mining and quarrying and in manufacturing.[25] Even in the subordinate levels of white collar employment in the clerical grades, a preponderant percentage of employees were Chinese and Indians with some secondary education in English, a privilege which very few Malays enjoyed.

But this trend could not go on indefinitely. In fact, as early as in 1952, the British authorities, realizing this racial inequality, had introduced a quota system for both Malays and non-Malays. The ratio of non-Malay Federal citizens who were admitted into the Malayan Civil Service was limited to "one for every four Malays". The quota system was introduced as one of the safeguards to ensure that "the special position of the Malays" would be retained in the Civil Service.[26] Consequently, in the early years, due to difficulties of recruiting adequately qualified Malays for posts in the professional and technical services, a lop-sided higher civil service existed: there was a concentration of Malays in the administrative and semi-professional service and a concentration of non-Malays in the professional and technical services. However, in 1970, it was found that in terms of the ownership of the national wealth, foreign interests owned the largest portion of the share capital — 60.7 per cent. The Chinese came next with 22.5 per cent, and the Malays and Indians had holdings of 1.9 per cent and 1.0 per cent respectively.[27] Chinese participation was highest in construction, then in transport, and next in commerce.

The racial imbalance in both the civil service and the private sector may be attributed to the Malays' low level of education. Different educational opportunities at the primary and educational levels for the various ethnic groups led to different results at the tertiary level. In 1967, nearly three-fourths of the university enrolment consisted of Chinese students, while the Malays only made up one-fourth.[28] No Malay secondary school existed in Malaya until 1957. Thus, not only were the Chinese and Indians ahead of the Malays in literacy in 1957, but the former ethnic groups also increased their lead during the period 1957 to 1970.[29] Malays in the rural areas also suffered high infant mortality and lower life expectancy than non-Malays in urban areas. In terms of mean household incomes, the average income of *rural* Chinese households was greater than the average income of *urban* Malay households, while ethnic and urban-rural distribution of household monthly income of less than Malayan $100, showed that the Malay poverty level was the highest.[30]

"Pluralism" in the Educational Policies, 1957–70

New directions in the administration's educational policies had aroused further suspicions of the "ultra-nationalist" Malay critics. The previous British policies on education had allowed for a "plural" system, i.e., Malays, Chinese and Indians had attended racially segregated schools using different language media, although they were allowed the choice to come together and attend any English-language school under one roof. But from an integrationist's point of view, it meant that apart from the English-language schools, the whole British system of education was racially divisive. It allowed for schools to exist racially and linguistically without "national schools", with a common curriculum, to integrate the students, build up a common national identity and bond a nation. Therefore, the policies of the Tunku's Minister for Education, Datuk (later Tun) Abdul Razak, were aimed at replacing these British policies and establishing a national education system, so that national unity could be fostered.

As a transitional move, Razak had allowed the colonial policy of multi-lingualism to continue temporarily in all the primary and secondary schools. This had come into force just before Malaya's independence. At the same time, to assuage Malay feelings, and to create national unity, Razak had taken the first step to elevate the Malay language to a position of importance in the primary schools. He made the Malay language a compulsory subject of study alongside the English language. This was in line with the government's intention to make Malay the National Language, the language of national unity, a policy that had been agreed to by the MCA and the MIC leaders. In the primary schools, knowledge of Malay was to be a compulsory requirement for admission to secondary schools that were wholly or partly run by public funds.

In the secondary schools, Razak also made both Malay and English compulsory subjects of study for the recently-introduced Lower Certificate of Education (LCE) and the National Certificate of Education, (the latter was later known as the Federation of Malaya Certificate of Education or FMCE). To satisfy the Chinese, he also allowed Mandarin (*Kuo Yu* — China's National Language) to continue to be used as the main medium of instruction in Chinese secondary schools. However, the content of their curriculum had to change and start reflecting independent Malaya's education syllabus. Prior to this, the topics and themes in Chinese school textbooks related to China's history and culture. But like in the English secondary schools, Chinese secondary schools had also to make Malay language a compulsory subject of study.

The Chinese community expressed mixed feelings about the Razak policies. About half of the Chinese secondary schools found them acceptable, although there were discordant voices from the Chinese School Teachers'

Association. The government's policies, however, angered the Malays. Some Malay legislators were particularly incensed that Malay was not made the sole medium of instruction in all schools. Answering these critics in the Legislative Council in 1956, [i.e., a year before Independence], the Minister for Commerce and Industry, Dr Ismail bin Dato Abdul Rahman, had said that such ambition was tantamount to posing as "imperialists with no considerations for the Chinese and Indians who are already in this country". Other legislators, mostly non-Malays, spoke in support of the Razak scheme, describing it as "a shining example of Malay liberalism" and as "a pattern for the weaving of what may in time truly become a virile Malayan culture".[31]

However, in the next 1959 general elections, the Tunku's administration yielded further to pressures from the MCA and the Chinese School Teachers' Association. He made an election promise to encourage and sustain the growth of the languages and cultures of the "non-Malay" races. He also agreed to recognize Chinese secondary school examinations results as equivalent to the government's Lower Certificate of Education (LCE) examinations. To fulfil these election promises, in February 1960, the Tunku's Alliance Government appointed a Committee under the new Minister for Education, Abdul Rahman bin Haji Talib, to review the Razak education policies. Its report said that there was still a long way to go before the ultimate objective of making the Malay language the national language could be fully realized. While allowing the system of multi-lingualism to continue in the primary schools, it recommended that only Malay or English should be used exclusively as the medium of instruction in secondary schools.

This latter recommendation again failed to satisfy the Malay critics, but this time it was also not welcomed by Chinese educational groups, including the Chinese School Teachers' Association. The latter saw this policy as threatening the very existence of Chinese secondary schools. These schools were required to conform to government policy and re-organize their structure of courses in such a way that their students who had completed their primary school education could move into a "Remove Class". This class was preparatory to their transfer to the first year of the national Malay or English-medium secondary schools. If they did not do so, these students would remain within their respective Chinese secondary schools, but these schools would not be supported by public funds, and their school certificates would not be recognized. Those Chinese secondary schools that converted to the national education system could no longer hold their own school examinations but would have to sit for the government's LCE and the FMCE examinations.

"Opponents of these proposals denounced the scheme as a calculated onslaught against the non-Malay languages and rejected them as a breach of the promises made by the Alliance on the eve of the 1959 general elections", commented one scholar, B. Simandjuntak (1969, p. 201), who went on to say: "Clearly it was technically inefficient to allow primary education to be carried on in one language and then to shift to another at the secondary level. But this seemed to be one of the dilemmas of Malaya's plural society, and only some form of racial compromise could provide an answer. Primary education in the mother tongue was a concession to the demand for free cultural development of each community, while secondary education in the two official languages [Malay and English], eventually solely in the Malay language, was intended to integrate the several communities and to promote a common Malayan outlook."

The Tunku's Alliance Government, having given way on multi-lingualism in the primary schools, felt it could not give way any further in the secondary schools, as it would undermine its objective of building a common national identity based on the Malay language. Most of the Abdul Rahman Talib committee's recommendations were accepted by the government and incorporated in the Education Act of 1961. As of 1962, free education was extended to all schools that received grants-in-aid from the government. There were minor changes over the years, but by and large the official policy embodied in the Education Act of 1961 has been held steadfastly to and constitutes the basis of the present national education system today — a legacy of the Tunku's administration. It is reaffirmed in Malaysia's Education Act of 1996, which incorporates all the changes in educational policies since 1961 as well as providing for new directions, including the establishment of private colleges and universities in the country, despite "ultra-nationalist" Malay opposition. Under the revised Education Act of 1996, the Minister for Education no longer has power to convert vernacular schools into national schools. The fourth Prime Minister

Datuk Seri Dr Mahathir Mohamed is on record as assuring the Chinese community that his government had no plans to close down any Chinese language schools, and that any such move would be against the law and if it made such a move, it could be taken to court. (*The Star*, 30 March 2002, p. 3; *New Straits Times*, 15 March 2002). Needless to say, when the Bill was presented, it aroused concern among Chinese opposition politicians and Chinese educational groups, but the MCA leaders in the government agreed to accept the government's assurances.

Inter-ethnic Tensions over the 1959 General Elections

As communal rivalries and tensions intensified, the Alliance Party began to lose influence and public support. This is best reflected in its dismal performance in both the June and August 1959 state and general elections respectively. Its policies of compromise and the contradictions between its "pluralism" and "Malay nationalism" policies had displeased many Malay voters, who accordingly gave their votes to the opposition PMIP. The internal challenges faced by the Alliance Party over how many candidates were to be allocated between the UMNO and the MCA also gave rise to inter-ethnic tensions. At one stage the Alliance came very near to dissolution. In the 1959 elections many non-Malay voters, particularly the Chinese, were so put off that they voted for other non-Malay parties like the Socialist Front and the predominantly-Chinese People's Progressive Party (PPP) of Ipoh.[32]

Unlike the 1955 elections, the elections of 1959 showed the Alliance suffered a tremendous loss of public support. In the state elections it won only 206 of the 282 constituencies contested. In the parliamentary elections it won 74 of the 104 seats contested. The PMIP won 13, the Socialist Front eight, the PPP four, the Party Negara led by Dato Onn Jaafar one, the Malayan Party one, while Independents won three. According to one detailed study of the 1959 election results,[33] "The most disturbing factor, however, was not the mere decline in popular support, but the fact that votes were largely lost to communal parties: the PMIP and the PPP. In 1955 the Alliance had won 79.6 per cent of the valid votes cast; in 1959 this was reduced to 51.5 per cent. The PMIP and the PPP, having won 3.9 per cent and 0.1 per cent respectively in 1955, now obtained 21.2 per cent and 6.4 per cent of the total vote." Altogether the Alliance polled just over 859,000 votes, which was just more than half the 1,583,000 votes cast, compared with nearly 320,000 for the PMIP, and 150,000 for the Socialist Front. The Alliance also lost control of the states of Kelantan and Terengganu to the PMIP.

Even before the elections, the Alliance was aware that the erosion of public support had started and that something had to be done. The Tunku had resigned temporarily from his office in April 1959 to prepare for the polls. Tun Razak had taken over as Prime Minister. According to one source, however, his resignation was due to "a spirit of dissension within the Alliance", over the allocation of seats for the three Alliance partners. UMNO wanted to have more candidates and reduce the number of MCA and MIC candidates, while these latter two parties had demanded a proportionate allocation of seats, now that registered Chinese and Indian voters had increased to 42 per cent.[34] In the 1955 general elections "non-Malay" voters had constituted only 10 per cent while 90 per cent were Malay voters.

At a meeting of the National Alliance Council, an arbitrary apportionment of the 104 constituencies was decided as follows: UMNO 74, MCA 28, and MIC two. But the central committee of the MCA at a stormy meeting refused to accept the decision and demanded instead that the MCA be given 40 seats. The MCA under its new president, Dr Lim Chong Eu, faced a revolt from some members of his central committee. The rebels included Yong Pung How, the MCA's Publicity Chief, who was reported in the Press as saying, "If we do not succeed in getting what we think is fair, the MCA Committee will on 12 July decide whether we fight under the Alliance banner or on our own." An angry Tunku regarded this as "an ultimatum" and a "stab in the back". He announced that the Alliance was prepared to go it alone and contest everyone of the 104 seats without Dr Lim Chong Eu's MCA. As the Tunku stood firm, one by one of the MCA "militants" resigned from the MCA. Finally, even Dr Lim Chong Eu stepped down from his office, allowing the "old guard" of Tun Tan Cheng Lock and his son, Tan Siew Sin, to return to the leadership and recapture the party.[35] By the middle of July, after further negotiations in the Alliance, the Tunku announced that the final distribution of candidates for the 1959 general elections was as follows: UMNO 69, MCA 32, and MIC 4. Thus, once again, a compromise was reached, for the sake of Malay-Chinese-Indian co-operation and peace and prosperity in the country.

The 1959 elections showed that the PMIP's appeals for a "Melayu" nationality, for a theocratic state based on the tenets of the Hadith and the *Qur'an*, and their resentment at the Alliance Government's inability to solve Malay rural economic backwardness had reflected the true feelings of large numbers of rural Malays. The newly-formed Party Negara of Datuk Onn Jaafar, which had been in the political wilderness since its defeat in the 1955 elections, also campaigned on largely Malay issues, and Datuk Onn won the party's only parliamentary seat in rural South Terengganu. Clearly, the backward eastern states of Kelantan and Terengganu did not support the Alliance's "pluralism" policy and its too generous citizenship terms to the "non-Malays".

On the other hand, the Socialist Front's calls for "equality for all" and the PPP's championing of Chinese rights apparently struck deep chords of "non-Malay" hearts. The PPP's two prominent Indian leaders, the brothers Seenivasagam D.R. and S.P., became Chinese "folk heroes" because they campaigned blatantly on Chinese dissatisfaction with the policies of the Alliance Government. Overall, the 1959 general elections showed a certain political maturity of the electorate and also that democracy worked. Political scientist K.J. Ratnam has stated that the Alliance Government deserved some credit for having facilitated the success of the electoral system. In spite of the communal divisions within its society, he observed that the Alliance had not resorted "to any electoral device aimed at ensuring some degree of communal representation". Since communal co-operation was the best way to maximize its own power, "it had every reason to want to make the system workable and realistic".[36] But this was probably the last general election in which it would allow for this free play of democratic forces. Thereafter, it would resort to constitutional gerrymandering of constituencies to ensure communal representation. An amendment in 1962 to the Constitution provided for rural weightage in the determination of electoral districts. As the majority of the rural population was Malay, this provision ensured a high representation of Malays in Parliament.[37]

The Formation of Malaysia: A New "Nation-State", 1961–63

The Tunku's second claim to greatness as nation-builder is the formation of the new enlarged federation of Malaysia comprising Malaya (a federation of 11 states), Singapore, Sarawak and North Borneo (later re-named Sabah).[38] Malaysia was inaugurated on 16 September 1963.[39] This brought together a total of 14 states comprising about nine million people. However, "Malaysia Day" or "Independence Day" is celebrated in the country on *31 August* and not on 16 September because Malaysia's inauguration was initially set for 31 August 1963, the Independence Day of the Federation of Malaya. But it was temporarily postponed to coincide with the announcement of the findings of the UN-conducted survey on whether the peoples of Sarawak and North Borneo wished to join Malaysia. The results were positive.

Malaysia is a fragmented multi-ethnic "nation-state". Not only is it fragmented geographically, but the multi-ethnic diversity of its population has presented problems of economic, social and political integration for the Federal Government. Largely because of some of these problems, predominantly-Chinese Singapore was separated from the federation on 9 August 1965. But its departure, however, was not followed by Sarawak and Sabah, although their separatist tendencies surfaced in the wake of Singapore's exit.

There are several reasons why Malaysia was formed. But the most significant from the viewpoint of the Tunku's administration was the ethnic factor. As the 1957 Census for Malaya had shown, the racial balance in Malaya was fairly equal between the Malays and the "non-Malays", but in the enlarged federation of Malaysia the Malays and "natives" of Malaya, Sarawak and Sabah would outnumber slightly the Chinese, Indians and other "non-natives" and "non-Malays". Sarawak had a population of 750,000 people, and North Borneo (later Sabah) 400,000. Singapore had 1.5 million people, of which the Chinese constituted 1.3 million. In Sarawak and Sabah, the Chinese and Malays were significant minorities. The majority of the people in Sarawak were the indigenous communities of Ibans (or Dayaks) and Bidayuhs, while the majority peoples in North Borneo were the indigenous Kadazan-Dusuns, and the rest were Muruts and Bajaus.

The Tunku had dropped his earlier opposition to merger with predominantly-Chinese Singapore and accepted it within Malaysia because the overall ethnic "indigenous" factor was now in the Malays' favour. In his memoirs, he said that, in a Malaya-Singapore merger, the Malays "might, without the protection of the Constitution, find themselves at a total loss in the only homeland they had. This might eventually mean trouble as an outcome. And who wanted that? ...Singapore *vis-à-vis* Malaya was not as simple as idealists might think."[40] Recalling the reasons given by the Tunku for rejecting merger, Lee Kuan Yew, in his memoirs, said that, to the Tunku, "...the political thinking in Singapore, like the racial make-up, was very different from that in the Federation, and the addition of the 1.3 million Chinese on the island would confuse Malayans and ruin the calm atmosphere there."[41]

Lee himself believed that "the Federation was anxious not to upset its own racial balance and it suspected that too many Singapore Chinese had communist sympathies".[42] The Tunku agreed that Singapore's security was being threatened by the communists who were creating problems for Lee's ruling People's Action Party (PAP). But he did not feel that Malaya should get involved in these problems. Lee, however, needed merger, if not Malaysia, for his own political survival. He wanted the Tunku's Government to take over responsibility for the island's security as he was reluctant to act against the communists who had supported the PAP and helped it come to power. According to the Tunku, Lee feared that "independence without merger would be disastrous, for an independent Singapore meant a Communist Singapore...."[43]

However, under the Malaysia plan, the Tunku's fears over Singapore's predominantly Chinese population would be allayed. The total population of the Malays and the "indigenous races" of Sarawak, North Borneo and Brunei (if it joined) would outnumber the Chinese. This ethnic factor is important in understanding why the Tunku agreed to form Malaysia. It shows how far-sighted he was in constructing a nation-state in which Malays and the "indigenous" races would predominate and ensure that the "indigenous" races were not swamped by the other races. Secondly, Malaya would expand its territorial area, and acquire valuable economic and mineral resources from the new member territories of Borneo, very much like what happened under the Melaka Sultanate in the 14th and 15th centuries. But in the end Brunei did not join Malaysia.

To show how much the ethnic Malay factor weighed on his mind, the Tunku later agreed to the "Maphilindo" concept temporarily. His role over this issue established him as a Malay nationalist at heart who has had to suppress his true sentiments as leader of a multi-racial society. During 1961–62, the Tunku, in order to overcome the opposition of both President Macapagal of the Philippines and President Sukarno of Indonesia to the Malaysia plan as a "British neo-colonial plot" to encircle both their territories, agreed to their proposal for a wider "Malay" confederation comprising the proposed Malaysian territories, the Philippines and Indonesia, called "Ma-phil-indo". Such a large Malay-based confederation would constitute a unity of the Malay world in Southeast Asia. This idea, however, raised concern among a few states in the Southeast Asian region, especially Thailand whose Foreign Minister, Thanat Khoman, opposed the idea. As Macapagal and Sukarno began to embellish the concept further, the Tunku had doubts about the feasibility of the project to construct "Ma-phil-indo", and quickly abandoned the idea. But this idea later inspired him to seek regional co-operation and join with other countries in the region to form, first, the Association of Southeast Asia (ASA) and, later, the Association of Southeast Asian Nations (ASEAN).

Initially, the charge that Malaysia was a "neo-colonial" plan seemed to have some validity in British diplomatic and imperial initiatives. Political progress in Singapore and Malaya was ahead of Sarawak and North Borneo, but the Malaysia plan accelerated political activity in the latter two territories, causing many new political parties to mushroom overnight. It revealed that Britain had been slow in encouraging the political and economic development of Sarawak and North Borneo in the past. The Malaysia plan would allow Britain to divest itself of the colonies of Singapore, Sarawak and North Borneo into the hands of the political leaders of Malaya, a "trusted" British Commonwealth member, which had gained independence earlier. Although attempts were made during the negotiations to convey the view that Malaysia would be an equal partnership of the four territories, it was undeniable that Malaya would dominate the new "nation state".

Apart from the British, the other strong supporters of the Malaysia plan were the political leaders of Singapore and Malaya. For their own reasons, they found it beneficial to work together to bring it about. Initially, the community and political leaders of Sarawak and North Borneo were opposed to Malaysia. They preferred to seek independence first for each of their respective territories, and then form a federation of North Borneo states, that would include Brunei. But, as the political leaders of Singapore and Malaya convinced them of the benefits of Malaysia, many were eventually won over.

Sarawak and North Borneo were promised and given a large measure of autonomy. For instance, they were given powers over immigration to allay their fears that they would be swamped by migrants from the other parts of the Malay peninsula. Even today visitors from the Malay peninsula who wish to enter these two territories still have to obtain separate visas. It was also agreed that the use of the Malay language as the National Language would be deferred for ten years, and until then English, already in use in Sarawak and North Borneo, would continue. Although Islam would be the religion of Malaysia, there were constitutional guarantees for the various ethnic groups in the two territories to have religious freedom. While education was a federal subject, Sarawak and North Borneo would be allowed some leeway in the states' educational administration, especially in the recruitment of local personnel. With regard to citizenship, those who were born, naturalized or registered in Sarawak and North Borneo and ordinarily resident in these territories when Malaysia came into being would become citizen by operation of law. The Federal Government agreed to allocate generous sums of capital for development. Sarawak, for instance, was promised M$300 million during the first five years after Malaysia Day.[44]

The Malaysian Parliament's total number of seats would increase to 159. Singapore, Sarawak and North Borneo, like the states in the Malay peninsula, would also transfer powers of defence and internal security into federal hands. Singapore would be given autonomy in education and labour and some freedom to administer economic matters. Like Sarawak and North Borneo, it was allowed to keep a substantial part of its state revenue for day-to-day administration to support various services. However, unlike Singapore, which was allotted 15 seats in Parliament, Sarawak and North Borneo despite their smaller populations, were given over-representation in the federal parliament: 24 MPs for North Borneo, and 16 for Sarawak.

When it came to the Constitution of Malaysia, the same provisions and guarantees of Malay special status as in Malaya's Constitution were extended to the "natives of Borneo". Islam would remain the official religion, the Yang Di-Pertuan Agong would be the constitutional monarch of the country and the Malay language would be the National Language of the country. The special status of the Malays as *bumiputra* (sons of the soil) was also extended to the "natives of Borneo". It would appear that like the previous Federation of Malaya, Malaysia had also been framed as a "Malay" nation-state legally and constitutionally. However, would the greater multiplicity of ethnic groups in this new federation challenge this concept? How would political integration now be achieved — on an ethnic Malay basis, or on a multi-ethnic basis?

Not only did the Tunku try to resolve these doubts gradually, but he felt that the formation of Malaysia was justified on political and economic grounds. When he first announced the Malaysia plan, "whereby these three territories can be brought closer together in political and economic co-operation" in his speech delivered to the Foreign Correspondents' Association of Southeast Asia in Singapore on 27 May 1961,[45] he had a vision of a nation-state that would achieve unity in diversity. Despite the odds that Malaysia faced, including Indonesia's "confrontation" against Malaysia and the Philippines' claim on North Borneo, Malaysia did survive, despite Singapore's exit some two and a half years later.

Looking back, it should be remembered that Malaysia was the name that UMNO had originally desired for the Malay peninsula when it secured independence from Britain on 31 August 1957. It was a sudden, unexpected creation brought about by Malaya, Britain, Singapore and the representatives of Sarawak and Sabah. Their political leaders had decided to place their faith in the Tunku's vision, leadership, and ability to make Malaysia a success.

The "Malaysian Malaysia" Campaign and Singapore's Exit, 1963–65

Besides the formation of Malaysia, the Tunku is also responsible for the decision on Singapore's departure from Malaysia. The Tunku's decision is described in Singapore's official version of the story as "expulsion", while some scholars have adopted terms like "separation" and "departure" to adopt a more objective approach to the issue. Despite Singapore's departure from Malaysia, one cannot but conclude that the Tunku's decision has enabled Malaysia to remain further within the mould of the "Malay nation-state" than when Singapore remained in Malaysia. It has also strengthened the peninsular Malays' control of Malaysian politics, especially in extending the Malay nationalist party UMNO's influence in the territories of Sarawak and Sabah. UMNO leaders in the Federal Government today have the Tunku to thank for this.

In the Singapore-Malaysia conflicts, the Tunku and his team matched the Singapore PAP leaders in the cut-and-thrust of politics. Having always been hesitant if not reluctant about merger with Singapore, Singapore's final departure from Malaysia did not constitute a serious loss to him. Before Malaysia was even inaugurated on 16 September, there were indications of future trouble ahead. On 31 August Lee Kuan Yew had personally declared Singapore's independence. He had refused to comply with the decision of the Malaysian Parliament to proclaim Malaysia on 16 September. Lee in his memoirs explained that Sarawak had already declared *de facto* independence and North Borneo had proclaimed the establishment of the state of Sabah. As these territories had assumed self-government in advance of merger, confiding federal powers in the interim to their respective governors, so in Singapore "all federal powers over defence and external affairs would be reposed in our Yang Di-Pertuan Negara who would hold them in trust for the central government".[46]

The Tunku's government and the British Government, however, did not agree with Lee's action. Lee was forced to brief angry British Ministers and officials about his move. Lee explained: "The Tunku and his colleagues believed that I had instigated the defiance of the North Borneo states in the face of his express wishes, because the week before, I had met the leaders of the Sabah and Sarawak Alliance in Jesselton [now renamed Kota Kinabalu]. Indeed I had urged them to do something dramatic on 31 August to prevent any further postponement."[47] This was, in fact, a violation of the Malaysia Agreement. Britain as the colonial power, however, decided to keep mum publicly on the matter, although in private correspondence British Ministers and officials had some nasty things to say about Lee.[48] But Lee and the Borneo states were allowed to get away with their actions.

The Tunku, however, was not to be outflanked. On the day of Malaysia's inauguration, he announced the appointment of two Bornean politicians to his Federal Cabinet. They were Temenggong Jugah anak Barieng as Minister for Sarawak Affairs and Peter Lo as Minister for Sabah Affairs.[49] But no Singapore leader was appointed to the Federal Cabinet. It was the unilateral proclamation on 31 August that probably caused this omission and started the thorny relationship between the Alliance Government and the PAP government, that eventually led to Singapore's exit from Malaysia. Lee was rebuffed, despite his desire to share power at the Federal level. Strangely, Lee makes no reference to this snub by the Tunku in his memoirs. Privately, however, Lee had made it known that he wanted to be in the Federal Cabinet, if not to displace the MCA, at least to be accepted as an equal partner. [50] Within the first six months of the formation of Malaysia, further differences flared up publicly between the PAP and Alliance leaders over a number of issues. These began with the general elections in Singapore on 21 September, five days after Malaysia was inaugurated. The PAP won 37 of the 51 seats in the Singapore Legislative Assembly, while 13 seats went to the left-wing Barisan Sosialis and one seat to another opposition party, the United People's Party. The Alliance Government had announced support for the Singapore Alliance candidates, followed by the Tunku personally arriving in Singapore to address an Alliance rally. This angered Lee and the PAP. The electoral defeat of all the Singapore Alliance's candidates was a severe blow to the Tunku. What riled the Tunku even more was that his own party, UMNO, did not win even a single seat. The day after the election, newspapers reported him as attacking the Malays who had voted for the PAP as "traitors". According to one source, "Failing even to congratulate Lee Kuan Yew on his party's electoral success, the Tunku instead warned that 'Singapore must appreciate that the political set-up of states on this side of (sic) of the Causeway is not the same as Singapore' ".[51] It was clear that the Singapore elections had sown the seeds of race politics between the two territories.

The Federal Government then dragged its feet over the proposed common market between Malaya and Singapore which had been agreed to in the Malaysia Agreement. The Tunku decided to get Lee out of the country. He appointed Lee to head a Malaysian delegation overseas to canvass support and recognition for Malaysia. It was not totally disadvantageous for Lee, who was allowed to build up his international image. But things came to a head when the PAP decided to participate in the April 1964 Malaysian general elections. The PAP opened several party branches in peninsular Malaya and fielded 11 candidates. The election results, according to Lee, "came as a shock".[52] The Alliance won 89 of the 104 seats contested, garnering 51.8 per cent of the votes. Every Alliance Minister had been returned with a bigger majority, while the PAP won only one seat. The resounding victory of the Alliance is believed to have been due to the Tunku's leadership and his call for patriotism and public support in the face of Sukarno's "Confrontation".

As the war of words went on between the Federal and Singapore leaders, inter-ethnic tensions rose in Singapore. In July of 1964 racial riots broke out in Singapore. Ninety-three people were killed, some six hundred injured and 1,700 were arrested.[53] Lee blamed UMNO's secretary-general, the late Syed Jaafar Albar, whom he labelled an "ultra" for having stoked up Malay feelings against the PAP government. UMNO, however, counter-charged that Lee's government was making Singapore "an Israel where Muslims are pressed down and suppressed". Police had discovered that, on the eve of the riots, leaflets signed by a so-called "Singapore Malay National Committee" had urged Malays to kill Chinese.[54] Although peace and calm returned, there was a second minor outbreak of racial violence in Singapore in September 1964.

It was a speech that Lee made in January 1965 that alarmed the Federal Malay Ministers and made them conclude that he was challenging the "special position" of the Malays. Lee was reported to have said that the Malays in Malaysia only constituted 40 per cent of the entire population and that they still retained strong feelings of closeness to the Sumatran, the Javanese and the Boyanese. According to one source, his statement was taken to mean that the Malays were a minority in Malaysia.[55]

This was followed on 8 May 1965 by a big opposition get-together comprising the PAP, the United Democratic Party led by Dr Lim Chong Eu of Penang, the PPP led by the Seenivasagam brothers in Perak, the Sarawak United People's Party and the United Pasok Momogun Kadazan Organisation — all "non-Malay" parties — which signed a declaration calling for a "Malaysian Malaysia" as follows:

A Malaysian Malaysia means that the state is not identified with the supremacy, well-being and interests of any one particular community or race. A Malaysian Malaysia is the antithesis of a Malay Malaysia, a Chinese Malaysia, a Dayak Malaysia, an Indian Malaysia or Kadazan Malaysia and so on. The special and legitimate interests of different communities must be secured and promoted within the framework of the collective rights, interests and responsibilities of all races.

This was the most serious threat ever to the framework of a "Malay nation-state". Thereafter there were calls by Malay leaders for the arrest and detention of Lee. His effigies were burnt at rallies. It was largely at that moment that the Tunku felt that the security situation in Malaysia was daily deteriorating that made him decide on Singapore's separation from Malaysia. On 7 August 1965 both parties signed the separation agreement. It was ratified at an emergency sitting of the Malaysian Parliament, which was hurriedly convened on 9 August 1965. In Singapore at a televised press conference on the same day, Lee said the separation was for him "a moment of anguish". He was so "emotionally affected" that he broke down, and the conference was terminated.

The 13 May 1969 Racial Riots and the Tunku's Departure

Not long after Singapore's exit, Indonesia underwent a *coup d'état* led by General Soeharto on 30 September 1965. This soon led to President Sukarno's overthrow and began the end of Indonesia's "Confrontation" against Malaysia. Malaysia and Indonesia normalized relations. Indonesia thereby formally recognized the existence of Malaysia, which President Sukarno had refused to do. The Philippines' opposition to Malaysia also abated after President Marcos took office in early 1966. He, too, began to drop the Philippines' claim to Sabah. Thereafter, Malaysia was relatively at peace with her neighbours.

Internally, however, the repercussions of Singapore's separation still took a while to abate in Malaysia, especially as Sarawak and Sabah leaders were not happy at the way the Tunku had handled Singapore's exit. They criticized the Tunku for failing to consult them and expressed fears that their own states' autonomy would be undermined. In 1965 owing to serious disagreements between the federal and the Sarawak state government, the Tunku engineered the removal of the Sabah Chief Minister, Donald Stephens. It was believed that the latter had sought greater autonomy for his state, and that his dismissal was related to his alleged intrigues with remaining expatriate British officers in Sabah. In 1966 the Chief Minister of Sarawak, Stephen Kalong Ningkan, was also removed for expressing dissatisfaction at the Federal Government's intervention in the state's autonomy. Clearly, the Federal Government's actions were motivated by fear that the two territories might follow Singapore's path.

In 1967 as the country approached its tenth-year anniversary of independence when Malay would officially be made the National Language, both Malay and non-Malay groups began to put pressure on the Tunku's administration. One Chinese educational group, the United Chinese School Committees' Association (UCSCA) asked the government to establish a Chinese-language university known as the Merdeka University. The opposition DAP supported it. The idea was initially supported by MCA leaders, such as T.H. Tan and Khaw Kai Boh, and later reluctantly "endorsed" by its president, Tun Tan Siew Sin. But Tun Tan feared Malay resentment and thought it might trigger Malay chauvinist demands.[56]

True enough, Malay groups demanded that the government should begin implementing fully Malay as the National Language. Various teachers' unions, national writers' associations and lobbies, such as the University of Malaya's powerful Malay Language Society started their campaign to urge the government not to compromise on the issue. A National Language Action Committee to co-ordinate nation-wide activities was formed under the leadership of Syed Nasir bin Ismail, the director of the Dewan Bahasa dan Pustaka (Council for Language and Culture). The agency itself had been holding month-long and six-month-long National Language rallies and parades and publicity in the media to promote support for its cause.

But apparently Syed Nasir, an UMNO member, went too far, in the eyes of some party officials. In October 1967 he began criticizing the use of Chinese characters on signboards of shops and business firms.[57] A fortnight later he followed this up with a confidential 13-page memorandum which he sent to the Prime Minister, the Deputy Prime Minister, all Cabinet Ministers, all *Mentri Besar* (state Chief Ministers) and all members of the UMNO Executive Council, "somewhat reminiscent", according to one source, "of the pronouncements of the [expelled] Aziz bin Ishak".[58] The memorandum criticized the government's policies to accommodate the Chinese and accused it of sidelining the Malay language:[59]

> For the importance of national unity and racial harmony, the Malays who are the sons of the soil (*bumiputra*), have agreed to compromise with non-*bumiputra*, especially the Chinese, on the question of their language, one of their few remaining properties. They agreed to compromise and allow citizenship rights to these non-Malays and agree to uphold the status of the Chinese language and other non-official languages, where the question of compromise need not arise at all, because, ... the question of Malay becoming the National

language and the official language of this country is a logical fact and a right of the language.

After independence what do we see? Not only is the status of Chinese preserved, it is now more widespread than before Independence....

There was some disagreement as to the wisdom of the timing of Syed Nasir's criticisms. Among the allies of Syed Nasir were Dr Mahathir Mohamed, Dato Harun Idris, the *Mentri Besar* of Selangor and Abdul Rahman bin Yaakub, Minister for Lands and Mines. But the Tunku would not allow Syed Nasir to destabilize the situation. He had decided not to make further concessions to the Malays on the language issue, but was more concerned that the MCA would become "vulnerable to charges by the Chinese communal elements of having sold out to the Malays". The Tunku, therefore, decided that the form of the National Language Bill was to be "balanced". "While it would in any case grant a slight edge to the Malays by reinterpreting the ten-year minimum to that of a maximum provision, the previously accepted protection of secondary languages also would have to be restated," said von Vorys.[60] In this regard, the Tunku was supported by his deputy, Tun Razak, and Dato (later Tun) Dr Ismail. "Tun Dr Ismail, who was about to retire on grounds of ill-health, spoke in favour of Tunku's Act. When the debate ended, Syed Nasir and some of his closest supporters, Dato' Harun Idris, Dr Mahathir Mohamad and Abdul Rahman Yaakub preferred to be absent," says the Tunku's biographer.[61] After the Bill passed through Parliament, Syed Nasir was told to leave government service. But following intervention by Tun Razak, he was allowed to apologize to the Prime Minister and resign from UMNO'S Executive Council. "Thus, Syed Nasir, the Malay folk hero, was permitted to remain in the party and for some time retain his post in the *Dewan Bahasa dan Pustaka*," observed von Vorys. "Unlike Aziz bin Ishak, he had made his point and managed to survive."[62] Another scholar interpreted his fate as follows: "... the UMNO leadership disciplined Syed Nasir for his outspoken and embarrassing criticism of the government's bill by removing him from his position in the party's executive council".[63] However, according to the Tunku's biographer, this problem did not end and had unforeseen consequences because "Malay opposition to the Act continued to weaken the support of school teachers for the Alliance with grave results in the 1969 elections".[64]

On the National Language Bill, the Tunku had gone to the rescue of the MCA which had asked for a "more liberal use" of the Chinese language in government notices, forms, signboards and announcements. The Tunku agreed that an Alliance Committee would be established to resolve disputes and "to solve the language problem". In the end, the National Language Act further delayed the "full" and wider use of Malay as the national language. Most Malays received this news with great disappointment. The delay allowed English to be used in translation of official government documents for "such purposes as may be deemed necessary in the public interest". This meant it would continue to be used in government departments, the law courts and even in Parliament and in state legislatures. Many Malays saw these as further concessions to the "non-Malays".

The Malaysian general elections in 1969 brought all these latent inter-ethnic tensions into the open. When the election results were announced, the Alliance won only 66 of the 104 seats in West Malaysia, polling only 48.1 per cent of the total votes. It thereby lost two-thirds of its majority for the first time. Several Alliance Ministers and even UMNO stalwarts like Dr Mahathir Mohamed lost their seats. Dr Mahathir lost to a PAS candidate. During his campaign it was reported he had asked the Chinese in his constituency not to vote for him, as he would not represent their interests in Parliament.[65] The opposition parties not only increased their votes but won the biggest number of seats ever since 1955 — the Democratic Action Party won 13, PAS 12, PPP four and Gerakan eight. In the state-level elections, the Alliance swept five states but in four others suffered serious setbacks. It did not secure a majority in the Selangor and Perak state assemblies, and it also lost control of the state of Penang to the Gerakan Rakyat Malaysia and the state of Kelantan to PAS. Two days after the results were announced, inter-racial riots broke out in various parts of the country.

The Tunku's strategies of nation-building, of accommodation and compromise had met with a serious setback. First, by pleasing the Malays, and then the "non-Malays", he had hoped to satisfy both Malays and non-Malays. But each group had felt even more dissatisfied. The riots have been attributed to many causes, but the most important was Malay dissatisfaction over "non-Malay" threats and challenges to Malay rights and Malay political primacy. The MCA's withdrawal from the Alliance Government was also an indirect cause. The MCA had done so because 20 out of its 33 candidates had been defeated, but many Malays saw this as an act of betrayal of UMNO in the Alliance. The MCA president, Tun Tan Siew Sin, was largely held responsible for this decision done ironically to "punish" the Chinese voters. Instead his decision raised serious implications for the constitutional contract. According to one observer, "By implication, this move raised the spectre of no-bargaining mechanisms being in place in the new government."[66] The *Mentri Besar* of Selangor, Dato Harun Idris, had called for a pro-government demonstration to counter opposition party celebrations on the evening of 13 May 1969. The area near his residence was one of the first areas where armed Malay gangs first gathered and violence broke out. The government's official report said he had lost control of the situation. Despite the imposition of curfews and the intervention of the military, killings, arson and looting continued for two days in Kuala Lumpur city. Disturbances also spread to various parts of the country.

However, following the declaration of an Emergency by the *Yang Di-Pertuan Agong*, who also suspended the Malaysian Parliament, the rioting subsided. Although the government tally put those who were killed at 178, journalists had reported that it was higher. To deal with the situation the government established a National Operations Council under the directorship of the Deputy Prime Minister, Tun Abdul Razak. It ruled jointly with the Cabinet under the Tunku, but all power in reality rested with Tun Razak.

The riots led to mounting criticisms of the Tunku's rule. Leading the attacks on the Tunku were those branded as "ultras". They included Dr Mahathir bin Mohamed. Malay student groups led by a charismatic leader Anwar Ibrahim burnt effigies of the Tunku. Perhaps the crisis within UMNO best reflects the orchestrated Malay criticisms and opposition towards the Tunku. One incident involved Dr Mahathir and led to his dismissal from the UMNO Executive Council and later from the party. On 5 June the Malay newspaper *Utusan Melayu* had published a joint letter by Dr Mahathir, Syed Nasir and Dato Syed Albar Jaafar, advocating the continued exclusion of the MCA from the government. Within the same day the Tunku had written each of them a letter, advising them to restrain themselves from issuing such statements which could worsen the situation in the country. Syed Nasir and Dato Syed Albar decided to pay heed to the advice, especially Syed Nasir who had earlier been disciplined for his stand on the national language issue. But Dr Mahathir decided to proceed further by replying to the Tunku.[67] It was the public circulation of his letter to the Tunku which led to his expulsion from the UMNO later on. Dr Mahathir's reply was later regarded by the UMNO Executive Council as "offensive", although it claimed to reflect the mood of the Malays. Dr Mahathir said that the Malays "hated" the Tunku, accused him of pandering to the Chinese, blamed him for the riots and urged him to resign.[68]

The Tunku was "deeply wounded by this personal attack, but apart from sending a copy of the letter to Tun Razak "for such action as he thought fit", he took no other action.[69] Dr Mahathir's letter was soon leaked to the public. "Thousands of copies were later cyclostyled and distributed all over the peninsula by others", claims the Tunku's authorized biography.[70] When this was discovered, Dr Mahathir denied that he had released it, but the damage had been done. The majority of the UMNO Executive Council, including Tun Razak and Dr Ismail, closed ranks behind the Tunku. "Tunku's senior colleagues were staunchly loyal and supportive. Tun Abdul Razak, although recognized as Tunku's heir apparent, made it known that Tunku must be allowed to decide for himself if or when he wished to retire," says the Tunku's biographer. "To Tunku, retirement, at this crucial instant, would be tantamount to abdication at a time of the gravest crisis the nation had ever experienced."[71]

Dr Mahathir was summoned before the UMNO Council, which was presided by Tun Razak. The Tunku decided to stay away. After presenting his case, Dr Mahathir left the meeting. Twenty-two members of the Council voted for his expulsion, while five members dissented. The government then banned Dr Mahathir's letter. Dr Mahathir's expulsion was followed by anti-Tunku student demonstrations in the campus. Soon after, the Tunku also sacked Musa Hitam, Tun Razak's Assistant Minister. As the UMNO opposition petered out, the Tunku began to be back in control.

However, a year later when the situation had returned to normalcy, the Tunku decided to step down from office. The decision was partly due to his decision to come to terms with Malay dissatisfaction with his rule, partly because King Faisal of Saudi Arabia offered him the prestigious post of Secretary-General of the Islamic Secretariat in Jeddah, and partly precipitated by the pending assumption of his nephew as the next *Yang Di-Pertuan Agong*, a prospect he did not cherish as he did not think it proper that as the latter's uncle he should remain as Prime Minister.[72]

Malay criticisms of the Tunku's policies centred around the main charge that he was "pro-Chinese".[73] "Non-Malay" criticisms of the Tunku were more muted.

The Making of a "Multi-Racial" or "Plural" Nation

Several social, economic and political forces were at work towards the integration of a multi-racial nation during this period. The Tunku's Alliance administration, while a major player in nation-building, had to compete with other players in resolving issues such as: What kind of a nation-state was to be formed? How much would political ideology, ethnicity, language, and religion play in the formation of nationhood? Was the state to be a just, equal and civil society? Would the Rule of Law be upheld?

Had a nation, a strong spirit of nationalism or an identifiable national identity emerged by the end of the Tunku's administration? It is not necessary to assume that there must be a consensus of all the parties and social groups on these issues before accepting the reality of a nation or a nation-state. A nation or nation-state is not something fixed or permanent, but one which is constantly evolving and changing. State formation is always in a state of flux. Although the Alliance Party won a landslide victory in the 1955 general elections, this did not mean that it had a monopoly of ideas on how to make a nation. However, its policies were certainly crucial in setting the agenda for nationhood to which various groups had to respond to.

The Tunku as the "Founding Father of the Nation"

The Tunku's claim to be "Father of Malaya's Independence" (*Bapa Malaya*) and "Father of Malaysia's Independence" (*Bapa Malaysia*) is generally accepted throughout the country, even by his severest critics.[74] He was also responsible for giving the country its National Anthem, National Flag and National Flower (Hibiscus). As his erstwhile critic has said, ".... he was 'Bapa Kemerdekaan' (Father of Independence) and the creator of Malaysia and whose personification was clearly reflected in the nation's policies."[75] The former Deputy Prime Minister, the late Tun Dr Ismail, has described the Tunku in his yet unpublished memoirs as "the personification of Malaya and Malaysia".[76] The best testimony of his great standing with the people and of how much they loved him was seen on the occasion of his death in 1992. There was an unprecedented outpouring of grief from people of all ethnic groups and all walks of life, from the ordinary man-in-the street to the sultan.

As the country's first Prime Minister, the Tunku set the pattern of administration for future Prime Ministers. The early years of Malaya's independence were crucial, fragile years, but the Tunku achieved political stability and multi-racial harmony, which were essential for the country's survival, until 1969 when the bloody inter-racial riots broke out. His Alliance government had been based on compromise, consensus and reciprocity. As one writer has observed, "the essence of Alliance bargaining was not equality but mutual dependency combined with a willingness to cooperate and accommodate".[77]

One of the ways by which he promoted national unity and national identity was to blend both Tradition and Modernity. He was not a reformer. Coming from a royal background, with a rich cultural tradition, he had a great respect for culture and customs, which he felt should be incorporated within the country's national identity. On the other hand, he was also a modernist in his ideas of government, democracy and education for nationhood. As a royalist, however, he believed the Malay monarchy was a unifying factor of all races and attempted to inculcate non-Malay loyalties to the Malay monarchs. The Tunku, however, had a common touch. He never allowed his royal background to stand in the way of his relationship with the ordinary people.

The Tunku was élitist in a traditional sort of way, like a patrician, who saw society as hierarchical. While he welcomed political participation by the lower strata of society as part of modernization and democracy, he himself still believed in a ruling class characterized by wealth, high status and high office. The left-wing Labour Party of Malaya described his government in 1956 as "mainly a Party of Privilege", who "by subtle and skilful propaganda, have led the Malay masses to believe that their interests are identical with those of the Malay Royalty and Ruling Classes". He was greatly opposed to the Labour Party's socialist ideology, to class conflict, or to any of its proposals for nationalization of industries and calls for "equality of rights". Fear of this socialist ideology caused him to dismiss one of his Cabinet colleagues, the socialist-inclined Aziz Ishak, who was Minister for Agriculture, when the latter tried to set up a scheme by which agricultural co-operatives would produce cheaper urea fertilizers for peasant cultivators. He feared that such a move would frighten foreign capital away. The Tunku's Alliance government was not only anti-communist, but also supportive of foreign capital which it needed in its industrialization programmes. Consequently, his government provoked the ire of left-wing political parties. In the international communist press, and especially over Radio Peking, his government was often described as comprising "feudalists and compradore capitalists".

The Tunku's transformation from a Malay exclusivist to that of a multi-racial inclusivist was due to his consciousness that as the Prime Minister of a multi-racial country, he could no longer just represent his UMNO party or the Malays but that of the whole multi-racial society, the majority of whom had chosen the Alliance Party to lead them. He, therefore, had to distance himself from the exclusivist faction in UMNO. This faction was bound always to be present. It would challenge his policies, if he deviated or neglected Malay demands; it would press for the strengthening of a Malay national identity, a Malay national culture and a Malay nation-state. The Tunku could not ignore this faction totally. He would have to accommodate their demands, wherever possible or whenever he felt that their position or their pressures were getting stronger. And, in the end, it was this faction that was responsible for expediting his retirement from office in 1970.

As the Tunku's erstwhile critic, Dato' Abdullah Ahmad, has recalled, "The Tengku [sic] ....had to walk a 'political tightrope and achieved up to a point, what had seemed an impossible thing to do, that of defending crucial Malay rights while simultaneously maintaining co-operation with the non-Malays.... He was... a friendly and generous man with a multi-racial image: a good mediator among competing races. He wanted Malay political dominance without submerging the other races; this brought him success for 14 years but this 'formula' failed him in 1964 (though the political and racial casualties came only in 1969). He attained success and racial harmony at first because the demands being articulated by the leaders of the various races were not so competitive or intense that they could not be accommodated until the Singapore leaders taught the non-Malays in Malaysia how to fight the Malays politically."[78]

Tunku's Inclusivist Pluralism

The Tunku in his early years of administration did attempt to evoke or formulate national integration through multi-racial co-operation. He attempted to inculcate loyalty to the nation-state by promoting the Malay king, the *Yang Di-Pertuan Agong*, as the king of a multi-racial nation, Malay as the national language, religious tolerance and the use of Mandarin and Tamil languages in primary schools and in private use. His agenda of nationalism was simple: each race should cultivate its own culture and try and mingle not only in the market-place, but also in several "national activities" such as sports, especially soccer and badminton, as well as participate in each other's cultural activities like the Hari Raya, Chinese New Year, Thaipusam and Christmas festivals, which were all declared as national holidays.

In the interests of sports, quite early in his administration he built the Merdeka Stadium — "the massive edifice of concrete and steel", at a great cost of public expenditure, and which served as the "centre-piece during the Independence celebrations".[79] A sportsman in his youth, the Tunku took up golf later in life; he was a horse-racer, but soccer was always his first love. The Tunku believed that when the people supported their home team in a national tournament, they would display their national unity and loyalty and forget their racial differences. Through sports, he tested national loyalty. In the early years, however, it was not always certain, during the annual *Merdeka* (Independence) soccer competitions, that the "true" loyalties were forthcoming. However, the Tunku himself ensured that he never failed to support these functions and, if possible, showed up in person at the games.

On such occasions, whether the local team won or loss, the Tunku was present to share the crucial moments with the local crowds. He is on record as saying that he preferred these activities to making rhetorical speeches and appeals to nationalist sentiments, like President Sukarno of Indonesia, who was famous for his fiery oratory. In contrast, the Tunku's speeches were always brief, monotonous, rambling and delivered with a drawl. Yet he lacked any pretensions. The people were comfortable with his simple and down-to-earth attitude.

In one of his memoirs, published in 1978, the Tunku recalled, "When I was being fair and impartial, Malay 'ultras' accused me of being pro-Chinese. Dr Mahathir, the new Deputy Prime Minister, was one of them, so the Chinese are now sceptical of his feelings towards them, hence the wild speculation on his attitude towards others. But those were popular words to gain the popular support of hot-headed youths in days gone by.... As he himself has said in a television interview, he is being labelled an 'ultra-nationalist' by his political foes. He has stressed that he will clean his image. Let him prove his words, for he knows full well that the peace and security of our country hang completely on Sino-Malay understanding and friendship."[80]

Like the Tunku, Dr Mahathir, too, tried to juggle between "pro-Malay" and "pro-Chinese" policies.

NOTES

1 See the end of millennium survey of Malaysia's four Prime Ministers in the Malay newspaper, *Utusan Malaysia,* 31 December 1999, p. 25. The Prime Ministers were described as follows: Tunku Abdul Rahman *Bapa Kemerdekaan* (Father of Independence), Tun Abdul Razak Hussein *Bapa Pembangunan* (Father of Development), Tun Hussein Onn *Bapa Perpaduan* (Father of Solidarity), and Datuk Seri Dr Mahathir Mohamad *Bapa Pemodenan* (Father of Modernization).

2 Cynthia H. Enloe, *Multi-Ethnic Politics: The Case of Malaysia,* Research Monograph Series, Centre for South and Southeast Asia Studies, University of California, Berkeley, California, August 1970, p. 1.

3 *Ibid.,* p. 35.

4 Reinhard Bendix, *Nation-Building and Citizenship* (Berkeley: University of California Press, 1964), pp. 89–90. He cites T.H. Marshall's *Citizenship and Social Class* and summarizes the latter's threefold typology of rights of citizenship as follows: "- *civil* rights such as 'liberty of person, freedom of speech, thought and faith, the right to own property and to conclude valid contracts, and the right to justice'; - *political* rights such as the franchise and the right of access to public office; - *social* rights ranging from 'the right to a modicum of economic welfare and security to the right to share to the full in the social heritage and to live the life of a civilized being according to the standards prevailing in the society'." See Bendix, *ibid.,* p. 92. The essay referred to is reprinted in T.H. Marshall, *Class, Citizenship and Social Development* (New York: Doubleday & Co., 1964), pp. 71–72.

5 Dato' Abdullah Ahmad, *Tengku Abdul Rahman and Malaysia's Foreign Policy, 1963–1970* (Kuala Lumpur: Berita Publishing Sdn. Bhd, 1985), pp. 21–22. In this chapter, I shall use this work to represent the views of of the Malay "exclusivist" group, whom the Tunku later identified as "ultras" identical to the term which was used earlier by Singapore leader, Lee Kuan Yew, who also faced criticisms from this group after he brought Singapore into Malaysia from 1963 to 1965. Individuals who were later identified as 'ultras' by both the Tunku and Lee were Dato Syed Nasir Ismail, Dato Syed Jaafar Albar, Dr Mahathir Mohammed and a young student leader named Anwar Ibrahim. Their names will crop up again later in this and other chapters.

6 K.J. Ratnam, *Communalism and the Political Process in Malaya* (Kuala Lumpur: University of Malaya Press, 1967), p. 1.

7 See the interesting discussion of the negotiations in Tan Liok Ee, *The Politics of Chinese Education in Malaya* (Shah Alam: Oxford University Press, 1996).

8 The official termination was not only for political reasons to score a psychological victory over the communists, but was also necessitated by economic and

commercial considerations. For instance, insurance companies had different policies and premiums to cover situations like "emergency," "war" or "peacetime" periods. One of the reasons the period was called an "emergency" and not "war" was due to such considerations.

9   Dato' Abdullah Ahmad, *Tengku Abdul Rahman's Foreign Policy*, p. 18.

10 *Ibid.*, pp. 23–24.

11 For personal details of Lim Lian Geok and his role, see Tan Liok Ee, "Descent and Identity: The Different Paths of Tan Cheng Lock, Tan Kah Kee and Lim Lian Geok", *Journal of the Malaysian Branch of the Royal Asiatic Society* LXVII, Part I (1995); see also Tan Liok Ee, *The Politics of Chinese Education in Malaya, 1945–1965* (Kuala Lumpur: Oxford University Press, 1995), p. 273.

12 See Visu Sinnadurai, "The Citizenship Laws of Malaysia", in *The Constitution of Malaysia: Its Development, 1957–1977*, ed. Tun Mohamed Suffian et al. (Kuala Lumpur: Oxford University Press, 1978), pp. 68–100.

13 Tan Liok Ee, *The Politics of Chinese Education in Malaya*, p. 273.

14 Karl von Vorys, *Democracy without Consensus: Communalism and Political Stability in Malaysia* (Princeton, New Jersey: Princeton University Press, 1975), p. 217. Von Vorys' book was "prohibited" from sale and distribution by the Malaysian Government for its daring disclosure of the views of UMNO dissidents and critics of the Tunku, whose statements and criticisms of government policies in the wake of the 13 May 1969 inter-racial riots were fully reported and commented upon. Some of these documents were banned by the government. The "prohibition" has given it an unfair reputation, but it is generally a well-balanced and critical account — in fact, it is one of the best academic accounts — on the 13 May 1969 riots. Von Vorys had taught for a while at the Economics Faculty of the University of Malaya in Kuala Lumpur. The prohibition meant that his book could not be imported but did not mean it could not be read or owned individually. A list of such "prohibited" books is available in most Malaysian university libraries, but permission to use them has to be obtained first from the relevant authorities, usually from a head of a university department.

15 *Ibid.*, p. 221.

16 *Ibid.*

17 *First Malaysia Plan 1966–1970*, p. 103, cited in von Vorys, *Democracy without Consensus*, p. 231.

18 See the arguments presented in *ibid.*, pp. 227–39. See also Ungku Abdul Aziz, "Who Will End This Rural Poverty?" *Straits Times*, 16 October 1963. With regard to middlemen, von Vorys states: "With respect to the racial composition of middlemen, perhaps the key element in the economic control of the rural sector, no definitive and comprehensive data were available. They continued to form

a mixed group of money-lenders, shop-keepers, landlords, merchants, and others. One authority, Mokhzani bin Rahim, however, estimated that no more than 30 per cent were Malays. Among the money-lenders, for example, the Indians formed a heavy majority, 1,471 out of 2,001 officially listed by the government in the spring of 1969. There were also 496 Chinese and 1 Malay."

19 Ungku Abdul Aziz, "Co-operative the Key to Rural Success", *Straits Times*, 17 October 1963. Cited in B. Simandjuntak, *Malayan Federalism, 1945–1963*, p. 242.

20 The Tunku's friendship with Aziz bin Ishak began long before they were Cabinet colleagues in the Alliance Government. Aziz was a well-known journalist who wrote the first biography of the Tunku.

21 *Ibid.*, p. 230. According to one source, following his dismissal from his cabinet post in 1962 and from UMNO in 1963, Aziz formed a left-wing party, Parti Perhimpunan Kebangsaan or National Convention Party (NCP). "Its avowed objective was to organize a so-called 'Malay left', composed of the poorest peasants, the most insecure fishermen, and other discontented rural dwellers as part of a left of centre coalition to oppose the Alliance." See B. Simandjuntak, *Malayan Federalism, 1945–1963*, p. 117.

22 J.E. Jayasuriya, *Dynamics of Nation Building in Malaysia* (Colombo: Associated Educational Publishers, 1983), pp. 75–88.

23 Based on *General Report. Population Census of Malaysia, 1970*, Vol. 1, Kuala Lumpur, 1977. Adapted from Table 7.15a, in Jayasuriya, *ibid.*, pp. 81–82.

24 Based on Milton J. Esman, *Administration and Development in Malaysia* (Ithaca: Cornell University Press, 1972). Table 5, cited in Jayasuriya, *ibid.*, p. 83. Von Vorys makes the same point with some interesting figures and notes the impressive performance of Indians in relation to Malays: "Shortly before the 1969 general elections, medical practitioners included 65 Malays, 808 Chinese, 771 Indians, and 249 others, presumably mostly Europeans. The total number of West Malaysian lawyers [i.e., in Malaya] included 92 Malays, 241 Chinese, 190 Indians, and 47 others. Incidentally some 67 of the Malays but only 14 of the Chinese were in the government's legal service. And the last item: the racial background of the University of Malaya teaching staff in 1969 included 51 Malays, 143 Chinese, 75 Indians, and 199 others." See von Vorys, *ibid.*, p. 244.

25 Based on *General Report. Population Census of Malaysia*. Kuala Lumpur, 1970, Table 7.12 (a), cited in Jayasuriya, *ibid.*, p. 81.

26 See Mavis Puthucheary, *The Politics of Administration: The Malaysian Experience* (Kuala Lumpur: Oxford University Press, 1978), p. 53. The quota system was introduced by General Gerald Templer, the British High Commissioner at this time.

27 Based on *Mid-Term Review of the Second Malaysia Plan, 1971–1975* (Kuala Lumpur, 1973). Table 4.7, cited in Jayasuriya, *ibid.*, pp. 87–88. With regard to ownership of banks, von Vorys observes: "Among the commercial banks registered in 1965 twenty-two were foreign, including seven European and three American, three Indian, and one Pakistani....There were also sixteen Malaysian banks: all but the state subsidized Bank Bumiputra were in Chinese hands (three of them with substantial Singapore capital)." See von Vorys, *Democracy without Consensus*, pp. 242–43.

28 Based on Howard Hayden, ed., *Higher Education and Development in South-east Asia*, Vol. 2 (Paris, 1967), extracted from Tables 24 and 25, cited in Jayasuriya, *ibid.*, pp. 79–80.

29 Based on Malaysia. *General Report. Population Census of Malaysia 1970*, Vol. 1 (Kuala Lumpur, 1977). Table 4.8, cited in Jayasuriya, *ibid.*, pp. 77–78.

30 Based on Malaysia. *Mid-Term Review of the Second Malaysia Plan, 1971–1975.* (Kuala Lumpur, 1973). Table 1.2, cited in Jayasuriya, *ibid.*, pp. 85–86.

31 B. Simandjuntak, *Malayan Federalism, 1945–1963* (Kuala Lumpur: Oxford University Press, 1969), p. 201.

32 This party was formed in Ipoh and fared badly in the 1955 general elections. The party's secretary-general in 1955 was D.R. Seenivasagam, a lawyer. He was elected to the Ipoh and Menglembu Town Council in 1954, but lost his deposit in that constituency in the 1955 general elections. However, at the by-election held there in 1956 he won the seat. In the 1959 general elections, he and his brother S.P. Seenivasagam were elected with big majorities in the Ipoh and Menglembu constituencies, each of which had a predominantly Chinese electorate. Due to their support of Chinese issues, they continued to be elected MPs of these two constituencies for several more terms. For biographical details of D.R. Seenivasagam, see K.J. Ratnam, *Communalism and the Political Process in Malaya*, p. 229.

33 K.J. Ratnam, *Communalism and the Political Process in Malaya* (Kuala Lumpur: University of Malaya Press, 1967), pp. 203–204.

34 K.J. Ratnam provides two reasons for this substantial increase in the strength of the non-Malay vote in the 1959 general elections: "First,... about 75 per cent of Chinese and Indian Federal citizens in 1955 had been under twenty-one years of age [the eligible age to become voters]. Since the 1959 elections were conducted on the registers of electors revised in the second half of 1958, those who had been between eighteen and twenty-one in 1955 had by this time qualified to register as electors. Secondly, the Constitution of 1957 had made it easier for non-Malays to become citizens by registration and naturalization." See Ratnam, *ibid.*, p. 201.

35   For a blow-by-blow account of this MCA conflict, see Heng Pek Koon, *Chinese Politics in Malaysia: A History of the Malaysian Chinese Association* (Kuala Lumpur: Oxford University Press, 1988).

36   Ratnam, *ibid.*, p. 207.

37   J.E. Jayasuriya, *Dynamics of Nation-Building in Malaysia*, p. 91.

38   Brunei was supposed to join Malaysia, but at the last minute decided not to do so. Several reasons have been given for its decision. Among these are its large reserves of oil which its Sultan feared would be used by the Federal Government in the form of taxes and revenue sharing, and also because the Sultan had to wait in the line to become the King of Malaysia, which he was reluctant to agree to. See James P. Ongkili, *Nation-building in Malaysia, 1946–1974* (Kuala Lumpur: Oxford University Press, 1985), pp. 170–74.

39   It was originally agreed by all the relevant parties that Malaysia would be formed on 31 August 1963, the Independence Day of Malaya, but owing to opposition from Indonesia and the Philippines to the proposed federation, Malaya agreed to defer the date until later. Malaya had agreed to the proposal of the two countries that the United Nations be asked to conduct an inquiry to ascertain whether the elections which had recently been held in Sarawak and North Borneo indicated the wishes of the majority of the population in those two territories to enter Malaysia. The UN report, based on the findings of its mission, was released on 14 September 1963. It confirmed that a large majority of the people wished to join Malaysia. It was, therefore, decided that two days later Malaysia would be proclaimed officially. However, this did not end the immediate opposition of Indonesia and the Philippines to Malaysia. Singapore held a referendum on 1 September 1962 but it was not for the people of Singapore to determine whether they were for or against merger, but which type of merger they favoured. About 71 per cent of the electorate voted for constitutional arrangements contained in a white paper "giving Singapore autonomy in education and labour". See Ongkili, *ibid.*, pp. 160, 174.

40   Tunku Abdul Rahman Putra, *Looking Back*, p. 79.

41   Lee Kuan Yew, *The Singapore Story: Memoirs of Lee Kuan Yew* (Singapore: Singapore Press Holdings, 1998), p. 362.

42   *Ibid.*

43   Tunku Abdul Rahman, *Looking Back*, p. 84.

44   Ongkili, *Ibid.*, pp. 161–70.

45   Tunku Abdul Rahman Putra, *Looking Back: Monday Musings and Memories* (Kuala Lumpur: Pustaka Antara, 1977), p. 81.

46   Lee, *The Singapore Story*, pp. 498–99.

47   *Ibid.*, p. 499.

48 British Minister Duncan Sandys in his report to British Prime Minister Harold MacMillan said: "He [Lee] realises that his declaration has no legal validity and that the British Government would not tolerate any attempt by him actually to exercise powers which he purports to have assumed. On the other hand, this act of public defiance towards Britain and Malaya has no doubt helped to strengthen the public image of himself which he wishes to create....Therefore, if we were to humiliate him publicly, he would, I believe, retaliate with further acts of defiance of one kind or another and we might very quickly be forced to suspend the constitution....The concessions which I hope to persuade the Malayan Government to make may induce Lee to go into Malaysia quietly. But unless I mistake his character, he will bluff, bully and blackmail up to the eleventh hour." This report has been reproduced at length by Lee Kuan Yew in his memoirs, *The Singapore Story, op.cit.*, p. 502.

49 Ongkili, *op.cit.*, fn., p. 209.

50 Ongkili cites several instances of Lee expressing this wish which came to the knowledge of the Tunku, but the latter was steadfast in his refusal of Lee. See Ongkili, *op.cit.*, pp. 181–86.

51 See Tae Y. Nam, *Racism and Nation-building in Malaysia and Singapore* (India: Sadhna Prakashan, Meerut, 1973), p. 62.

52 Lee Kuan Yew, *The Singapore Story*, p. 547.

53 Tae Y. Nam, *op.cit.*, p. 79.

54 *Ibid.*

55 *Ibid.*, p. 80.

56 For an interesting discussion of this episode, see von Vorys, *Democracy without Consensus*, pp. 283–84. Earlier, before endorsing the idea, Tun Tan had said, "It would be easier for hell to freeze over than for the Merdeka University to be established under prevailing circumstances in Malaysia." See also his comments in the *Straits Times*, 9 April 1969.

57 Von Vorys, *Democracy without Consensus*, p. 203.

58 *Ibid.*, p. 203.

59 Extracts of Syed Nasir's document reproduced in von Vorys, *op.cit.*, p. 204.

60 *Ibid.*, pp. 204–205.

61 Mubin Sheppard, *Tunku: His Life and Times*, p. 157.

62 *Ibid.*, p. 210.

63 Cynthia H. Enloe, *Multi-ethnic Politics: The Case of Malaysia*, p. 93.

64 Mubin Sheppard, *Tunku: His Life and Times*, p. 157.

65 Von Vorys, *Democracy without Consensus*, p. 284.

66 Gordon P. Means, *Malaysian Politics: The Second Generation* (Kuala Lumpur: Oxford University Press, 1991), p. 7.

67   The above account is based on von Vorys, *Democracy without Consensus*, p. 372. It is interesting to observe that although the author of an authorized biography of the Tunku, Mubin Sheppard, does not cite von Vorys' book, yet his own account is almost identical to that of von Vorys' for this episode of the "ultras" attack on the Tunku. This means that he had used it. A comparison of both accounts will confirm this, despite the fact that von Vorys' book had been banned by the Tunku. It probably means that von Vorys' account was closer to the truth and that was why it could not be allowed to be publicly sold and distributed. See Mubin Sheppard, *The Tunku: His Life and Times (The Authorized Biography of Tunku Abdul Rahman Putra al-Haj)* (Kuala Lumpur: Pelanduk Publications, 1995), pp. 169–70.

68   *Ibid.*, p. 373.

69   Mubin Sheppard, *The Tunku: His Life and Times*, p. 170.

70   *Ibid.*, p. 169.

71   *Ibid.*, p. 170.

72   *Ibid.*, p. 171.

73   Dato' Abdullah quotes the following statement from the late Tun Ismail's memoirs: "The people [apparently he meant the Malays] were secretly cursing the Tengku for holding onto office when he had outlived his usefulness", and also the recollection of Dato Harun: " 'The Tengku's pro-Chinese posture, utterances and actions both as Prime Minister and leader of UMNO angered the Malays. The accumulation of Malay grievances against him and the Malay economic frustration and the incomparable economic supremacy of the non-Malays; their arrogance, the Chinese in particular, precipitated the riots'." See Dato' Abdullah Ahmad, *Tengku Abdul Rahman and Malaysia's Foreign Policy*, pp. 16 and 17.

74   What seems a curious aberration was that the Tunku during his retirement took umbrage against a book edited by a Malay university historian, Professor Zainal Abidin bin Wahid, which was entitled *Glimpses of Malaysian History*, a collection of essays by a group of Malaysian historians which had earlier been broadcast over Radio Malaya. It was published in 1974 (?). The Tunku took particular exception to the essay by Prof. Zainal Abidin on the independence of Malaya, in which the Tunku's name was not mentioned at all. The Tunku has written about his unhappiness over this article several times. It finally prompted him to start writing his memoirs in an English-language newspaper, *The Star*, which later appointed him chairman of its company. The Tunku only stopped writing in 1987 when *The Star* was banned by the Malaysian Prime Minister, Datuk Seri Dr Mahathir Mohamed for publishing criticisms of government policies, but it was later allowed to publish again. However, the Tunku's

column ceased as apparently he had been critical of Dr Mahathir. Nevertheless, his articles were extremely popular and were later collected and re-published in several books. Among them are *Looking Back: Monday Musings and Memories* (1977), *Viewpoints* (1978), *As A Matter of Interest* (1981), *Lest We Forget: Further Candid Reminiscences* (1983), *Challenging Times* (1984?) and *Contemporary Issues in Malaysian Politics* (1984). In his Foreword to *Looking Back*, the Tunku wrote: "One academic writer did write a book in Malay on Malaysia's Independence, a work which was actually distributed to schools for our boys and girls to read, but the author had completely omitted to associate me with events leading to Independence. My service needs no more to be remembered — I am a 'has been'." See Tunku Abdul Rahman, *Looking Back: Monday Musings and Memories* (Kuala Lumpur: Pustaka Antara, 1977), p. vii. In *Lest We Forget*, pp. 35–36, he identified the historian: "One book was written and used as a textbook for the schools by Professor Zainal Abidin, compiled from his lectures given to the university students. When I read the book, I realised it was obviously an attempt to put party politics above the historical facts. On my return from Jeddah, where I had been working in the Secretariat Islamic for two years, I lodged a protest and the Government was kind enough to withdraw the book from the schools. It was not because I was omitted from all mention, but the facts in the book were so misleading in that it did not give proper emphasis to the important incidents and events which led to independence."

75 Dato' Adullah ahmad, *Tengku Abdul Rahman and Malaysia's Foreign Policy*, p. 24.
76 *Ibid.*, p. 25.
77 D.K. Mauzy, *Barisan Nasional: Coalition Government in Malaysia* (Kuala Lumpur: Maricans, 1983), p. 143.
78 Dato Abdullah Ahmad, *Tengku Abdul Rahman and Malaysia's Foreign Policy, 1963–1970*, pp. 14–15.
79 See S. Durai Raja Singam, ed., *Tribute to Tunku Abdul Rahman*, published by the author (Kuala Lumpur, 1963), pp. 95–98, chapter entitled, "The Tunku As a Sportsman — by Alex Soars".
80 Tunku Abdul Rahman, *Viewpoints* (Kuala Lumpur: Heinemann, 1978), p. 91.

CHAPTER FOUR

1970–76
Malay Dominance, Economic Integration
and National Unity under Tun Razak

... the government policy on national unity is not by process of assimilation but by integration, that is, by mutual adjustment of diverse cultural and social traits, acceptable to all races in the country.
Tun Abdul Razak, *Straits Times* (Malaysia), 16 May 1972

Due to his strong determination in championing the cause of the Malay peasants when he was Minister of National and Rural Development, he was branded by the non-Malay communities as racialist, as biased against the Chinese, as a religious fanatic who would discontinue, even reverse, the liberal and humanitarian policies so wisely pursued by the Prime Minister, Tunku Abdul Rahman.... Eventually, using wisely and honestly the great power conferred upon him by his office, he finally won the acceptance and respect of his fellow countrymen."
Paridah Abd. Samad, *Tun Abdul Razak:*
A Phenomenon in Malaysian Politics, p. 213

THE GROWING assertion of Malay political primacy during Tun Abdul Razak's administration marked the most radical change from the Tunku's administration. However, given the mixed ethnic composition of Malaysia, and in the wake of the 13 May inter-racial riots in 1969, he still felt that an official declaration of Malay political primacy or a statement claiming Malaysia was a "Malay" nation-state would cause further tensions. Consequently, this was not done.

In view of this, Tun Razak's nation-building efforts take on a difficult, tragic dimension. Although a Malay nationalist at heart, and anxious to please the Malay nationalists within and without his UMNO party, he also desired to preserve and strengthen Malaysia as a plural, multi-ethnic nation. He could have opted for an all-Malay government, but did not do so. A devoted and loyal Deputy to the Tunku, he probably hesitated to dismantle the latter's national integration policies entirely. He had waited for at least 15 years to take over from the Tunku. Unlike the Tunku, he was an indefatigable administrator, who seldom took time off to relax. His nation-building efforts are all the more remarkable when it is realized that when he became Prime Minister in 1970, he had already been diagnosed as suffering from leukaemia. Paridah Abd. Samad, in her intimate biography of the man, reveals that doctors gave him less than six years to live. Realising the short time he had left to accomplish as much as he could for the nation, he became a "man in a hurry".

His illness was kept a secret from all except from one or two persons. One of them was his Deputy, Tun Dr Ismail, a medical doctor, who, however, did not survive him. Tun Ismail died of a heart attack on 2 August 1973 at the age of 57. His successor as Deputy Prime Minister was the Minister for Education, Datuk Hussein Onn, Tun Razak's brother-in-law. In mid-1975, says Paridah Abd. Samad, Tun Razak's health deteriorated. People close to him observed that he had been losing weight rapidly. He looked tired and gaunt. His bush jackets hung loosely on his shoulders. His jowls had begun to sag. Rumours spread about his health, yet the public was not told a word. One night in December 1975 a critically ill Tun Razak quietly boarded a French aircraft specially diverted from Singapore to pick him up. While Kuala Lumpur was officially claiming he was on holiday, he was making a desperate dash to Paris and from there to London where he entered a clinic. On 14 January he died following a relapse from which he never recovered.[1] He was 53. His sudden death brought shock and dismay to the nation.

Tun Razak died in the same week as China's Prime Minister Zhou En-lai. "Asia had lost two prominent regional figures at one time," recalls his biographer.[2] "The two men had much in common. It was said that both were singularly free from egotistical ambitions of most politicians, were very loyal when they were Deputies, but showed their charismatic capabilities when they held top leadership. Both practised arduously their beliefs that actions spoke louder than words and were essentially executives, efficient implementers rather than creators of policies." This assessment was based on a *Far Eastern Economic Review* commentary of 26 January 1976.

Tun Razak's leadership left several important legacies: the New Economic Policy which was aimed at helping the Malays, the formation of an enlarged ruling coalition of political parties and a "Government of National Unity", a National Culture policy based on Malay culture, Islam and "suitable elements from other cultures",[3] massive infrastructures of roads and development in the rural areas and new directions in Malaysia's foreign policy. The last enabled Malaysia to emerge as the leader and spokesman of the Third World in the next two decades and into the new millennium.

It was under his administration that 94 square miles of the greater Kuala Lumpur area, which had for decades served as both the state capital of Selangor and the Federal capital, became in 1974 a separate metropolis for the whole nation. The area was created a Federal Territory (*Wilayah Persekutuan*), by detaching five "decidedly anti-government [parliamentary] constituencies from Selangor state, thus effectively reducing the threat of the opposition coming to power in the state".[4] It was also during his administration that major changes took place in local government in Malaysia. The government had earlier suspended elections to local councils.[5] State governments took over municipal authorities and appointed members to such authorities by an Act of 1973.[6]

Tun Razak was responsible for generating agricultural growth on an unprecedented scale to bring Malays into the main stream of the economy. During his ten years as Minister for National and Rural Development more than 80,000 acres of virgin jungle were opened up for Malay agricultural settlement and farming under the Federal Land Development Authority (FELDA). For his outstanding contribution to national and rural development in Malaysia, he was awarded the Magsaysay Award by the Philippines on 13 August 1967. Some of these achievements led him to be called Malaysia's "Father of Development" and the "Architect of Peace" by the local media after his death. Yet, it is ironical that since his death in 1976, only five books have been published on him, one of which is a pictorial biography in Malay.

Perhaps this was largely due to his own quiet character and not so genial personal style, which made him appear inaccessible and aloof. He was a very private person. He was forced to devise new nation-building strategies following the Tunku's failures, which came largely at the end of the latter's administration when the latter could not satisfy the demands of both Malay and non-Malay interests. Ironically, a similar fate later befell the fourth Prime Minister, Datuk Seri Dr Mahathir Mohamed, whose policies in 1998–2002 while going through the end of the second decade of his administration had also begun to experience serious divisions within the Malay community and occasional disagreements with the Chinese community. Since communal interests weigh heavily in a multi-racial nation-state, every Prime Minister has had to walk a tightrope between these competing groups. Despite Malay political primacy being enshrined in Malaya's Constitution, the Tunku had been reluctant to project it strongly. His "pluralism" and "balancing" or "give and take" strategies on national integration, rights of citizenship and full participation in administration, while they aroused resentment among Malays, did not go far enough to satisfy the non-Malays, either. The Tunku had thereby tested the parameters and limitations of nation-building, and was found wanting.

National integration must be viewed mainly as an evolutionary process, one of trial and error. Tun Abdul Razak, therefore, had to start where the Tunku left off. His new policies did, in fact, begin *just before* the Tunku retired from office. It was when Tun Razak was appointed by the Tunku as the Director of the National Operations Council (NOC) following the outbreak of inter-racial riots on 13 May 1969, that he became the most powerful man in the country.

This public image helped him tremendously. As the disease of leukaemia sapped his strength, he needed to appear strong. When he became Prime Minister, he faced various challenges. Communist guerrillas had intensified their assaults and bomb explosions in urban centres of peninsular Malaysia, including the Federal capital, threatening national security and embarrassing the government. The attacks, partly fanned by rivalry amongst breakaway communist groups, grew serious just before his death.

His toughness, despite being in ill-health, emerged most clearly when he faced student protests and demonstrations. He crushed the student revolts on various campuses with an iron hand, especially during the period of NOC rule when student disturbances were directed at former Prime Minister Tunku Abdul Rahman. At the forefront of student demonstrations were the students' unions and their various cultural and language societies. They agitated on a wide variety of issues, such as language policy, implementation of the New Economic Policy (NEP) and rural poverty, especially the plight of Malay peasants and rural squatters in Johor, Perak and Kedah in 1974 whom they alleged were starving due to the sudden drop in rubber prices. These disturbances came mostly from Malay students, who were beneficiaries of government scholarships yet who felt alienated from the national élite or who felt that the government was too slow in helping the disadvantaged rural Malays. This coincided with a world-wide phenomenon of student radicalism. Even non-Malay radical students in the universities, especially at the University of Malaya, were drawn in. Apparently they were experiencing frustrations, too, with government policies especially with limited access to university education and the system of discrimination in government service. They had joined in some of the Malay student disturbances by presenting a common front.

The government suddenly began to divert its attention to the non-Malay radical students. It published a White Paper which alleged infiltration by the Communist Party of Malaya in the University of Malaya's Chinese Language Society as the cause of the troubles. "Even though most of the arrested demonstrators were Malay students, it became convenient to attribute the conflicts to the conspiratorial manipulative capabilities of the Malayan Communists from their jungle hide-outs in the Thai-Malaysian border area", observed one source cynically.[7] The Minister for Education Dr Mahathir Mohamed warned the Malay students that their scholarships would be revoked if they continued to become involved in further demonstrations. To quell these troubles, Tun Razak's Deputy, Tun Dr Ismail, who was also Minister for Home Affairs, invoked the Internal Security Act to arrest and detain several student leaders and university lecturers on charges of being involved in these disturbances.[8] But, in most cases, the government resorted to a massive show of force to suppress the campus disturbances. Police moved in force to occupy several campuses. In suppressing the largest student demonstration on 3 December 1974 police detained some 1,100 students, mostly Malays, to face charges of participating in an unlawful assembly.

The situation led the government to introduce amendments to the Universities and University College Acts in 1975 to curb political activities at all institutions of higher learning. Students could no longer hold office in any political party, or trade union, or express support, sympathy or opposition to any political party, or trade union. The UCCA had far-reaching consequences. It not only stifled student dissent but created political apathy, a creeping lethargy and a tendency to bookishness among the students. They only rose to defy the authorities occasionally, especially in the 1999–2001 period following the ouster of Anwar Ibrahim, deputy of the fourth Prime Minister, Datuk Seri Dr Mahathir Mohamed, but much of their steam had gone, as the UCCA restrictions were extremely severe and punitive.

It was clear that throughout his administration Tun Razak was under siege from numerous fronts. His doctors ordered him to follow a limited work schedule, but he refused to follow suit. "At that time, he had many urgent agenda that simply could not be ignored," says his biographer.[9] Challenges to his authority came from within his own UMNO party, especially from the ambitious Selangor Mentri Besar (Chief Minister), Datuk Harun Idris, who was said to aspire to being Prime Minister. Tun Razak also encountered problems from Sabah's recalcitrant Chief Minister, Datuk Mustapha, who championed state rights *vis-à-vis* the Federal Government.

Upholding the Constitutional Contract, 1969

The first major move of Tun Razak as NOC Director was to return to the constitutional contract to uphold and implement Malay political primacy more vigorously. In this way, he appeased the forces of Malay nationalism. To pacify the non-Malays, he recognized their rights to citizenship and their participation in the economy and the administration, but warned that the "democratic excesses" of the Tunku's system had to be curbed.[10] The non-Malays would no longer be allowed to challenge the constitutional contract. The Malays would be entitled to full government assistance to achieve economic and social integration. There would be no more attempts at "pluralism" and "balancing acts of compromise and accommodation", or as the Malay ultras had called it, "policies of give and take" to delay this course of action in the interests of social justice.

The economic disparities of the "haves" and the "have-nots" (i.e., the "non-Malays" and "Malays", or *bumiputra*) would be narrowed. These terms were to become Tun Razak's favourite catch-phrases. The Malays would no longer be excluded from the modern sector of the economy. There was to be a more egalitarian distribution of income and a reduction of Malay unemployment through economic restructuring.

If these objectives had been set out for a Marxist government through the means of nationalization and the redistribution of income, critics would probably have said, "That's to be expected." But these were the objectives of a developing capitalist state operating within a global free market economy. The plan, therefore, seemed somewhat bold and ambitious. Could it be achieved? How much had Tun Razak been influenced by Fabian socialism to which he had been exposed in London while he was a law student there in the 1950s?[11]

Tun Razak's early life might throw some light on his later nation-building policies. He was born on 11 March 1922, the son of a Pahang aristocrat. He was of Bugis descent and traced his lineage to a warrior prince from Macassar. He studied at the Malay "Eton", the Malay College, Kuala Kangsar (better known as MCKK). Later, he went to Raffles College in Singapore, where his university mates included Lee Kuan Yew, Maurice Baker and others who were later to emerge as part of the ruling élites of Singapore and Malaysia. Like Lee, Tun Razak's studies were interrupted by World War II, but were resumed in 1946 in London. After completing his law studies, he returned to Malaya in 1950 and became active in politics. In

1951, he was Deputy President of UMNO and became the right-hand man of Tunku Abdul Rahman. Four years later, after being elected in the country's first general elections, he was appointed the Tunku's Minister for Education. After independence he became Deputy Prime Minister and Minister for Defence, later taking on a third portfolio, Minister for National and Rural Development. In the last post, he was responsible for opening up large rural areas to development, an achievement on which his fame partially rests. Although his biographer would claim that his policies in favour of Malay peasants when he was Minister for National and Rural Development made non-Malays view him as a "pro-Malay" politician, it was, in fact, his earlier role as Minister for Education and the architect of the "Razak Education Report of 1955" that first created this image. "Despite coming from an aristocratic family," says his biographer, "he was born and brought up in the midst of a kampong (village) environment, moulding a strong desire in his character to improve the hardship and difficulties of the mainly Malay rural people in earning their livelihood".[12]

Besides the New Economic Policy (NEP), Tun Razak also adopted other measures to achieve social and cultural integration. In 1970 he approved a policy to make the Malay language the main medium of instruction in the educational system. This policy was "squeezed through" while he was the Director of the NOC. The then Minister for Education, Abdul Rahman Yaakub, who was in the Tunku's emergency cabinet, had announced that from 1970 onwards, all subjects except English would be taught in Malay. This policy would be introduced one year at a time, at a graduated level, beginning from Standard I in the primary schools and culminate at university level ten years later. A pro-Razak man, Abdul Rahman Yaakub's seemingly spontaneous act displeased the Tunku, who complained to Tun Razak to restrain him. The Tunku especially resented the strong remarks Abdul Rahman Yaakub had made in relation to his new policy. "All this while", Abdul Rahman Yaakob was reported to have said to the Malay newspaper *Utusan Melayu*, "the government has been very lenient, persuading certain sectors to learn and use Bahasa Malaysia [the National Language].... But if persuasion still does not provide results, then we must resort to the whip. The human psychology is such that if we leave it to their intelligence to choose, they do not make the correct choice."[13] Although angry with him, the Tunku conceded defeat as he did not feel strong enough to delay it. The policy became a *fait accompli*.[14]

To demonstrate his intentions further, Abdul Rahman Yaakob had returned letters that were sent to him and written in the English language by the teachers' unions. The Tunku had, in 1967, ten years after independence, when the language policy came up for review under the "historic bargain", delayed the full implementation of Bahasa Malaysia by allowing the continued use and teaching of English as an official language. In contrast, Tun Razak, the integrationist, seemed impatient to create and inculcate a national identity through the national language. He desired to achieve national integration by making the non-Malays use Malay widely, so that it could become the sole National Language for all citizens. While these strategies were being adopted, he also attempted to form a "government of national unity" for the first time in the country.

Accommodating Left, Right and Centre

Initially, it seemed as though Tun Razak was pursuing diametrically opposed policies by placating one race and then antagonizing the others. But until his death in 1976, these strategies seemed to achieve racial harmony, national integration and political stability. Tun Razak allowed for debates in the NOC but behind closed doors. He consulted with representatives from a wider range of ethnic communities, non-government organizations and opposition political parties than in the Tunku's tripartite Alliance government before 1969. Tun Razak also tapped advice and talents inside and outside government circles from a cross-section of the entire political spectrum — from the Left, Right, and Centre. During his administration, one of his confidantes and speech-writers was a former political detainee and journalist A. Samad Ismail, while another former political detainee, James Puthucheary, a lawyer, was appointed to the NOC.[15] Another left-wing intellectual, Abdullah Majid, was appointed a Deputy Minister.

"Although Tun Abdul Razak was easy to talk to and he was always calm, he had somehow managed to give the impression of being calculating, powerful but friendless. It took a little time to shed that impression,"[16] says his biographer, Paridah Abd. Samad, adding that unlike the Tunku, he "never did develop a genial political style". She observed that despite hundreds of occasions in which he had been in contact with newspapermen and radio reporters, the latter had not warmed towards him, as they had done towards Tunku Abdul Rahman.[17]

This aloofness, which had been developed over the years while he held several ministerial posts, never left him. However, remarkably, despite this, as Prime Minister, he succeeded in winning over several opposition parties to join the government. He had arranged the deals so neatly that he took everyone by surprise. The difficult negotiations had involved disparate and opposing groups. He was able to cajole and influence each of the political leaders. But the public knew nothing of what had happened behind the scenes except when the Opposition parties fell one by one under his influence.

As an indication of his "no-nonsense" style, Tun Razak in August 1970 had decided to move against corruption in high places. He set up the Anti-Corruption Agency (ACA) under a government prosecutor, Datuk Harun Hashim, who would later earn a fearless reputation for the agency's investigations of prominent politicians. Not long after the ACA had begun its work, the *Mentri Besar* of Perak, Dato Ahmad Said, and the *Mentri Besar* of Terengganu, Ibrahim Fikri, both of whom had "public image problems" in relation to corruption, were forced to resign. In September 1970, a Federal Minister, Tan Sri Khaw Kai Boh, who had "a similar predicament", according to von Vorys, was dropped from the Government.[18] In November 1975 the *Mentri Besar* of Selangor, Datuk Harun Idris, was brought to court on charges of corruption.

A Wind of Change: Or, almost a "Coup"?

Although the transfer of power from the Tunku to Tun Razak occurred peacefully, it had all the makings of a "coup". This public image enabled Tun Razak to consolidate his authority and meet any challenge to his rule. In the eyes of most non-Malays he was a "pro-Malay" politician. He was remembered as the architect of the 1955 Education Report which made

Malay an official language. The Tunku's weakening position in government conveyed this impression further. It was reinforced by the belief that a major shift of power to the Malays had occurred, especially as the MCA had lost its representation in the government by its withdrawal from the Cabinet. In the wake of the riots on 13 May 1969, the Tunku had initially carried on for a while as head of an emergency cabinet, but later virtually handed over the administration to Tun Razak as the Director of the NOC. This took place after the King had proclaimed a national emergency and suspended the Malaysian Parliament.

This sense of crisis that surrounded Tun Razak's appointment as a kind of "supremo" made him a feared and over-powering figure in the country, a fact not lost on both Malays and non-Malays. Among the non-Malays it led initially to a mood of despondency and political apathy, causing even some to migrate to other countries. The experience of the 13 May 1969 riots had revealed to the non-Malays "Malay superior political power backed up by overwhelming Malay-controlled force," says a historian of the MCA.[19] "Having observed the efficacy of the armed forces in quelling the fighting and restoring peace at the time of the rioting," she added, "the Chinese became keenly aware that in a show-down they lacked the means to impose their will on any issue of fundamental concern to the Malays."

The NOC's primary task was to restore law and order throughout the nation. It had nine members comprising three politicians from UMNO, one Chinese politician (formerly in the MCA) and one Indian politician (from the MIC), two Malay top civil servants and the Malay heads of the military and police forces. The members of the NOC were: Director of Operations, Tun Abdul Razak; Tun (Dr) Ismail bin Datuk Abdul Rahman; Datuk Hamzah bin Datuk Abu Samah; Tun Tan Siew Sin; Tun V.T. Sambanthan; Tan Sri Abdul Kadir Shamsuddin (Civil Service); Tan Sri Muhammad Ghazali Shafie (Civil Service); General Tunku Osman Jewa (Armed Forces); and Tan Sri Mohamed Salleh (Police).[20]

The NOC was largely a Malay, if not an UMNO, caucus. But the police and military had been given a higher profile in the wake of the 13 May riots. Besides General Tunku Osman Jewa, Tun Razak appointed Tan Sri General Ibrahim Ismail as Chief Executive Officer of the NOC. To supplement the police and military forces, the new *Rukun Tetangga* scheme (Neighbourhood Vigilantes) was aimed at involving all able-bodied male adults in neighbourhood security throughout the country. Such public participation in neighbourhood security was aimed at fighting crime and any political acts of violence and terrorism. The 1969 riots forced the government to increase its defence expenditure, including expansion of the armed forces to withstand any internal or external threats. Tun Razak would bring about changes in the country's foreign policies in line with Malaysia's new defence and internal security needs.

Although Tun Razak could have been a dictator, he chose instead government *by consensus* through the NOC and the National Consultative Council (NCC), which took the place of Parliament. To the NCC he had appointed a cross-section of public opinion such as political parties, the mass media, religious groups, ethnic communities, business associations, and trade unions. Opposition leaders from the PAS, Gerakan, and the PPP accepted their appointments, but the DAP chose to stay out in protest at the continued detention of its secretary-general, Lim Kit Siang. On the other hand, the NOC functioned very much like the semi-martial law colonial government of the 1948–55 "communist" emergency period. The Tunku was reported to have said, "During the Emergency period the Cabinet is playing a secondary role to the National Operations Council."[21] This showed how much the Tunku had lost his authority.

Restrictions on "Sensitive Issues", 1970

The first decrees and directives from the NOC showed the direction that politics was heading. The NOC announced that it would restrict certain "sensitive" provisions of the Federal Constitution from public discussion. These related to Articles 71, 152, 153 and 159 pertaining to the "special position of the Malays" and the "legitimate interests" of the non-Malays over citizenship; and the rights and prerogatives of the Malay Rulers. These provisions, Tun Razak argued, were to be found within the pre-independence "historic bargain" or constitutional contract, between the UMNO, the MCA and the MIC leaders. The NOC would undertake to reinforce and consolidate

Malay political primacy. When the Parliament resumed in 1971, one of its first acts was to amend the laws to incorporate these provisions.

A Department of National Unity was also set up to study ways and means of restoring inter-racial goodwill. It was later empowered with the task of drafting the *Rukunegara* (National Ideology), which was felt to be necessary. The final draft emphasized five principles: Belief in God; loyalty to King and Country; Upholding the Constitution; Rule of Law; and Good Behaviour and Morality. The *Yang Di-Pertuan Agong* proclaimed the document on National Day on 31 August 1970. A special preamble, which elucidated the third principle, "Upholding the Constitution" restated the constitutional contract. A Bill on the *Rukunegara* was presented for parliamentary approval in 1971, and later worked into the educational curriculum to be taught to schoolchildren. Comparison has been made between this document and the *Pancasila* of the Indonesian Republic. This attempt at using a national ideology in nation-building lasted only temporarily. The *Rukunegara* today is no longer strongly emphasized in the school curriculum, although calls for its revival have occasionally been made by ruling party politicians whenever tensions arose in race relations.

Despite the restrictions on "sensitive issues", Malay intellectual groups, especially those in Malay literary associations and the universities, were emboldened and inspired by Tun Razak's increasingly pro-Malay government policies to convene a Malay cultural congress in 1971. The congress formulated a policy on National Culture, which was later officially endorsed by the Ministry of Culture, Youth and Sports, that National Culture should be based on the culture of the Malays and other indigenous peoples, of which Islam was an important element, and that it could also include "suitable elements of other cultures". Over the years, several Malay Ministers defended this policy, but it had not received public endorsement by non-Malays or their political parties. As far as most of the Malay intellectuals were concerned, the issues of National Culture, National Literature and National History had all to be decided on the basis of Malay society as the "base society", while the other races were viewed as "immigrants" or "splinters" from their own ethnic societies. Up to the 1980s, right into the administration of the fourth Prime Minister until the latter announced his

"Vision 2020" in 1991 for the creation of a future Malaysia as a just and egalitarian society, these issues were viewed as one-sided and generated opposition and heated debates among the non-Malays.[22]

Towards a "Government of National Unity", 1970–73

The formation of the "Government of National Unity" by Tun Razak came about more by accident than by design. This was based on his belief that once the non-Malays and their political parties realized that the Malays would not accept a government where the non-Malays played a dominant part, they could be accommodated and be involved in power-sharing. "In the heightened atmosphere of Malay intransigence after 1969, the threat of an all-Malay government was a real one," recalled Tun Razak's biographer; "hence, non-Malay elite motivation was to support the moderate UMNO leadership, to ensure that a greater number of non-Malay candidates would be elected on the Government ticket to provide a stronger influence on public policy, and to defend non-Malay cultural interests".[23]

In 1970 as the country was returning to normalcy, it was intended to reconvene the Parliament. But the NOC felt that before this could be done, it would test the political waters first through the holding of parliamentary and state level elections. When the emergency was declared in May 1969, the Alliance had won 66 seats in West Malaysia and 10 in Sabah, and thereby failed to gain a two-thirds majority in Parliament. There remained one seat to be contested in Malacca, six seats in Sabah and all the 24 seats in Sarawak. In June and July of 1970 the interrupted elections were held. The Alliance won all the six seats in Sabah, but was disappointed with the results in Sarawak. The Alliance parties secured 23 seats against the opposition's 24 — the Sarawak United People's Party (SUPP) winning 12 and the Iban-dominated Sarawak National Party (SNAP) 12, and thereby lacked a majority. Tun Razak, therefore, decided to negotiate with the predominantly-Chinese SUPP, instead of with the SNAP, which had earlier left the Alliance. He also planned to send back Abdul Rahman Yaakub, a Sarawak Malay, to serve as the state's Chief Minister. The SUPP agreed to form a coalition government with the Alliance. On 7 July 1970 their agreement was signed, ushering in the first "unity" government at a state level, under which the SUPP was given two Cabinet posts, including that of the Deputy Chief Minister. Later its president Ong Kee Hui was made a Federal Minister.[24]

The Malacca election result turned out to be favourable to the government, and it was followed by two cross-overs from the opposition. The Alliance Government had, therefore, secured the majority figure of 96 seats. Only then did it agree to reconvene the Parliament.

The first peninsular coalition was between the Alliance and the Gerakan Rakyat Malaysia (Malaysian People's Movement). The latter had started off as a party whose leadership comprised English-educated moderates, several of whom were former members of the MCA, the Labour Party and other parties. It was formed in May 1968. Despite being a new party, the Gerakan won 16 of the 24 state seats in Penang in the 1969 general elections. A few days after its leader Dr Lim Chong Eu had just formed a state government, the 13 May riots broke out. When the ban on politics was lifted in April 1971, the Gerakan party suffered a split. Dr Lim was left with only 12 supporters in the 24-man state assembly. When one of the Gerakan members who had resigned returned to the party's fold, the Alliance accepted the Gerakan's right to rule Penang. Negotiations on a coalition government culminated in an agreement between the two parties on 13 February 1972, under which an Alliance member would be co-opted and sworn into the Penang state Executive Council. There would be no Gerakan federal minister, but the Alliance Government pledged support to Penang's economic development, including the building of a bridge linking the island with the mainland.[25]

The next coalition was formed in Perak between the Alliance and the People's Progressive Party (PPP), which had been led by the Seenivasagam brothers. Although the PPP secured four seats in Parliament and a few seats in the Perak state assembly in the 1969 elections, due to its electoral pacts with the DAP and the Gerakan, its main political base was in Ipoh where it controlled the Municipal Council. Just before the elections, however, D.R. Seenivasagam died suddenly. When S.P. Seenivasagam failed to form an opposition coalition to take over the state government of Perak, he was willing to entertain overtures from the Alliance. On 15 April 1972 agreement was reached with the Alliance under which the PPP would get one position on the State Executive Council (Exco), and the Alliance would get three places on the Ipoh Municipal Council.[26]

Finally, on 5 September 1972, agreement was reached between PAS and UMNO, under which PAS and UMNO mutually co-opted each other into a coalition government in Kelantan, Terengganu, Perlis and Kedah. At the federal level, PAS was given a Minister's post, as well as that of a Deputy Minister, and other minor political appointments. The coalition, however, did not come into effect until 1 January 1973.[27]

It was clear in the bargaining with these opposition parties, the Alliance was prepared to make major concessions in order to secure their support and achieve a broad front of unity and co-operation. After having formed the "Government of National Unity" Tun Razak next moved towards the formation of a broader alliance of these "coalition" parties to replace the original tripartite UMNO-MCA-MIC Alliance which the Tunku had presided over since 1952.

The Transfer of Power, 21 September 1970

Just before the Parliament reconvened on 17 February 1971, the Tunku decided to leave office. Malay resentment against the Tunku was growing stronger so that his departure was expected. On National Day (31 August) 1970 the Tunku announced that his last day in office would be 21 September, the day the new *Yang Di-Pertuan Agong* would take office. He had indicated that it would be difficult for him to remain as Prime Minister when his nephew was the new king. However, another reason was that King Faisal of Saudi Arabia had asked him to take up an appointment as Secretary-General of the Islamic Secretariat in Jeddah, if and when he wished to retire. The Tunku declared that Tun Razak would succeed him. He also announced the lifting of the one-hour curfew in several areas of the country and the ban on politics. Not long after this, the DAP leader, Lim Kit Siang, and leaders of the Party Rakyat were released from detention.

However, the day after the Tunku relinquished power he attended a hastily-organized meeting of UMNO, of which he had been president for 19 years, to say farewell and to introduce his successor. It would have been better had he stayed away. UMNO gave him a cold reception, which amounted to a rebuke. It indicated that he was unwanted and unwelcome. The Tunku's recollection of the mood at that last meeting has been well-captured by his biographer Mubin Sheppard:

> Tunku was a man of deep emotions, emotions normally hidden from even the closest of his colleagues. To onlookers, near and far, he maintained the familiar appearance of a still dominant leader, genial and gentle....

> Very soon afterwards, Tunku and Tun Razak drove to the headquarters of the Language and Literature Institute [*Dewan Bahasa dan Pustaka*], where four hundred leaders of UMNO had assembled in its largest conference room. Tun Razak, with the inspiration of his newly-conferred premiership, addressed the assembly, announcing his cabinet appointments, including the return of the MCA members to Cabinet posts, and his plans for the future government of the country. It was a stirring speech and when Tunku rose to say farewell, the sense of anti-climax recalled Tennyson's "authority forgets a dying King", and robbed his remarks of any prospect of a favourable reception. There was little applause and he left the hall almost unescorted.[28]

The "Exclusivists" Are Absorbed into Government

The Malay exclusivists who were branded as "Malay ultras" by the Tunku and whom he had sacked from the party could not restrain their jubilation when he stepped down from office. They had been waiting in the wings for this moment to occur. For Tun Abdul Razak was really their man, their patron. Although Tun Razak had served the Tunku loyally as Deputy Prime

Minister, he was sympathetic to the UMNO dissidents who were critical of the Tunku's policies. Yet he had played his game so skilfully with both sides that none of them seemed to distrust him. As expected, he resurrected the Malay dissidents to high office in UMNO and in his government.

Many of them had formerly worked for him. Musa Hitam, who had served him as an Assistant Minister, returned to UMNO and was elected as Deputy Chairman of UMNO Youth, and in 1973 appointed Deputy Minister for Trade and Industry. Expelled UMNO Executive Council member, Dr Mahathir Mohamed, was also brought back to UMNO, appointed a Senator and in 1974 appointed Minister for Education. Abdullah Ahmad, Tun Razak's former Political Secretary, who had also been forced to resign during the Tunku's administration, became a Deputy Minister in the Prime Minister's Department. On the other hand, some of the Tunku's loyal colleagues like Mohamed Khir Johari and Senu Abdul Rahman were dropped from the Cabinet. Tun Tan Siew Sin (MCA) and Tun V.T. Sambanthan (MIC) were retained, but before long they would leave office to be replaced by younger leaders from their respective parties.

Dato' Abdullah Ahmad, the Tunku's erstwhile critic, who had been a close confidante of Tun Razak, revealed that Tun Razak had confided to his inner circles, "Never again would the non-Malays be allowed to threaten the political future of the Malays," and assured them that he would entrench the "pattern of Malay political supremacy which had always existed in the Constitution".[29]

Parliament Approves "Sensitive" Issues Bill, 17 February 1971

One of the first duties of the reconvened Parliament was to discuss a White Paper explaining the need to amend the Constitution to entrench the "sensitive" provisions adopted by the NOC to put them beyond the pale of public discussion. During the debate on the White Paper and the amendments to the Constitution, members acquitted themselves creditably by conducting affairs in an affable manner. Strong differences were aired by the DAP and PPP members, who felt that the government was trying to muzzle free speech. Tun Razak, who moved the amendments which was seconded by Tun Tan Siew Sin, said: "We are what we are — a multi-racial nation still imperfectly united. We are a relatively young nation and our experience of parliamentary democracy is less than two decades. We are not yet fully an economically developed country and there exist pronounced economic disparities between the racial groups in the country...There are also unscrupulous individuals who seek to ride to power by inciting and exploiting racial emotions, fears and mistrust...."[30] Tun (Dr) Ismail, in closing the debate, pledged that the Alliance members would scrupulously interpret the spirit and letter of the bill. Those who did not do so would be severely punished. In turn, those who attempted to obstruct the government would be dealt with "effectively and mercilessly". When the votes were counted, the Bill was passed with 125 in favour and 17 against. Only the DAP and PPP voted against it.

Parliament Approves New Economic Policy, July 1971

The ideas of the New Economic Policy were first outlined in a paper, dated 18 March 1970, which was prepared in the Department of National Unity. It identified the economic priorities as follows: "(i) the promotion of national unity and integration; (ii) the creation of employment opportunities; and (iii) the promotion of overall economic growth". This was then passed on to the economists, who included some experts from the United States, Britain and Norway in the Economic Planning Unit of the Prime Minister's Department who were asked to work on them.[31] Finally, "after draft after draft was submitted, revision after revision considered" the final version appeared before the NOC which was anxious to implement quickly the economic terms of the constitutional contract. At a meeting of a NOC Sub-Committee chaired by Tun Razak, Tun (Dr) Ismail suggested that, whatever the flaws in form, the Malays insisted on a new economic policy and would not tolerate further delay, procedural or otherwise. No one objected to this but some, like Tun Sambanthan, echoing views in one of the papers presented, felt that the question should not be communally but economically defined. There were poor Indians and Chinese as well, and they too had the right to become beneficiaries of the new policy. Only Dato Asri (PAS), an NOC member, and another Malay councillor responded by pointing to the constitutional contract. In the end, the report was approved.[32] The various views were incorporated but drafting still took another year before the report went into the Second Malaysia Plan which was submitted to the reconvened Parliament in July 1971 and approved.

The Second Malaysia Plan called specifically for a two-pronged approach. One prong was the reduction and ultimate elimination of poverty "by raising income levels and increasing employment opportunities for all Malaysians, irrespective of race", while the second was for a restructuring of Malaysian society "to correct economic imbalance, so as to reduce or actually eliminate the identification of race with economic situation". In his analysis of the Plan, von Vorys concluded that, despite the priority of economic integration of the Malays, the Plan had again showed a compromise. Tun Razak, in his Foreword to the Plan, had said "no one will experience any loss or feel any sense of deprivation of his rights, privileges, income, job or opportunity".[33]

However, it was made clear that redistribution of wealth was imperative. For this reason, the largest share of public development expenditure went to agriculture and rural development. The government hoped that the steady advance of the economy (GNP had grown at 6.1 per cent) was to be sustained primarily by the private sector. Under the Plan, the government would create government corporations whose job was to form new business ventures and, when these had turned successful, offer them to the Malays. The National Corporation (PERNAS), which was set up in 1969, offered the initial capital for all types of new companies in the fields of manufacturing, finance, transportation, insurance, mining, and other business areas. An Urban Development Authority (UDA) was set up in 1971, ostensibly to change the "Chinese" face of Malaysia's cities and towns. It would provide capital for the construction of new office buildings, shops and commercial facilities in areas where municipal 99-year leases had expired and which could be taken over for urban renewal. Tun Razak, in launching the UDA, said the government had no intention of adopting the policy of "robbing

Peter to pay Paul". The MARA Unit Trust, which was set up during the Tunku's administration and Bank Bumiputra would now provide financial assistance to Malays for their entry into more urban, sophisticated trades and commercial activities.

Later, after Tun Razak's death, owing to the shortage of *bumiputra* capital, the government set up the National Equity Corporation (PNB) and the National Trust Fund (ASN) in 1978 and 1981 respectively to purchase ownership of properties or shares in the name of the Malay community. Shares in these corporations were to be limited to Malays. It was these corporations which were later involved in buying British companies that controlled the mining and plantation sectors — such as Dunlop, Sime Darby, Guthrie, Harrison and Crosfields and the London Tin Company — during Prime Minister Dr Mahathir Mohamad's administration in the early 1980s.

Specifically, the goal of the NEP was to increase Malay share ownership from around 3 per cent in 1971 to 30 per cent over a 20-year period. This involved a massive government effort to bring the Malays into the modern urban economy. As long as economic roles were determined by race, it believed, economic integration of the Malays could not be achieved. Although the government intended to make the percentages of the jobs and economic opportunities reflect the percentages of the population, initially it still felt that the Malays would remain mainly in the agricultural sector — their traditional area. But this outlook would later change in the late 1980s and 1990s when the government of Dr Mahathir decided to move the Malays into the financial, manufacturing and hi-tech technology areas.

Between 1971 and 1973, Tun Razak's policies had begun to succeed in injecting dramatic changes. More government corporations were created to help Malays in the urban sectors of commerce and industry. From 1970 onwards through affirmative action the employment quotas of Malays in the government service began increasing by leaps and bounds, so that by the time of Tun Razak's death in 1976, Malay confidence had been restored. Their economic and social integration within the nation had become a reality.

NEP's Success in Economic Integration and Affirmative Action, 1971–85

On the basis of several socio-economic studies, the progress of the NEP in the areas of economic and social integration between the years 1971 and 1983 can be chartered, as part of the thread of national integration and nation-building. Almost all the relevant studies confirm the success of the NEP during Tun Razak's administration and in the period thereafter. Researcher Lim Teck Ghee has done a summary of these studies.[34] He began with Milton Esman's study (1987) which showed that by 1983 (when the NEP was just two-thirds of the way into its projected 20-year plan) Malay ownership had grown from 2.4 per cent to 18.7 per cent, a feat that would never have been possible without the NEP. The NEP also spawned an "increasingly confident Malay bourgeoisie with middle-class incomes and a modern lifestyle, plus a small group of politicians, members of the royal families, and retired civil servants which had accumulated considerable economic assets, in large measure due to their connections with the government". Esman noted that a new Malay "managerial bourgeoisie" had emerged "holding middle-class positions in government agencies, state enterprises, and to a lesser extent in the private sector. It owed its new status, middle-class incomes and modern life-style not to the ownership of properties but to occupational roles resulting primarily from collective action." This had also been achieved not through "an inflationary fiscal policy or the expropriation of assets but by external borrowing and increments of economic growth which were deployed in a deliberate and openly preferential way on behalf of the Malays".[35] But the NEP had begun to carve out a substantial segment of the modern economy for the Malays.

In their 1991 study, Salleh and Osman Rani also identified the unprecedented expansion of the public sector in the first two decades of the NEP as the cornerstone of the racial redistribution strategy. The shares of *bumiputra* individuals and trust agencies rose from 2.4 per cent of the total $5.6 billion in 1970 to 12.5 per cent of $32.4 billion in 1980 and 17.8 per cent of $76.1 billion in 1985. They noted that the increase in the share of *bumiputra* ownership was largely at the expense of foreign ownership which declined in importance from 63.3 per cent in 1970 to 56.7 per cent. Meanwhile, the

Malaysian non-*bumiputra* share increased from 34.3 per cent in 1970 to 56.7 per cent in 1985.

In his 1986 study on the restructuring of Malaysian banks, Benny Liow showed that by 1983, *bumiputra* individuals, government and *bumiputra* trust agencies were already holding 75 per cent of share ownership in commercial banks, 68.4 per cent in merchant banks, and 49.9 per cent in finance companies. The share of non-*bumiputra* Malaysians was 16.6 per cent, 8.5 per cent and 47.2 per cent in the commercial banks, merchant banks and finance companies respectively, while the share of foreigners was 8.4 per cent, 23.1 per cent and 12.9 per cent respectively.

After 1970, *affirmative action* programmes in favour of the Malays was intensified. Tai Yoke Yin's study showed that between 1970 and 1980, a total of 260,000 additional *bumiputra* employees had been recruited in the government services. Malay share of the new recruits in the public sector rose from 68 per cent of the total between 1970–78 to 93 per cent by 1979–80. Over 1970–80 the public sector undertook three major revisions of salaries, making it not only the largest employer but also one of the highest paying. Affirmative action programmes were also taken to increase *bumiputra* corporate ownership.

A 1985 study by Sieh Lee Mei Ling and Chew Kwee Lyn examined the role of the *bumiputra* trust agencies which were set up by the government to promote *bumiputra* equity investments, such as the National Equity Corporation (*Permodalan Nasional Bhd.* or PNB) and the National Unit Trust Bhd. (*Amanah Saham Nasional Bhd* or ASN). As of March 1984, PNB held investments in 139 companies, of which 91 were listed on the Kuala Lumpur Stock Exchange. Together, PNB and ASN were majority shareholders (over 50 per cent) in 17 companies operating in various sectors, and minority shareholders (between 20–50 per cent) in another 17 companies.

Tun Razak's Legacy: Problems in Social and Ethnic Integration, 1971–85

Some studies have indicated that although the economic policies, especially the government's affirmative action, have brought about a successful improvement of the socio-economic position of the Malays, the problems which had arisen as a result of this implementation might not promote overall multi-ethnic or national integration. Given the significance of the NEP on Malaysia's multi-racial politics and society, it may be useful to look at the findings of the studies made over the past two decades.

Lim Teck Ghee in his survey has referred to a study by Ong Puay Liu on "Ethnic Quotas in Malaysia — Affirmative Action or Indigenous Right?" which revealed that ethnic relations had deteriorated as a result of the implementation of the NEP. Non-Malay students interviewed in a survey saw themselves as being discriminated against and not being treated as equal citizens. Lim Mah Hui in a 1985 study revealed that the NEP's success had not created a "harmonious and unified society". He argued that if the central purpose of the affirmative action was social and economic justice and redistribution in favour of the discriminated, then the primary consideration for receiving assistance should be based on needs, a universalistic criterion, rather than ethnicity, a particularistic criterion. Gordon Means (1991) also argued that, although tremendous progress had been made towards reducing ethnic disparities, the ethnic preferential system had also reinforced ethnicity by defining more and more issues in ethnic terms. He highlighted the silence over a very salient question — the time frame of Malay Special Rights which has, over the years, constituted one of the most volatile issues in ethnic relations in Malaysia. Jomo (1986) has argued for the discontinuation of ethnic-based affirmative action on the grounds that the Malays had reached — or even surpassed — the targets set for them. He echoes the same view as Gordon Means that, far from promoting national unity, the implementation of the NEP had engendered ethnic polarization.

A fuller debate involving both Malay and non-Malay views appears in Chapter 5 of their 1990 book, *Growth and Ethnic Inequality* by three of the NEP economic planners involved, Just Faaland, J.R. Parkinson and Rais Saniman.[36] They made an interesting observation that the Malays "are standing pretty much alone in their defence of the NEP". The authors were surprised that the Malays had not come out more strongly in defence of the NEP, locally or abroad. "Indeed," they went on to say, "the Malays are beleaguered with nowhere to turn for help or sympathy for their cause in face of the onslaught sustained by the well-organised and economically advanced non-Malays and their allies." One reason for this is attributed to the disunity among the Malays themselves. They claim that this goes a long way to explain Malay inability to put their act together for the improvement of their common destiny. Frequent conflicts among themselves, especially the split in UMNO in 1986, had been blamed for this state of affairs.[37]

In brief, what these findings reveal is that although the NEP had improved the livelihood of the Malays through large-scale employment in the public sector, and had been provided with financial assistance in the business and agricultural sectors, it had not disadvantaged the non-Malays except cause them some unhappiness. The economic power of the non-Malays, especially the Chinese, was still untouched, and their dominance was still evident in industries, properties, banking, and insurance. The NEP would first cut into the foreign equities of the economic cake.

The Formation of Barisan Nasional, 1972–74

As the "Government of National Unity" was being formed, the Alliance partners of UMNO, MCA and MIC were undergoing stresses and strains. By February 1970 the MCA had agreed to rejoin the government. But it had lost Chinese support, especially from the Chinese associations. In January 1971 both the MCA and the MIC received a shock from the Deputy Prime Minister, Tun Dr Ismail, when he said that it would be better for UMNO to break with the MCA and the MIC if the two Alliance partners continued to be "neither dead nor alive".[38] Of the three, UMNO was the strongest, although it was itself beset with internal problems. As the coalition in Sarawak had shown, the personal intervention of Tun Razak had played a crucial role and it was partly motivated by the moribund state of affairs in UMNO's two Alliance partners, the MCA and MIC. Tun Razak needed to find more suitable partners than these two. The MCA was stung by Tun Ismail's statement, but Tun Razak pacified the leaders of the two component parties by saying that they would remain partners as long as he was Prime Minister.

The sorry state of affairs in MCA, for instance, had been largely due to the MCA leader Tun Tan Siew Sin's personal decision to withdraw the MCA from the Tunku's emergency Alliance Government. He had done this to "punish" the Chinese community for rejecting the MCA in the 1969 elections. That decision did more harm than good for both the Alliance and the ethnic Chinese community, observers believed, because it was one of the contributory factors that led to the riots. It caused the Malays to feel "let down" by the MCA's withdrawal of support at the critical hour, especially as the Alliance had already lost its two-thirds majority. The other was the Chinese community's incomprehension of the "sulkish" behaviour of Tun Tan himself.

It became apparent from the end of the riots till the Parliament reconvened, that the UMNO Malays had need of Tun Tan more than the Chinese members of his own party. While MCA was out of the Cabinet, Tun Tan was in. Similarly, with the MIC's Tun Sambanthan. As a result, their respective parties lost respect and standing within their respective communities. Both leaders were seen more and more as individuals who had abandoned their parties, so that by the time Parliament reconvened, they virtually no longer had parties.

Both Tun Tan and Tun Sambanthan desperately needed to revive their parties once more, but found the going tough and their lieutenants had gone missing. As a desperate attempt to garner Chinese support, Tun Tan appeared at a "Chinese unity" gathering which was organized by a Chinese lawyer and MCA member, Alex Lee, in 1973. At the meeting he urged the Chinese community to let "bygones be byones" and even offered to resign his Cabinet post, if the community wished it. There were doubts raised in the Chinese newspapers whether he was sincere about this. The MCA appeared to be willing to work with other Chinese organizations, and other Chinese-based political parties such as the DAP and the Gerakan. However, the Chinese Unity Movement did not last long because soon Tun Tan claimed it had been "hijacked" by young radicals like Alex Lee, an MCA "rebel" who was sacked from the party. But the truth was more galling — the Chinese Unity Movement had drawn criticisms from UMNO. "Not only had the Seditions Act 1970 been used to arrest two of the Movement's leaders in April 1971 but Tan Tan himself had also withdrawn his patronage of the Movement," says one source. "Moreover, UMNO was also becoming extremely critical of it."[39]

In the MIC, Tun Sambanthan was being challenged by his deputy, Tan Sri V. Manickavasagam. The mood for change within the MIC was so strong that branch elections gradually showed that the former had lost the support of a majority of the party's members. In 1973 due to a deal mediated by Tun Razak, Tun Sambanthan stepped down and was succeeded by Tan Sri Manickavasagam.

Tun Razak, however, could not wait for these two leaders to put their respective houses in order. Instead, he initiated his own moves and succeeded in forming coalitions at state levels with other opposition parties who were apparently willing to form a wider alliance with UMNO. Although Tun Razak announced in August 1972 — about six months before the Alliance coalition with PAS — that there was the possibility of a "national front among political parties", it was not until the early months of 1974 that the front took shape. The parties were working out a common strategy and platform for the general elections expected sometime in 1974. It was then announced, in piece-meal fashion, that there would be a common symbol for all the national front political parties. There would be no more individual party symbols, no more Alliance "sailing boat" but the scales of justice (*dacing*) instead. In early May, a massive "Barisan Nasional" (National Front) rally was held in Alor Star, and on 1 June 1974, the Barisan Nasional was registered by the Registrar of Societies. The nine parties listed in the Barisan Nasional were UMNO, MCA, MIC, PAS, PPP, Gerakan, SUPP, Parti Pesaka Bumiputera Bersatu (PBB), and the Sabah Alliance Party. Tun Razak was the chairman, Encik (later Datuk) Michael Chen was Secretary and Datok Asri was Treasurer.

It was clear that these coalition agreements between the Alliance and the opposition parties had undermined the positions of the MCA and MIC as the sole spokesmen of their respective communities for the government. In fact, in the midst of these coalition agreements, in August 1973, the Deputy Prime Minister and Deputy President of UMNO, Tun Dr. Ismail, died. A major Cabinet shuffle occurred, in which his position was occupied by the Minister for Education and an UMNO vice-president, Datuk Hussein Onn. Unknown to the public, Tun Tan Siew Sin had requested as the senior Cabinet Minister after Tun Razak to be appointed as a Deputy Prime Minister, if not as one of two Deputy Prime Ministers. But Tun Razak refused him, explaining that the Malays would not stand for a Chinese being named Deputy Prime Minister, even though there were no constitutional barriers to it. "He (Tun Tan) was angry about being by-passed," says Diane Mauzy. "This incident was hushed up and it did not appear in any Malaysian newspapers".[40]

In the 1974 general elections Tun Razak was supremely confident that the Barisan Nasional would win. He even predicted that it would garner about 80 per cent of the votes, but it turned out the BN was able to obtain only 59 per cent of the votes. Still, the performance was impressive. It captured 135 out of 154 seats in Parliament, while the opposition obtained 19 seats. Just prior to the elections, Tun Razak had established diplomatic relations with China and made an official visit to China. During the election campaign large Barisan Nasional billboards were erected showing Tun Razak shaking hands with China's Communist Party chairman Mao Zedong during his visit to China. This was to show that the meeting was well received by Chinese Malaysians. "The euphoria generated by its (BN's) first success did much to cement the component groups together," says a Singapore observer. "Divisive signs were quick to resurface again in the next few years."[41]

Trouble within UMNO: Datuk Harun's Challenge

Conflicts within UMNO emerged in 1975 when Tun Razak's health began to deteriorate. As if they were aware of this, his opponents within UMNO had intensified their challenge to his leadership. Tun Razak was forced to retaliate. Although he had purged the "pro-Tunku" elements within his Cabinet, and infused "new blood" into the top ranks of UMNO, Tun Razak faced a new challenge from Datuk Harun Idris, Selangor Mentri Besar and UMNO Youth leader. The latter was under investigation by the ACA and was also "perceived to be a threat to the party establishment because of the ultra-Malay stand he took on popular issues".[42] It was also believed in UMNO circles that he was extremely ambitious and that he aspired to a vice-presidential position in the party, after which he would contest for the deputy presidency or the presidency. He had used the UMNO Youth movement to organize protests and demonstrations and create a new image of itself as a watchdog of government policies until it began to create uneasiness among government bodies and the private sector.

At the June 1975 UMNO General Assembly, where triennial elections were scheduled to be held, the battle was joined. Focus was on elections to the party's three vice-presidential posts. Incumbent Ghafar Baba and standing vice-president Tengku Razaleigh were regarded as strong favourites. The real contest was for the third post between Dr Mahathir Mohamed and Datuk Harun. Tun Razak decided to show his personal support by calling on the delegates to support the "government team" of three candidates: Ghafar Baba, Tengku Razaleigh and Dr Mahathir. "In his speech, Tun Razak repeated several times that the most important prerequisite was honesty, a reference not lost on the delegates," says one source, "and he told the delegates that their choices would have far-reaching effects on the political system."[43] When the delegates' votes came in, the government team had won. Datuk Harun came in a poor fourth.

Despite his defeat, Datuk Harun was given an honourable way out. He was asked to step down and accept the offer of the ambassadorship to the United Nations. Datuk Harun knew that this was the exit route for the pro-Tunku stalwarts like Encik Khir Johari and others. "He procrastinated and finally announced that he was only prepared to go if the corruption charges against him were dropped," says a Singapore source. "This condition was unacceptable to Tun Razak."[44] The offer was withdrawn. He was charged in November 1975 on several counts of corruption involving the misuse of UMNO's funds, and the misappropriation of Bank Rakyat's stock and share funds, totalling nearly RM8.0 million. He was alleged to have used the money to finance the World Heavyweight Boxing Championship match between Muhammad Ali and Joe Bugner in Kuala Lumpur. Despite this, he continued to pose a major problem when he refused to step down from office. He was given leave of absence to fight the court case. Thus, when Tun Razak died in January 1976, he left behind the unfinished business of the prosecution against Datuk Harun which fell within the responsibilities of his successor and brother-in-law Datuk Hussein Onn.

Foreign Policy Initiatives

Tun Razak had embarked on a series of dazzling initiatives in foreign policy largely to move Malaysia from its pro-Western, anti-communist stance, which had been adopted since independence under the Tunku's leadership. He felt this was necessitated by its national security needs, which required Malaysia to live in peaceful co-existence with all countries, communist or non-communist. In 1971, the year he took over as Prime Minister, he had to face the problem of Britain's withdrawal of its armed forces in Malaysia scheduled for completion in 1971. Britain had underwritten Malaysia's defence needs since its formation in 1963. Even earlier Britain had given similar commitments to Malaya since 1957 and to both Sarawak and Sabah, its former colonies, until they joined Malaysia in 1963. In the superpower race, Britain had begun to lag behind the United States and the Soviet Union. Britain was no longer capable of maintaining itself as a global power due to the dismantling of its colonial empire, and a slow-down in its economy. Although Britain indicated it might participate in a Five-Power Commonwealth defence force, it would not provide anything like its former number of troops. Both New Zealand and Australia confirmed they would maintain a military presence in Malaysia after 1971, but the extent of their commitment was uncertain. At the international level, U.S. President Nixon had announced two important changes in U.S. foreign policy. In 1969, after three decades of Cold War, he said he would withdraw U.S. troops from South Vietnam, and in 1971 he recognized Communist China.

It was in this context that Malaysia took the lead in Southeast Asia by adopting a non-aligned image and advocating regional détente. Tun Razak proposed the neutralization of Southeast Asia as a Zone of Peace, Freedom and Neutrality (Zopfan), which was to be guaranteed by the United States, China and the Soviet Union. He expounded this idea at the Non-Aligned Nations Conference in Lusaka, Zambia in August 1970. In fact, this was an idea of Tun Dr Ismail who had raised it in 1968 in a speech in the Malaysian Parliament when he was a backbencher, but it had been spurned by then Prime Minister Tunku Abdul Rahman. The Zopfan proposal was adopted by the ASEAN Foreign Ministers' meeting on 27 November 1971.

The Zopfan proposal won the support of both North and South Vietnam, and was even endorsed by China. When the last U.S. troops withdrew from South Vietnam on 29 March 1973, in line with the Paris Peace Agreements, Malaysia announced the establishment of diplomatic relations with North Vietnam. In 1972 after President Nixon had visited China, Malaysia announced its recognition of China. This was soon followed by Tun Razak's visit to China. Malaysia viewed China's links with the communist insurgency in peninsular Malaysia as a threat, and Tun Razak's visit was to urge Beijing to stop giving aid to the Communist Party of Malaya. Chinese leaders replied that the government had no such links, which existed only between China's ruling Communist Party and the CPM on a party-to-party basis. Tun Razak raised with Chinese leaders the status of some 200,000 "stateless" Chinese in Malaysia. China's response was that since quite a number of them had been born in Malaysia but did not have documents to prove it nor did they want to return to China, the law of *jus soli* (citizenship by country of birth) should apply, or they could be allowed to migrate elsewhere. It was an internal matter for Malaysia to decide, and it would not interfere. Tun Razak's trip was viewed as a success by both sides in promoting cordial ties between the two countries.

When Saigon fell to the North Vietnamese forces on 30 April 1975, Tun Razak was the first leader to greet the victory as an end to a civil war between the peoples of Vietnam. The following year, Vietnam reciprocated by assuring Malaysia that it would abstain from giving support to the on-going insurgency of the pro-Beijing CPM.[45] Despite these foreign policy postures, in the 1975–76 period, Malaysia's arms purchases from the United States exceeded all previous levels, implying fear of external aggression, largely due to the communist victories in Laos, Cambodia and Vietnam. Malaysia's policy of non-alignment and peace gradually won the respect and trust of not only its ASEAN partners, but other states in the region which began to use its diplomacy increasingly to settle their conflicts with one another. Malaysia's standing in the Non-Aligned Movement also increased as Zopfan won wide support and allowed her to distance herself from the superpowers.

The Communist Challenge

While Malaysia's foreign policy had been devised to ensure long-term security externally, the immediate and vital threat was internal. A major victory was scored in Sarawak in March 1974 when one of the Sarawak Communist Organization's leaders, Bong Kee Cheok, was persuaded to surrender with 481 followers, about 75 per cent of the total communist force.[46] On the other hand, communist activities in peninsular Malaysia showed no signs of a let-up. On 23 May 1974 about a hundred CPM guerrillas planted explosives which blew up earth-moving equipment along the East-West Highway near Grik, North Perak. This followed soon after Tun Razak's visit to China, to show its independence and that Beijing had not curbed its activities. However, following Tun Razak's death, about 250 guerrillas were reported to have crossed the Thai border into peninsular Malaysia, and clashed with security forces. In March 1977 a new border agreement was signed with Thailand allowing Malaysian security forces to cross into Thailand in pursuit of the communist guerrillas. Communist groups carried out a bomb attempt to destroy the National Monument, a grenade attack on a Police Field Force Platoon Heaquarters in Kuala Lumpur, and the assassination of the Chief Police Officer of Perak. These activities were caused by the split of the CPM into three factions, totalling about 2,000 members, with each faction trying to rival the other in militancy and violence.[47] Communist influence on Malay politicians, especially within UMNO, was announced during the early period of the administration of Tun Hussein Onn, as part of the cut and thrust of local politics, but his Government took the matter seriously and arrested and detained several journalists and two UMNO Deputy Ministers under the ISA.

Secession Threat from Sabah under Tun Mustapha

The threat of secession from Sarawak or Sabah had always been present since the day Malaysia was formed. It had loomed large when Singapore left Malaysia, and the Federal Government under Tunku Abdul Rahman was forced to deal firmly with the leaders of the two states, Stephen Kalong Ningkan in Sarawak and Fuad Stephens in Sabah who had raised the issue of state rights. Rumours had indicated that if their demands were not met, they might follow Singapore's departure, but instead the Tunku had forced them out of office.

Politics in Sarawak became tolerable for the Federal Government after negotiations with SNAP in 1975 had indicated that it would join the Barisan Nasional state Government, a possibility which materialized in March 1976. This came after its long-time President and former Chief Minister Datuk Ningkan had been defeated in party elections for the top leadership. It also followed the announcement that its Deputy President Datuk James Wong Kim Min had been released from detention, which had been related to Datuk Ningkan's opposition to Malaysia in the wake of Singapore's departure.

Relations between the Sabah government under Tun Mustapaha and the Federal Government, however, began to deteriorate. Once again, there was talk of secession. Since Tun Mustapha took over as Chief Minister from Fuad Stephens, he had practised a dictatorial style of government, to which the Federal Government had initially closed an eye. Tun Mustapha had been giving support to the Moro Rebellion in the southern Phillipines in conflict with Malaysia's foreign policy. Although Sabah was rich in timber resources, Tun Mustapha had so mismanaged the state's resources, allowing a programme of ruthless exploitation by timber companies that Sabah was in financial difficulties. His attempts to negotiate a financial loan with Libya were blocked by the Federal Government. In order to remove him from office, he was appointed to a federal post of Minister for Defence, but Tun Mustapha refused to accept it. Relations between the state and federal governments soured further as the undercurrents of political discontent spread in the state. By the end of 1975, it was rumoured he was talking about secession.

For a while, it appeared as if Kuala Lumpur had exhausted all constitutional measures against Tun Mustapha. Then, in July, the Federal Government acted to curb the heavy-handed tactics of Tun Mustapha by withdrawing the extraordinary police and internal security powers in Sabah which had been given to him in the wake of the 13 May 1969 riots. This development was soon followed on 12 July 1975 with the registration of a new Sabah multi-ethnic party Berjaya, formed mainly by former members of Tun Mustapaha's party, United Sabah National Organization. Two weeks later, the Yang di-Pertuan Negri (Governor) of Sabah, Tun Mohd. Fuad Stephens, resigned, accusing him of secession and was named president of Berjaya.[48]

As the Sabah Alliance under Tun Mustapha had had disagreements with the Barisan Nasional headquarters in Kuala Lumpur regarding the proposed amendments to the Front Constitution, its joining of the Barisan Nasional was being held up. In August Tun Razak admitted Berjaya to the Barisan Nasional. Likewise, he said, the Sabah Alliance would be admitted if it accepted the rules and provisions of the Barisan Nasional. Then came the surprising announcement that Tun Mustapha would resign on 31 October 1975. Although for the moment, secession had been stemmed, the challenge was still far from over, as Tun Mustapha attempted to influence the Sabah Alliance government under the Acting Chief Minister Datuk Keruak, from behind the scenes. It was not until after the death of Tun Razak in January 1976 that the Sabah Legislative Assembly was dissolved, and state elections were called for the 48 seats. The elections, held during the administration of Tun Razak's successor Datuk Hussein Onn, saw the election victory of Berjaya which won 28 seats to 20 seats by Tun Mustapha's USNO.

Tun Razak's Death

As Tun Razak's political problems were multiplying, his illness took its final toll on him. When he died in London on 14 January 1976, the "shroud of secrecy" which had been thrown around his illness lingered after his death, says his biographer. "It was many hours after he had died that it became known that acute leukaemia had claimed him."[49] The body was brought to the Malaysian High Commission in Belgrave Square where it lay in state. The Sultan of Selangor, who was in London, was the first to sign the book of condolence, while back in Malaysia a sobbing Datuk Hussein Onn, his brother-in-law, was sworn in as his successor. The body of Tun Razak was later flown back to Malaysia for a state funeral. Like the funeral of Tunku Abdul Rahman, the first Prime Minister, thirteen years later, his funeral generated a spontaneous outpouring of grief by Malaysians of all races. While millions watched on television or listened to the radio, thousands thronged the streets to follow the gun carriage which bore his casket to its final resting-place, the Heroes' Mausoleum in the grounds of the National Mosque in Kuala Lumpur.

NOTES

1   The details of his last few weeks have been taken from his most recent biography, which was written with the assistance and support of his family. See Paridah Abd. Samad, *Tun Abdul Razak: A Phenomenon in Malaysian Politics* (Kuala Lumpur: Affluent Master, 1998), pp. 145–54.

2   *Ibid.*, p. 146.

3   The policy was adopted at the National Culture Congress in 1971. See Kementerian Kebudayaan, Belia dan Sukan, Malaysia, *Asas-Asas Kebudayaan Malaysia* (Kuala Lumpur, 1973); Aziz Deraman, *Masyarakat dan Kebudayaan Malaysia* (Kuala Lumpur: Kementerian Kebudayaan, Belia dan Sukan, 1975); and also Kua Kia Soong, *National Culture and Democracy* (Kuala Lumpur: Kersani, 1985).

4   Diane K. Mauzy, *Barisan Nasional: Coalition Government in Malaysia* (Kuala Lumpur: Maricans, 1983), p. 143. Mauzy remarked further that the five constituencies in the Federal Territory were so delimited that, "despite the urban, Chinese, and pro-opposition character of the Territory as a whole, the Barisan Nasional had a fair to good chance in several of the seats". Tun Razak's biographer, Paridah Abd. Samad, has clarified further that, "While Kuala Lumpur may have irreversibly fallen into the hands of the opposition parties [as in the 1969 general elections], the political isolation of Kuala Lumpur from Selangor has great significance in that the Alliance Party could continue to dominate the State Government of Selangor and that racial tragedies such as the May 13 incident would not recur." Datuk Harun Idris, the former Mentri Besar of Selangor, she added, "foresaw that since Kuala Lumpur is politically dominated by the Chinese, continued poor performance of the Alliance in future General Elections could make Selangor fall into the hands of the opposition". See Paridah Abd. Samad, *Tun Abdul Razak*, pp. 60–61.

5   In local government elections, Alliance parties frequently fared badly. Most of the town and district Councils fell under the control of opposition parties.

6   This was based on the recommendations of the Report of the Royal Commission of Inquiry headed by Senator Athi Nahapan. The Report was submitted in

1965, but not published until late 1967. See Paul Tennant, "The Decline of Elective Local Government in Malaysia", *Asian Survey* XIII, no. 4 (1973).

7   Gordon P. Means, *Malaysian Politics: The Second Generation* (Singapore: Oxford University Press, 1991), p. 37.

8   Among those arrested under the ISA were Anwar Ibrahim, Gurdial Singh Nijar, Ibrahim Ali, Syed Husin Ali, Lim Mah Hui and Tengku Shamsul Bahrain. The first three were student leaders, and the last three lecturers at the University of Malaya. Anwar Ibrahim later became the founder and president of the Angkatan Belia Islam Malaysia (Islamic Youth Movement of Malaysia), which is better known by its acronym, ABIM. For an account of his detention, see S. Husin Ali, *Two Faces: Detention without Trial* (Kuala Lumpur: Insan, 1996).

9   Paridah Abd. Samad, *Tun Razak*, p. 149.

10   D.K. Mauzy, *Barisan Nasional: Coalition Government in Malaysia* (Kuala Lumpur: Maricans, 1983), p. 24.

11   For his early background and interest in Fabian socialism, see W. Shaw, *Tun Razak and His Times* (Kuala Lumpur: Longmans, 1977), p. 73.

12   Paridah Abd. Samad, *Tun Abdul Razak*, p. 1.

13   Von Vorys, *Democracy without Consensus*, p. 397.

14   *Ibid.*, p. 397: "And Rahman Yaakub got away with it. The Prime Minister was displeased with him not so much because of the policy he enunciated, but what he considered his unnecessarily provocative manner. Twice he instructed Razak to warn him, an assignment which the latter carried out with moderate zeal."

15   "As a national leader, Tun Razak was never a man who closed his mind to new trends of thought and ideas from any quarter," recalls A. Samad Ismail. "James was among those intellectuals whom Tun Razak and Tun Ismail would invite for an exchange of ideas on political and economic issues." See A. Samad Ismail, "Our James", in *James Puthucheary: No Cowardly Past*, ed. Dominic Puthucheary and Jomo K.S. (Kuala Lumpur: Insan, 1998), p. 62.

16   *Ibid.*

17   Paridah Abd. Samad, *Tun Abdul Razak*, p. 99.

18   Von Vorys, *Democracy without Consensus*, p. 393.

19   See Heng Pek Koon, *Chinese Politics in Malaysia: A History of the Malaysian Chinese Association* (Kuala Lumpur: Oxford University Press, 1988), p. 261. For similar views of MCA leaders, see G.P. Daniel, *Dr Ling Liong Sik and The Politics of Ethnic Chinese Unity* (Kuala Lumpur: Times, Subang, 1995), pp. 67–68.

20   See Goh Cheng Teik, *The May Thirteenth Incident and Democracy in Malaysia* (Kuala Lumpur: Oxford University Press, 1971), p. 27n.

21   James P. Ongkili, *Nation-Building in Malaysia, 1946–1974* (Singapore: Oxford University Press, 1985), p. 216.

22 For a fuller discussion of these issues, see Cheah Boon Kheng, "Writing Indigenous History in Malaysia: A Survey on Approaches and Problems", *Crossroads* 10, no. 2 (1997): 33–81.

23 Paridah Abd. Samad, *Tun Abdul Razak*, p. 122.

24 Diane K. Mauzy, *Barisan Nasional: Coalition Government in Malaysia* (Kuala Lumpur: Maricans, 1983), pp. 52–53.

25 *Ibid.*, pp. 55–59.

26 *Ibid.*, pp. 62–66.

27 *Ibid.*, pp. 67–73.

28 Mubin Sheppard, *Tunku: His Life and Times (The Authorized Biography of Tunku Abdul Rahman Putra al-Haj)* (Kuala Lumpur: Pelanduk Publications, 1995), p. 174.

29 Dato' Abdullah Ahmad, *Tengku Abdul Rahman and Malaysia's Foreign Policy, 1963–1970* (Kuala Lumpur: Berita Publishing Sdn. Bhd., 1985), p. 23. The author claimed he was present at the meeting.

30 The debate was fully reported in the Malaysian newspapers. See the *Straits Times*, 24–26 February 1971.

31 Von Vorys, pp. 401–12. Von Vorys apparently knew some of these economists or had access to their papers which he cites from indirectly, and, in some cases, mentioning them by name. Among these were D.S. Pearson from Britain and Just Faaland from the Chr. Michelsen Institute in Bergen, Norway. Just Faaland, J.R. Parkinson and Rais Saniman from the same institute in Bergen were later allowed to publish jointly their account of the NEP. See Just Faaland et al., *Growth and Ethnic Inequality: Malaysia's New Economic Policy* (Dewan Bahasa dan Pustaka in association with the Chr. Michelsen Institute, Bergen, Norway, c.1990). I am grateful to ISEAS research fellow, Dr Lee Hock Guan, for drawing my attention to the book by Faaland, Parkinson and Saniman.

32 The above is based on von Vorys who clearly had access to the confidential papers of the NOC Sub-Committee. See von Vorys, pp. 401–406.

33 Malaysia, *Second Malaysia Plan 1971–1975* (Kuala Lumpur: Government Printing Office, 1971), p. 3.

34 Lim Teck Ghee, *Social and Economic Integration of Different Ethnic Groups in Southeast Asia, with Special Reference to Malaysia: A Review of the Literature and Empirical Material* (Geneva: International Institute for Labour Studies, 1995), pp. 1–17.

35 *Ibid.*, p. 6. The study by Milton I. Esman is entitled, "Ethnic Politics and Economic Power", *Comparative Policies*, July 1987, pp. 395–418.

36 See Just Faaland, J.R. Parkinson and Rais Saniman, *Growth and Ethnic Inequality* (Kuala Lumpur: Dewan Bahasa dan Pustaka, 1990), pp. 152–210.

37   *Ibid.*, pp. 201–203.

38   Mauzy, *Coalition Government*, p. 41.

39   Loh Kok Wah, *The Politics of Chinese Unity in Malaysia* (Singapore: Institute of Southeast Asian Studies, Occasional Paper No. 70, and Maruzen Asia, 1982), p. 22.

40   Mauzy, *Coalition Government*, p. 161fn. Another source, however, confirmed the incident as follows: "Informed sources said Tun Abdul Razak would have been faced with a full-blown crisis if Tun Tan Siew Sin had left the Government then. The Minister of Finance's apparently rigid stance angered Tun Abdul Razak so much that sources said he was prepared to consider the immediate possibility of a Government without the MCA . Wisdom prevailed and Tun Tan Siew Sin backed down....UMNO sources said they were prepared to consider the possibility of more than one Deputy Prime Minister, in which case Tun Tan Siew Sin would have had a more than even chance to fill that post. However, the MCA's decision to leave the Government even for a while after the establishment of the NOC, since May 1969, had partly affected Tun Tan Siew Sin's chance of becoming Deputy Prime Minister." See Paridah Abd. Samad, *Tun Razak*, p. 157.

41   Ismail Kassim, *Race, Politics and Moderation: A Study of the Malaysian Electoral Process* (Singapore: Times Books International, 1979), p. 12.

42   *Ibid.*, p. 15.

43   Mauzy, *Barisan Nasional*, p. 101.

44   Ismail Kassim, *Race, Politics and Moderation*, p. 15.

45   For a discussion of Malaysia's policies towards Vietnam, see Danny Wong Tze-Ken, *Vietnam-Malaysia: Relations During the Cold War, 1945–1990* (Kuala Lunpur: Penerbit Universiti Malaya, 1995).

46   R.S. Milne and Diane K. Mauzy, *Politics and Government in Malaysia* (Singapore: Federal Publiciations, 1978), p. 316.

47   Documents captured by the Government revealed that the CPM, supported by Beijing, was the strongest numerically. The CPM (Revolutionary Faction) was set up in February 1970, after rejecting a directive by the CPM Central Committee to liquidate recent recruits as "enemy spies", while the CPM (Marxist Leninist) was established on 1 August 1974. See Milne and Mauzy, *ibid.*, p. 317.

48   See Diane Mauzy, *Barisan Nasional*, pp. 108–112, for an account of the federal-state level conflict in Sabah.

49   Paridah Abd. Samad, *Tun Razak*, p. 149.

1976–81
National Unity and Islamic
Fundamentalism under Hussein Onn

*We have a society in which people of various racial origins have been
brought up to be tolerant, understanding; we are a nation of people with
conscience. The Indians can be very magnanimous, so can the Malays, the
Chinese. The great diversity is a blessing, not a handicap. I don't say that
it is a handicap. It is a challenge and a blessing because no one race can
dominate the others. I would hate to see the day when any one race
dominates the others.*

Prime Minister Hussein Onn in an interview
reported in the *Far Eastern Economic Review*,
26 January 1979, p. 19

T UN HUSSEIN Onn's administration was the briefest of Malaysia's four
Prime Ministers. It was the most conservative, the most resistant to
change. The conservatism was most apparent in the shape of his Cabinet
itself: basically it was not more than an enlarged version of that bequeathed
to him by Tun Razak.[1] He continued the national integration policies of Tun
Razak and succeeded in maintaining political stability and racial harmony,
thus earning the title *Bapa Perpaduan* (Father of Solidarity) from the Malay
media. Although he is remembered for some tough and authoritarian
policies, he was also known as timid, over-cautious, "slow-moving", and a
"one-problem" man. A lawyer by training, he was said to be a stickler for
legalism. At the end of his tenure, as his heart problem wore him down, his

deputy, Dr Mahathir Mohamed, increasingly handled most of his "hatchet work" and was quite successful at that.[2]

Like his late brother-in-law, he took office as a sick man, but unlike the former, he found the duties of Prime Minister onerous and gave up the office after serving only one term. Opposition to his leadership within UMNO coalesced around the opponents of Tun Razak who attempted to topple him, but he survived the challenge. Fortunately for him, the Malaysian economy performed spectacularly. The NEP policies made further progress and exceeded their targets during his period, so that soon after he left office, his successor reaped the rewards and was credited with most of its achievements.

Hussein's administration faced the problems of communist insurgency, corruption, Islamic fundamentalism, secession from Sabah and the outbreak of riots in PAS-ruled Kelantan state. He was responsible for sacking PAS from the BN coalition. Overall, national security interests dictated the government's directions and led it to commit frequent abuses of human rights and democratic practices. A *Far Eastern Economic Review* report in 1979, just prior to his retirement, explained that his first two years in office saw the Communist Party of Malaya launching a terror campaign. This meant that his regime "had to be intolerably harsh" and "Draconian laws [had] to be passed to bring the terror to a halt".[3] Internationally, Hussein's foreign policies did not cast him as a dynamic figure. He moved cautiously, following his predecessor's footsteps closely.

Time's Verdict: "Gentler, but Still Repressive"

Although his administration ruled with "a gentler fist" than Tun Razak's, it was still viewed as "repressive", remarked *Time* magazine of 18 September 1978, largely because it continued to invoke security to thwart virtually any criticism. The ongoing communist insurgency still served as a convenient excuse for suppressing civil liberties. Emerging from a weak position in UMNO politics and due to his own poor health, Hussein was seen as a caretaker Prime Minister. Hence, he had to rely not only on the already wide powers available to him as Prime Minister, but acquired even more powers to suppress dissent.

"Unfortunately during Hussein Onn's term of office," recalled a former Opposition parliamentary leader,[4] "there had been an erosion of fundamental liberties." He was referring to the restriction in the Societies (Amendment) Act 1981, which was "a setback to the Rule of Law". It did not allow for dissent "which is an essential ingredient of parliamentary democracy".[5] Under this law, the government attempted to curb political comment by any society on government policies and activities unless it had registered itself as a "political society". Opposition to this law came from a large number of organizations, including the Angkatan Belia Islam Malaysia (ABIM), the Aliran Reform Movement, and the Bar Council. Over the years the successor government tried to soft-pedal the issue.

Hussein Onn's regime detained six prominent politicians without trial in November 1976 under the ISA. It introduced several amendments to the Malaysian Constitution to deprive arrested or detained persons of rights to legal representation, or to be brought before a magistrate 24 hours after their arrest, on the grounds that such action was a necessary weapon against communist subversion. But owing to strong public opposition, especially from the Bar Council, which said the Act infringed fundamental liberties, a few of the amendments were subsequently withdrawn. The lawyers in response to a call initiated by the Bar Council, boycotted cases under the Essential (Security Cases) Regulations, 1975 (ESCAR), because it allowed suspects for undefined offences to be arrested without a warrant and held for a week and a further 60 days for "questioning". In retaliation, the government decided to punish the lawyers by allowing foreign lawyers, especially from Commonwealth countries, to practise in Malaysia. It also decided to amend the Legal Professional Act to disqualify lawyers from registration unless they had been advocates and solicitors for seven years or more. At its 32nd annual meeting, the Bar Council adopted a resolution accusing Hussein's government of "the clear and wholly unworthy intention of muzzling the Bar", and also of "showing itself to be unwilling to accept valid and constructive criticism".

UMNO Factionalism Weakens BN Coalition

Unlike Tun Razak, Hussein found UMNO factionalism most troublesome. The pressures of factional politics within UMNO went beyond his control and affected his government's policies. The intrigues of rival UMNO politicians also made it impossible for the former opposition party PAS to remain for long in the BN government. Its departure fragmented the Malay coalition of the Government of National Unity, a creation of Tun Razak's nation-building efforts. The long-term consequences of this split did not become apparent until the next administration of Hussein's successor, Dr Mahathir Mohamed, who found PAS a formidable challenge. The exit of PAS from the Barisan Nasional coalition government in 1977 was precipitated by prolonged UMNO-PAS conflicts, especially UMNO politicians' interference in the affairs of the PAS administration of Kelantan state. The conflicts eventually led to riots, the declaration of an Emergency and the imposition of Federal rule in the state. The non-Malay communities could only watch as the two Malay parties fought it out and bruised each other.

UMNO dominance of the BN government and its influence over the non-Malay BN component parties like the MCA, the MIC and the Gerakan began to falter. This generated internal disaffection and division among the BN coalition's non-Malay parties. During Tun Razak's regime, UMNO had grown stronger, and so had Malay domination in Malaysian politics. UMNO had been able to check the influence of PAS. Malay support for UMNO seemed to be rock-solid. But the cracks within UMNO generated differences among BN non-Malay component parties over how best to advance their respective communities' rights and demands, as well as compete for UMNO support on relevant issues in the government. As we have seen in the previous two chapters, while UMNO needed Chinese and non-Malay representation in the government, submission to UMNO leaders and to UMNO concerns took priority. Owing to what one political scientist has described as its "patronage dispensing function",[6] UMNO distributed the political goodies to the other component parties.

In the wake of the 1969 riots, the MCA became a dormant party, weakened and discredited, having fared badly in the 1969 elections and temporarily withdrawn from the government. It soon became bogged down in leadership struggles. Tun Razak's decision to include another Chinese-based party, the Gerakan, in the Barisan Nasional meant that the MCA's influence as one of the three major components in the previous Alliance had been greatly reduced in the enlarged coalition. Its bargaining position was weakened, "since the MCA can no longer present itself as indispensable".[7] However, UMNO was initially guarded about the Gerakan leaders who were formerly in the MCA and had been involved with Chinese interests. Their activities had aroused a degree of suspicion among certain sections of UMNO. Both the MCA and the Gerakan were competing for the confidence of UMNO as well as the support of the Chinese. This was particularly crucial in the period before elections when seats were allocated by UMNO. "For this [reason] the MCA cannot afford to appear to UMNO as an expressly chauvinistic party," observed historian Lee Kam Hing. "Thus, the MCA has found it necessary as in the case of the Gerakan (and in fact because of it) also to present itself as a party with leaders who are moderate and possess technocratic ability and outlook."[8]

UMNO displeasure was evident after the MCA had joined with certain individuals and groups within the Chinese community, including the DAP, to form a "Chinese Unity Movement" between 1971 and 1973 to struggle for "Chinese rights" as a parallel concept to UMNO's struggle for *bumiputra* rights for Malays and indigenous peoples. Before long, the MCA had to withdraw from this movement. Not only had the MCA failed to gain control of the movement, but the movement's goals had met with UMNO criticisms. For the rest of the Hussein Onn years, the MCA sought to explore various economic and educational projects which would benefit the Chinese community together with other Chinese-based parties like the Gerakan and the opposition party, the DAP.

The 1978 general elections, however, revealed that the majority of the Chinese viewed the DAP and not the MCA as the party most committed to Chinese interests. At the parliamentary level, few MCA or Gerakan candidates were able to obtain more than 30 per cent of the Chinese vote. In all the constituencies where the Gerakan and the MCA won, "a very large proportion of support came from the Malay electorate",[9] largely due to UMNO support. Only in later general elections, especially in 1986, in areas where UMNO and PAS contested against each other (i.e., after PAS had left the coalition), and Malay votes were split, were Chinese and MCA votes crucial in determining UMNO victories.[10] But this had to await the UMNO-PAS split in 1979.

The MCA initially focussed its efforts on education because of the desire to preserve Chinese education and the realization of the increasing difficulty faced by qualified non-Malays to gain admission to Malaysian universities due to the *bumiputra* quota system. The MCA sponsored the formation of the Tunku Abdul Rahman College, with the blessings of the government. By 1980 the college had expanded to accommodate over 4,000 students. The success of this college inspired certain members of the Chinese community to initiate the formation of a privately-funded university to be called "Merdeka University". It would use Chinese as a medium of instruction and would cover all academic fields. Its supporters argued that the university would be a logical extension of the Chinese primary schools still financed by the government, and the privately-funded Chinese secondary schools. This proposal, however, met with opposition from Malay leaders, especially those from UMNO. In the 1978 UMNO General Assembly the proposal was rejected by the Education Minister Musa Hitam.[11]

During Hussein Onn's administration, the Industrial Co-ordination Act (ICA), which had been introduced in 1975 to extend the NEP racial employment quota system to the private sector, met with strong opposition from foreign and Chinese businesses. The ICA's aim was to require manufacturing firms to take out licences and employ 30 per cent Malays and promote some of them in suitable management positions. Foreign and non-Malay businesses would also divest at least 30 per cent of their equity to Malay shareholders. The Chinese chambers of commerce opposed the move, claiming it was difficult for most Chinese businesses, especially the more traditional family-based small business enterprises, to comply with the ICA's equity requirements. Dr Mahathir, who was the Minister for Commerce and Industry responsible for the implementation of this Act, initially took a tough line, but when even foreign investors expressed dissatisfaction, he went on several overseas trips to assure foreign investors that the Malaysian Government would implement the Act with pragmatism and great flexibility.

The government eventually relented. In 1977, the Act was amended to make it less onerous on foreign and Chinese interests. It was amended again a few more times until 1986, despite "great resistance" by the Malay-dominated bureaucracy of the government. After he was appointed Deputy Prime Minister by Hussein Onn, Dr Mahathir Mohamed expressed his dissatisfaction with the "bureaucratic obstructionism" and even publicly stated that the government was "on the verge of revoking the Act entirely".[12] Exemption from Malay equity participation, for instance, was given to Chinese firms employing 25 workers with a paid-up capital of more than RM250,000; in 1986, a further exemption was given to cover firms with more than 75 employees and RM2.5 million paid-up capital. "While most of the liberalization was aimed at export-oriented firms, some controls were also removed for small- and medium-sized Chinese businesses," observed one source further.[13] "Even so," observed another source,[14] "the government remained unwavering in pursuing the primary objectives of the ICA, since the Act was considered a mainstay instrument in achieving the target goals promised the Malays for improved employment opportunities and economic betterment under the New Economic Policy."

During this period, the MCA had become ineffective to Chinese businessmen who ventilated their grievances through the guilds and chambers of commerce and had begun making business arrangements with *bumiputra* partners to survive. In 1974, Tan Siew Sin resigned as party leader, and was succeeded by Lee San Choon who held the post until 1983. During his tenure of office Lee worked to establish the Tunku Abdul Rahman College to help Chinese secondary school graduates, who were unable to gain admission to state universities, to obtain tertiary education. He also helped set up the Multi-Purpose Holdings Berhad, an investment conglomerate, in 1977. The former was a success. But the second had a short meteoric rise and eventually failed due to Malay political and business opposition, the MCA's own internal party conflicts and mismanagement. "From that time," said a source, "Chinese business leaders found it more advantageous to deal directly with Malay patrons in UMNO, the royal families and the upper reaches of the bureaucracy."[15]

Like the MCA, the MIC was also beset with internal leadership struggles, and found that it "could not deliver many goods with limited government assistance".[16] Following in the MCA's footsteps, it started to form co-operatives and self-help projects to support the Indian community. In 1979 when Samy Vellu took over the leadership of the MIC on the death of the incumbent president Tan Sri V. Manickavasagam, he started working on an idea for an investment company for the MIC. This materialized in 1984 as Maika Holdings, and was identical to the MCA's project to set up KOJADI, a co-operative for educational purposes, and the Multi-Purpose Holdings.

In 1972 the MIC set up the Tan Sri Manickavasagam scholarship fund to assist Indian students at university level, and the MIC Education Fund in 1973 to help Indian students at the secondary school level. Like the MCA's TAR College, it set up the Maju Institute of Educational Development (MIED) in 1984. "Although scandal has tainted the MIED," says a researcher,[17] it had acquired two private institutions of learning, the Negri Institute of Technology (later renamed TAFE College) and the Vanto Academy (later renamed TAFE PJ). In 1985 when the MIC complained it did not get much support from the government,[18] it was allotted 10 per cent of the shares in the country's private Malay-owned TV station, TV3, with government backing. These shares were later sold in 1990 to reduce some of Maika's other problems. In that same year Maika was involved in a financial scandal. The Treasury had offered 10 million Telecoms shares to the MIC, which in turn allotted only one million shares to Maika. The rest were diverted to two RM2 (two ringgit) shell companies. The Anti-Corruption Agency later investigated and cleared MIC president Samy Vellu of any wrongdoing.[19]

Islamic Fundamentalism

Hussein Onn's phlegmatic administration was also characterized by social unrest and religious and inter-ethnic violence. The start of his administration saw a group of white-robed Islamic youths who called themselves "The Army of Allah" attack Hindu shrines at the Kerling Temple in Ulu Selangor.

The attackers were met by armed Hindu guards who killed four of them. Later, eight Hindu youths were charged in court with homicide. The case attracted the attention of all ethnic communities. Just before Hussein Onn retired from office in 1981 the Islamic calendar entered the 1400th year. A millenarian-oriented group of 20 white-robed armed men read it as an opportune moment for the arrival of the *Mahdi* (Saviour). They attacked the district police station in Batu Pahat, in the state of Johor. Chanting *Allahu Akhbar!* (God is Great!), the men led by a recent convert, a charismatic Cambodian refugee who claimed to be the *Mahdi*, charged into the town. They brandished long swords and slashed at the police staff and anyone who stood in their way, including a pregnant Muslim woman. The leader and his group had been involved in a series of escalating conflicts with the local authorities, as they migrated from Kelantan to Johor. In the ensuing skirmish with the police, eight of the attackers including the leader were killed and 23 men were injured.

These acts of violence were manifestations of the Islamic revival movement known as *dakwah* (meaning missionary or call to worship). The social and political turmoil which had begun to spread all over the world in the wake of the Islamic revolution in Iran in 1979, had arrived in Malaysia. This phenomenon was evident by the increasing mobilization of the Muslim community by various organizations pursuing the fundamentals of Islam. They posed both a threat and a challenge to the government. The demands and initiatives made by these organizations implied that the government seemed not to be pursuing enough of these fundamentals. On the other hand, the government was concerned that the world-wide situation allowed divergent or "deviationist" groups to emerge, and hence it attempted to nip in the bud their activities.

The *dakwah* movement for a "pure" Islamic way of life was largely an urban phenomenon. It influenced Muslims mainly in schools and higher institutions of learning, and in the civil service.[20] The reason why it did not spread to the large Muslim poor and illiterate peasant communities in the rural areas was that it relied heavily on educated élite groups and on knowledge in the basic Islamic texts. The new Malay intellectual élite from the universities, therefore, led the movement. There was great competition among them to prove Islamic credentials and claim superior religious knowledge, moral support and leadership of the Malay community.

For at least one whole decade from 1975 until 1985 the impact of this Islamic revival movement was great. Not only Muslim girls and women were forced to cover up their heads and, in some cases, their faces as well and adopt Arabic dress, but the Muslim men also took to wearing such garments in work sites and government offices. As diverse variants of the *dakwah* movement mushroomed, the Hussein Onn government appeared ineffective in stemming the tide. The movement was soon to influence and transform the opposition party, PAS. It soon fell under the control of a group of *ulama*, who ousted its nationalist-oriented leaders like the party president Datuk Mohammed Asri. Recounting the impact of this phenomenon at that time in Malaysia, a foreign observer wrote:

> In contrast with just over a decade ago, the Malaysian urban scene of today is remarkable for its highly visible Islamic consciousness, with widespread evidence of a new devoutness. Whether expressed through the observances of prayer or dress, or attention to strict dietary purity (for example, by eliminating anything of possible Chinese origin as unclean), or in personal morality, the new *dakwah* spirit pervades life among the city youth in general, beyond the confines of school and university.[21]

Among the more well-known established *dakwah* organizations at this time were *Perkim* (an acronym for Islamic Welfare and Missionary Association of Malaysia), which was founded in 1960 with Tunku Abdul Rahman as its head; *ABIM*, which was formed in 1972 primarily of Malay urban middle-class youth and led by Anwar Ibrahim, who played a leading role in the student disorders of 1975; *Darul Arqam* which was formed in 1971 under an *ulama*, Ustaz Ashaari Muhammad, to establish economically self-sufficient communes applying strict Islamic principles; and *Tabligh* a missionary movement originally founded in India which encouraged religious retreats and was confined almost exclusively to the Indian Muslim communities of Penang and Kuala Lumpur. A government survey in 1981 found that there were forty "deviant" Islamic organizations with an estimated following of 30,000. Most of these groups eschewed materialism and followed a simple way of life.

Another effect of this Islamic resurgence was its relationship with the ethnic question. As more and more Malays became drawn into what had been largely non-Malay and therefore non-Muslim areas of the cities, Islamic consciousness emphasized their different separate identities rather than a common solidarity or equality. It was clear that the government felt that there was little it could do to stop the phenomenon.[22] Hussein Onn, therefore, waited for this religious crisis to pass. He left it to his successor, Dr Mahathir Mohamed, however, to come to terms with it.

Federalism and East Malaysian Politics

Intra-ethnic and inter-party conflicts also occurred in the East Malaysian states of Sarawak and Sabah. These two states attracted much Federal Government attention, as it feared that their integration within the nation-state was fragile. Moreover, the two states had presented the threat of secession when Singapore seceded from Malaysia in 1965, but quick Federal Government action had nipped it in the bud. Although Kelantan state on the Malay peninsula had fallen to opposition party PAS, it had never threatened secession like Sabah and Sarawak.

The state elections in Sabah in 1976 had ushered in the new Berjaya government. The party was led by the veteran politician, Fuad Stephens, an ethnic Kadazan, who was installed as Chief Minister, with the Federal Government's blessings. Stephens had led Sabah to independence within Malaysia and was its first Chief Minister. He had earlier advocated Kadazan nationalism, and when Singapore withdrew from Malaysia in 1965, had expressed a desire to re-examine Sabah's continued participation in the Federation, but met with the opposition of Tunku Abdul Rahman, who was then the Prime Minister, and soon found himself under pressure to leave office.

Stephens later changed his policy, leading one academic to observe that it marked the "demise of Kadazan nationalism",[23] although this was a premature conclusion, as Kadazan nationalism later revived in 1985 under the Kadazan-based Parti Bersatu Sabah (PBS) led by Datuk Pairin Kitingan. The PBS was a break-away from the Party Berjaya. However, before this happened, Stephens changed his mind once more and began to incline towards multi-ethnic politics. Just before the elections in 1976 he had been Yang Di-Pertuan Negri (Governor) of Sabah, but stepped down to re-enter politics to fulfil a political need. Berjaya was a new party which had been founded by Harris Salleh, a little known lawyer. The latter gave up the party's presidency to allow Stephens to take over the leadership. In the ensuing elections Berjaya won 28 seats to 20 seats by the party USNO, under the former Chief Minister Datuk Mustapha Harun, who had been forced to resign after nine years in office just before the elections. His ouster is said to have been engineered by the Federal Government. He had ruled the previous Alliance government in Sabah with an iron fist. His administration was noted for corruption, nepotism and abuse of power and he had been increasingly showing signs of recalcitrance towards Federal rule. At one stage, he even threatened secession, but later withdrew the proposal. During his administration, he eliminated the Kadazan language in the schools in line with his policy to make Bahasa Malaysia the national and sole official language of the state. He also embarked upon a programme to Islamize the state.[24]

Tun Razak had apparently decided that Mustapha should go, but found it difficult to remove him, as he had entrenched himself well within the Sabah political network. Berjaya's account after it had won the elections revealed that "Tun Mustapha sought to perpetuate his dictatorship and realise his ambitions of turning Sabah into a serfdom (sic) under his tutelage".[25] It said the choice for the people of Sabah was "between continued totalitarian and ineffectual government on the one hand and democratic government and respect for fundamental civil liberties and progress on the other".

However, despite his party's electoral defeat, Mustapha remained active as the President of the party USNO, and plotted to recover his power. During his administration, he had permitted the illegal immigration of over 150,000 Filipinos and some 50,000 Indonesians to Sabah "in a bid to tip the demographic balance towards Muslim-Malay political identity being espoused by USNO".[26] These illegal immigrants remained grateful and fiercely loyal to Mustapha, who now used them to threaten the new administration. After the Berjaya government had been installed, there was an outbreak of violence in the state capital, Kota Kinabalu, during which bombs were set off. Police linked the incidents to Tun Mustapha's USNO. They raided a house behind Mustapha's residence and seized a cache of arms, weapons and explosives. Some 4,000 people, mostly Filipino supporters of Mustapha, were arrested.

The Federal Government reinforced the security forces and brought the situation under its control. Hussein Onn, who now had taken over the Federal Government from Tun Razak, felt his government was too weak to deal with local strongman Mustapha, who got away with only a slight reprimand. The death of Fuad Stephens in a plane crash on 6 June 1976, after being in office for more than a month, allowed his deputy Harris Salleh to take over as Chief Minister. The latter initiated development-oriented programmes as a contrast to Mustapha's regime of oppression and corruption. A chastened Mustapha withdrew to London, and despite his long absences from the State, still attempted to influence politics by "remote control".

Despite these political crises, Hussein Onn's administration weathered the storm. In Sarawak, another strongman, Abdul Rahman Yaa'kub, the Chief Minister, a former Federal Minister in Tun Razak's Emergency Cabinet, who decided to return to Sarawak politics, attempted to form a wider Malay-native-Chinese coalition of parties. He became Chief Minister in 1970, with federal support. "Using consummate skills of balancing and playing off coalition partners against each other," observed Means, "he gradually constructed a stable government." Yaakob first attempted to woo the Iban-based Party Pesaka to merge with his Malay-based Partai Pesaka Bumiputera Bersatu (PBB), and then with the largest Iban-based party, the Sarawak National Party (SNAP). The last behaved like an opposition party by remaining outside the BN state government, although it was accepted within the BN parliamentary coalition at Federal level. But the infighting among these parties was intense. By the time of the 1978 federal elections,

Yaakob was still able to keep the coalition together, although a faction of his party broke away to form a new party called Partai Anak Jati Sarawak. Better known by its shortened name of PAJAR, its leaders accused his government of nepotism and corruption. Three other minor parties also contested against the Sarawak BN in the state's 24 parliamentary constituencies, but the BN candidates won all the seats. In the 1979 state elections the SNAP retained its power within the Iban constituencies, while the PBB and the Sarawak United People's Party (SUPP), which was also in the BN state coalition, retained theirs in the Malay/Melanau and Chinese constituencies, respectively.[27]

UMNO Politics

Ironically, it was the lack of Malay unity within the coalition between UMNO and PAS that allowed the BN coalition to become stronger. Malay disunity weakened UMNO, but strengthened national integration. UMNO relied more heavily on non-Malay parties to rule. The first cracks appeared within the UMNO party itself. The UMNO factions during the latter period of Tunku Abdul Rahman's regime revived themselves during Hussein Onn's weak administration. They had lain low during strongman Tun Razak's administration, when their in-fighting had been shadowy, low-key and kept in check.

Hussein Onn's background might prove illuminating, as we move towards a discussion of UMNO politics. The son of the late Datuk Onn Jaafar, the first president of UMNO, Hussein Onn had served as UMNO youth leader under his father's leadership and shared his father's earlier "Malaya for the Malays" views. When Tun Razak appointed him as UMNO's Deputy President on the death of the incumbent Tun Dr Ismail, he had been one of the three vice-presidents of UMNO. This post automatically ensured that he succeed as Deputy Prime Minister. But the "succession" had been cleverly "master-minded" by Tun Razak, according to Hussein Onn's biographer. Tun Razak's action, says the biographer, "did cause some surprise because Hussein Onn had not as yet established himself as one qualified for this high office", although he "soon consolidated his position and convinced the critics that he was the right man for the right place at the right time".[28]

The tenure of Hussein Onn's Prime Ministership, observed one source, "involved no marked innovations or policy changes. It was a continuity of efforts initiated by his predecessor, Tun Abdul Razak".[29] Hussein Onn was an extremely indecisive man. He often allowed crises to solve themselves. Even his biographer noted, for instance, that in the industrial dispute between Malaysia's national airline (MAS, or Malaysian Airline System) and its staff union he was a "prisoner of indecision".[30] He allowed his own minister a free hand in the long drawn-out crisis until the latter resorted to arrests and detention of union leaders, and de-registration of the Airline Employees Union. The biographer further observed that Hussein Onn was not only aloof, but inaccessible to the public. Seen as reticent, cold and arrogant, he had been criticized for dilly-dallying. "Why is he so cautious in taking decisions?" asked the biographer. The biographer's guarded answer: "political prudence". Hussein was said to be so cautious that he took six months to go through the 430-page Third Malaysia Plan. He studied every chapter before approving it. He read it carefully "underlining page after page and checking and counter-checking facts and figures. He would seldom miss a footnote." Summing up, the biographer commented: "A cautious man — far too cautious sometimes — he takes time to make an important decision .... Explaining this habit of his to a journalist he observed, 'How can you be anything but cautious? An error of judgement may sometimes cause misery or unhappiness to many people....' ".[31]

Tun Razak's untimely death in January 1976 was such a shock to Hussein Onn and his close associates that they did not have time to consolidate their positions in the UMNO party hierarchy. Hussein Onn's inability to control the UMNO party to the same extent as Tun Razak generated serious internal dissent. The Malay national leadership who consisted mainly of Tun Razak's supporters was once more challenged by the old guard led by the Tunku and his associates and a loose coalition of disparate UMNO politicians and non-UMNO groups. These included Dato Harun Hj. Idris, a former Mentri Besar of Selangor who had been charged with corruption by Tun Razak in November 1975;[32] the recalcitrant Tun Mustapha, the independent-minded Chief Minister of Sabah whose wings were clipped by Tun Razak; and Syed Jaafar Albar, a veteran who led the UMNO Youth section. These were all individuals who sought revenge at Tun Razak by attacking his close associates and protégés. Ironically, the PAS and Singapore's Prime Minister Lee Kuan Yew also played supporting roles in these factional politics.

During most of Tun Razak's regime, Tunku Abdul Rahman had been away in the Middle East to head the Islamic Secretariat in Jeddah. The appointment, made by the Saudi Arabian Government, was in recognition of his services as a leading Islamic statesman. When his term of office ended, the Tunku returned to Malaysia to enjoy his retirement. But soon he found himself playing an influential role behind the local political scene. Appointed chairman of the board of directors of the English-language newspaper *The Star*, he began writing a widely-read weekly column which he used to comment on local politics and discuss his past role and experiences in government.

One of the first critics to attack Hussein Onn's government was Syed Jaafar Albar. He alleged that there were "communists" who had obtained positions of considerable influence in the UMNO party during Tun Razak's administration and that they were still directing policies. Since the communist rebellion was still on, this was a serious charge to make. The anti-communist theme was later taken up by the Tunku, by supporters of Datuk Harun, and in Singapore by Lee Kuan Yew. "Their targets included a number of politicians with left-wing backgrounds including Khalil Akasah, the Executive Secretary of UMNO, and Wahab Majid, Tun Razak's press secretary. Others named included James Puthucheary, a lawyer, and Samad Ismail, a well-known novelist who was also managing editor of *New Straits Times*", recalled Bruce Gale in his biography of Datuk Musa Hitam,[33] the former Deputy Prime Minister, who was also singled out for attack.

Hussein Onn's poor health, which had contributed in no small way to the rise in UMNO's factional conflicts, gave the appearance that he would be no more than an interim Prime Minister. Several factions were clearly unhappy when he passed over the more senior UMNO vice-president

Ghafar Baba and appointed Dr Mahathir Mohamed as the Deputy Prime Minister. Ghafar reacted by withdrawing from the Cabinet, although he continued to support the national leadership. Hussein Onn also alienated Tan Sri Ghazali Shafie and Tengku Razaleigh, who like Ghafar was an UMNO vice-president. Both had been hopeful of being promoted at some time or other.

With the possible exception of Tengku Razaleigh and Ghazali Shafie, all of the more important of Tun Razak's protégés were in some way opposed to the Tunku and the UMNO old guard. Some like Dr Mahathir Mohamed and Musa Hitam had been previously punished by the Tunku for reportedly challenging his authority after the May 1969 crisis. While Hussein Onn had not been involved in anti-Tunku activities, he had avoided serving in the Tunku's government. The Tunku was his father's (Dato Onn Jaafar's) political enemy. The old UMNO guard still held few positions of considerable influence. For more than a year Tun Razak's protégés had been on the defensive, struggling to maintain control of the party machinery in the face of a concerted attempt by the Tunku and his associates to remove or curtail the influence of certain persons towards whom they were opposed. The latter were determined to make a political come-back by capturing key posts in the UMNO and in the Government, and, if necessary by toppling Hussein Onn.

The conflict was probably initiated by Hussein Onn himself when he hauled Datuk Harun to court on corruption charges to complete a process that had been initiated by Tun Razak. Although in mid-1976 Harun had been removed as Mentri Besar of Selangor and expelled from UMNO, a concerted action by powerful supporters caused Harun to be readmitted into the party in October despite his conviction on corruption charges earlier. In June of the same year the UMNO General Assembly elected Jaafar Albar as UMNO Youth leader to replace Harun. This was clearly due to a pact between the two factions and despite Hussein Onn's support for Datuk Mohamad Rahmat, the Deputy Minister for Trade and Industry. "In the same month still more pressure was brought to bear on the national leadership with the arrest in Singapore of two Malay journalists who confessed to having been part of a communist scheme directed by Samad

Ismail," says Bruce Gale.[34] Some political observers saw this as the handiwork of Lee Kuan Yew who was determined to get back at some of his "old comrades in the PAP" like Samad Ismail who had apparently wormed their way into Tun Razak's government and within his protection.

But these arrests caused great disquiet within the Cabinet, especially among senior UMNO leaders like Mahathir, Musa Hitam, Razaleigh and Ghafar Baba. Hussein Onn's attitude was to allow things to move on at their own momentum without interference. The Minister for Home Affairs Ghazali Shafie, described by one opposition politician as "an arrogant and intellectually pretentious prima donna with over-inflated ambitions",[35] had failed to win election as one of the vice-presidents of UMNO. In trying to safeguard and promote his position within UMNO, he made his own move by ordering Samad Ismail's detention under the Internal Security Act. Abdullah Ahmad and Abdullah Majid, two Deputy Ministers in Hussein Onn's government, were also later detained for their links with Samad Ismail. Recalling this episode more than a decade later, Abdullah Ahmad wrote: "The Minister for Home Affairs during Tun Hussein Onn's administration (1976–1981), Tan Sri Ghazali Shafie, used the ISA as a means of revenge towards his political opponents especially this writer and Tan Sri Samad Ismail (the journalist) because this writer blocked his political career from moving upwards".[36] Because of Hussein Onn's dilatoriness in this matter, Abdullah Ahmad had castigated him in a book which he had written earlier after Hussein Onn had just stepped down from office:

> Hussein was very well-known for being gullible and the least clever of Malaysia's four Prime Ministers. He finds everything laborious and has a quick temper and an even quicker tongue.[37]

On the arrests, Hussein Onn had refused to intervene. There were unconfirmed rumours in the foreign press that senior Cabinet Ministers like Mahathir and Musa Hitam were likely to be detained.[38] But before long the anti-communist campaign had begun to lose its steam, especially following the death of Syed Jaafar Albar. In Sabah, Tunku Abdul Rahman's close associate, Tun Mustapha's party USNO was soundly defeated by a breakaway group Berjaya in the state elections, giving Hussein Onn another shot in the arm. The Tunku finally seemed willing to accept a partial reconciliation of the old guard with the new party leadership when he accepted an invitation to attend UMNO's thirty-first anniversary celebration. Although factionalism had been common enough in UMNO, it had not yet developed to the point where UMNO's own unity was at stake. But this time the factionalism planted the seeds for the party's serious split in 1988 when the then incumbent Prime Minister Dr Mahathir Mohamed was challenged for the post of party president.

The Economy

As the government's NEP policies began to achieve most of its targets, anxiety arose among the non-Malay communities whether these strategies might cut into their promised share and reduce their competitive edge. Under the inspiration of the NEP, the government had continued to recast the balance of power between the public sector and the private sector, in which the state played the leading role and laid down the agenda for private capital to follow. "The choice of this particular alternative expressed primarily the demands of the Malay business and intelligentsia network, many of the latter being in bureaucratic positions, who wanted the state to be interventionist in favour of 'Malay' interests", observed one researcher.[39] In implementing this policy, the state utilized state resources to sponsor a Malay capitalist class, which emerged eventually within public corporations acquiring assets for and on behalf of Malays, and run by political appointees and bureaucrats. The policies of the Hussein Onn regime remained essentially the same as had been formulated during the Razak era. But it was this period which saw the great extent of bureaucratization of the state, the creation of a Malay business class and the trend of Malay businessmen being given preference in obtaining licences, credit and government contracts. As the state sector expanded rapidly under the control of Malay bureaucrats and politicians, the ICA strategy to increase Malay participation in the modern economy forced Chinese and foreign enterprises to "restructure" themselves in such a way that 30 per cent of the shares were given to Malays. It was during Hussein Onn's regime that the NEP targets, formulated by Tun Razak's government, seemed suddenly to be within reach.

Fortunately, for both the Tun Razak and Hussein Onn regimes, the financial resources to finance Malay investments and corporations became available largely due to Malaysia's sustained economic growth rate for almost a decade. Real GDP averaged 7.6 per cent for the 1970–80 period, and 8.6 per cent for the 1975–80 period. It was further assisted by the world-wide increases in commodity prices and the discoveries of oil and natural gas off-shore from the Malay peninsular state of Terengganu. Petroleum revenues increased due to the rise in the oil prices announced by the OPEC countries in 1975.

The government was able to step up the transfer of corporate ownership to *bumiputra* and provide heavy investments for *bumiputra* trust agencies. The annual growth rate of *bumiputra* equity increased 23.5 per cent per annum for individual *bumiputra* ownership and by 39 per cent per annum for *bumiputra* trust agencies between 1971 and 1980. Malay employment in industry in the same period also rapidly increased, due to the ethnic employment quotas set by the ICA for the private sector. Even the incidence of poverty had been reduced from 43.9 per cent to 29.2 per cent in the same period, while household incomes of all communities also increased dramatically.[40] This meant that despite the NEP providing large state assistance to the Malays, the non-Malays were not totally disadvantaged.

The Kelantan Crisis and the UMNO-PAS Split

When PAS joined the BN it had been acknowledged that Kelantan state would remain a PAS stronghold, and UMNO would have a share in the PAS-dominated government. However, UMNO's promise of non-interference was not observed for long. Participation in the BN coalition appeared to benefit the PAS leaders more at the federal level than at the state level, as UMNO-PAS rivalries intensified in Kelantan, leading eventually to PAS' decision to remove the incumbent Mentri Besar (Chief Minister), Mohamed Nasir, for defying the party's instructions. Nasir appeared more a recalcitrant than an UMNO convert, but his defiant actions towards the PAS leadership gave UMNO great satisfaction. PAS called for his resignation, but he refused. He presented himself as the champion of honest and clean government against corrupt and self-serving politicians. A "no-confidence" motion was tabled in the Kelantan state assembly and carried by 20 PAS votes after 13 UMNO and one MCA assemblymen had walked out in protest. A legal impasse followed when Mohamed Nasir called for the dissolution of the state assembly. His followers gathered in the streets to demonstrate support for his cause, and violence and looting erupted. This later led the Federal Government to ask the *Yang Di-Pertuan Agong* (the King) to declare an emergency and a curfew in the state capital.

Before the declaration of an emergency, Hussein Onn and his UMNO ministers attempted to negotiate a settlement with the PAS federal leaders. After several proposals from the Federal Government had been rejected, Hussein Onn said he would impose federal rule in Kelantan. An emergency bill was rushed through Parliament and passed with 118 votes in support and 18 votes against, including 12 of the 14 PAS members and all six DAP members. PAS members who held office in the BN government resigned their positions but said they would remain in the BN. However, the BN Council met and decided to expel all members who had voted against the Kelantan Emergency Bill. Three months later, the Federal Government called a surprise election for the state which was set for 11 March 1978. The election was contested by UMNO, PAS, and a third party which was formed by Mohamed Nasir, the former Mentri Besar, called Barisan Jemaah Islamiah Se-Malaysia, or Berjasa for short. The results were unfavourable to PAS, which won only two seats in the 36-seat assembly, while BN won 23 seats and Berjasa 11.

The results meant that UMNO had succeeded in capturing Kelantan from PAS, which had been made possible by Berjasa splitting the votes, and had won the right to form the state government. The distribution of votes showed that the BN had obtained 36.7 per cent, PAS 32.7 per cent and Berjasa 27 per cent. PAS had paid dearly for participating in the BN coalition. At the same time, Malay UMNO-PAS national unity which had been achieved by Tun Razak with great effort lay in shambles. UMNO had gone for short-term gains, and disregarded PAS party's rights and interfered in its sphere of jurisdiction. Their enmity and rivalry now resumed with greater intensity. As Malaysia faced the challenge of Islamic fundamentalism, the PAS came under its influence and that of the *dakwah* groups. Its new leadership passed into the hands of *ulama* (religious leaders), which adopted as their objective an Islamic state along the lines of the new Islamic Iranian Republic and became a serious threat to UMNO.

The 1978 General Elections

Hussein Onn, apparently inspired by the BN's election victory in Kelantan and Malaysia's good economic performance, decided to call for general elections in 1978 about one and a half years before the government's mandate expired. He wanted to win public endorsement of his tenure of office as Prime Minister on his own terms. He was still Acting President of UMNO, and had yet to go before the party's General Assembly for election as its president. In the elections for the 154 seats of the recently enlarged Parliament, the BN won 130 seats, DAP 16, PAS five, independents two and a Sabah party, one seat. The DAP had gained eight more seats from its previous nine, while PAS had lost nine seats. "Clearly, Hussein Onn's leadership of the BN was reaffirmed, and the basic structure of its coalition remained intact", was the verdict of one observer.[41] Onn next convened UMNO's General Assembly to get himself elected as the party's president. However, he did not have it easy, as UMNO rival factions fielded a candidate against him — the first UMNO Prime Minister to be challenged for the post of president. Hussein Onn, of course, won, but the contest revealed that UMNO's internal conflicts were far from over. In February 1981 Hussein Onn went to Britain for a coronary by-pass operation, after which he decided to retire from office.

Conclusion

Hussein Onn failed to provide a strong and dynamic leadership in government, in the BN and in UMNO, yet the BN government managed to run itself smoothly, largely due to the continuity of policies from the Razak era and the institutional infrastructures which were in place. Fortunately, the economy did quite well and many of the government's policies achieved their targets. Despite the communist insurgency, national security and racial harmony were maintained. Hussein Onn's weak and ineffective leadership, however, led to repressive measures, frequent factionalism and internal conflicts among the BN parties and to the break-up of the UMNO-PAS coalition. In most cases, he allowed a crisis to resolve itself. And when he did intervene, as in Kelantan in 1977, the crisis had led to riots and he was forced to declare an emergency and impose federal rule. In most studies of his tenure of office, his government was seen as uninspiring, lacking in new directions and representing continuity from Tun Razak's era. He was a sick and tired man. When he stepped down from office, his successor, Dr Mahathir Mohamed, found in the Prime Minister's office 18 unopened red Cabinet boxes.[42] It showed how slow he had been in coping with his duties.

NOTES

1   *Asiaweek,* 18 November 1977, p. 21.

2   *Ibid.,* p. 21.

3   *Far Eastern Economic Review,* 26 January 1979, p. 18.

4   Tan Chee Khoon, *Without Fear or Favour* (Singapore: Eastern Universities Press, 1984), p. 40.

5   *Ibid.*

6   Harold Crouch, "Authoritarian Trends, the UMNO Split and the Limits to State Power", in *Fragmented Vision: Culture and Politics in Contemporary Malaysia,* ed. Joel S. Kahn and Francis Loh Kok Wah (Sydney: Allen and Unwin, 1992), p. 27.

7   Lee Kam Hing, "Three Approaches in Peninsular Chinese Politics: The MCA, the DAP and the Gerakan", in *Government and Politics of Malaysia,* ed. Zakaria Haji Ahmad (Singapore: Oxford University Press, 1987), p. 88.

8   *Ibid.,* p. 89.

9   *Ibid.,* p. 86.

10   According to an MCA analysis of the 1986 general elections, the MCA and Chinese voters were the deciding factors in UMNO's win in at least 19 parliamentary constituencies, where only UMNO and PAS contested, "that is, 23 per cent of all UMNO-won seats were ones in which the majority obtained was less than the number of Chinese voters in the constituency". Most of these

areas were in Kelantan, Terengganu and Kedah. See *The Future of Malaysian Chinese* (Kuala Lumpur: Malaysian Chinese Association, 1988), p. 32. Ironically, in each succeeding delineation of Parliamentary constituencies carried out by the Elections Commission, initiated and endorsed by the UMNO-dominated government, the proportion of Chinese majority seats had been reduced, from 33 in 1964 to 26 in 1986. This had produced a lop-sided weightage in favour of rural, Malay majority constituencies. It had not dawned on the UMNO that these were not necessarily given seats to UMNO, for when the PAS contested against it and split the Malay votes, non-Malay votes became crucial in determining who was the winner. The UMNO-PAS rivalry was most intense during the administration of Prime Minister Dr Mahathir. In the 1999 general elections the contests in peninsular Malaysia showed that more than half of the Malay electorate had deserted his UMNO party for PAS and his BN coalition's candidates were returned largely by Chinese and Indian voters.

11   Means, *Malaysian Politics*, pp. 60–61.

12   At this stage, Dr Mahathir was said to be already having ideas of imposing tighter controls over the bureaucracy, controlling the "subsidy mentality" of the Malays and developing a faith in private enterprise and competition. For an interesting analysis of his views and for the Act's impact on Chinese capital, see Khoo Kay Jin's article, "The Grand Vision: Mahathir and Modernisation", in *Fragmented Vision: Culture and Politics in Contemporary Malaysia*, ed. Joel S. Kahn and Francis Loh Kok Wah (Sydney: Allen and Unwin, 1992), pp. 69–70fn.

13   Heng Pek Koon, "Chinese Responses to Malay Hegemony in Peninsular Malaysia (1957–1996)", in *Cultural Contestations: Mediating Identities in a Changing Malaysian Society*, ed. Zawawi Ibrahim (London: Asean Academic Press, 1998), p. 73.

14   Means, *Malaysian Politics*, p. 59.

15   Heng Pek Koon, "Chinese Responses to Malay hegemony....," *op.cit.*, p. 68.

16   See Selvakumaran Ramachandran, *Indian Plantation Labour in Malaysia* (Kuala Lumpur: Institute of Social Analysis, 1994), pp. 310–11.

17   *Ibid.*, p. 313.

18   In Samy Vellu's words, "We could not go into banking, finance, insurance, transportation, or even distribution sectors. Could not even get an agency. Wherever you look, the word no, no, no was there. All we need was a small lift in life and the rest will be done by us." M. Magesvaran, "Malaysian Indians: Where Do They Stand?" *Malaysian Business*, 16 August 1994, pp. 5–9, cited in *ibid.*, p. 312.

19   "Nevertheless, the fact remains that even when Maika was given government support, albeit relatively paltry, this was abused by the MIC leadership for their

own advantage, and have consistently failed to deliver to the [Maika] shareholders," says researcher Selvakumaran Ramachandran, *ibid.*, p. 312.

20 See Judith Nagata, "Islamic Revival and the Problem of Legitimacy among Rural Religious Elites in Malaysia," in *Readings in Malaysian Politics*, ed. Bruce Gale (Kuala Lumpur: Pelanduk Publications, 1987), p. 121. Nagata claims that many of the urban young Malays who were influenced by ideas of Islamic revival had revealed that they been exposed to such ideas while abroad, "in such infidel outposts as Australia, the United Kingdom and North America, or else in the Middle East. Their mentors and mediators are colleagues and fellow students from other Muslim countries, particularly Pakistan, Saudi Arabia and Libya. Through these contacts, a form of non-traditional 'peer learning,' young Malays are suddenly made aware of their religious deficiencies...."

21 *Ibid.*

22 See Chandra Muzaffar, "Islamic Resurgence: A Global View (with illustrations from Southeast Asia," in *Readings in Malaysian Politics,* ed. Bruce Gale, p. 162.

23 Margaret Roff, "The Rise and Demise of Kadazan Nationalism", *Journal of Southeast Asian History* 10, no. 2 (1969): 326–43.

24 See Francis Loh Kok Wah, "Modernisation, Cultural Revival and Counter-Hegemony: The Kadazans of Sabah in the 1980s", in *Fragmented Vision: Culture and Politics in Contemporary Malaysia*, ed. Joel S. Kahn and Francis Loh Kok Wah (Sydney: Allen and Unwin, 1992), pp. 230–31.

25 Bill Campbell, *Berjaya's Success Story* (Kota Kinabalu: Chief Minister's Department, n.d. 1981?), p. 17.

26 Gordon Means, *Malaysian Politics: The Second Generation*, p. 65.

27 Jayum A. Jawan, *Iban Politics and Economic Development: Their Patterns and Change* (Bangi: Penerbit Universiti Kebangsaan Malaysia, 1994), p. 116.

28 J. Victor Morais, *Hussein Onn: A Tryst With Destiny* (Singapore: Times Books International, 1981), p. 33.

29 Aziz Zariza Ahmad, *Mahathir's Paradigm Shift* (Kuala Lumpur: Firma Malaysia Publishing, 1997), p. 1.

30 Morais, *Hussein Onn, ibid.*, p. 48.

31 *Ibid.*, p. 57. His penchant for detail is well known. An *Asiaweek* report of 18 November 1977, p. 21, says: "One habit from his days in law: using ballpoint pens in three or four colours to underline important points. If most politicians pay too little attention to detail, Datuk Hussein may well be paying too much."

32 Datuk Harun established his reputation as "a Malay saviour and nationalist" during the 1969 riots. The official enquiry report claimed that some of the rioters had gathered outside his residence in Kuala Lumpur, and that he had lost control over their activities. He was UMNO Youth leader when he organized

a World Heavyweight Boxing championship fight between Muhammad Ali and Joe Bugner in 1975. Harun's involvement in this fight with losses incurred by Bank Rakyat led to an investigation which revealed various corrupt and irregular practices. Tun Razak removed him as Mentri Besar. He was offered a post as ambassador to the United Nations, but a defiant Harun turned it down, whereupon corruption and criminal breach of trust charges were filed against him. "It was Hussein Onn who was left with the problem of facing the political consequences of that action," says Gordon Means in *Malaysian Politics: The Second Generation* (Kuala Lumpur: Oxford University Press, 1991), p. 56.

33 Bruce Gale, *Musa Hitam: A Political Biography* (Kuala Lumpur: Eastern Universities Press, 1982), p. 88.

34 *Ibid.*, p. 89.

35 See Fan Yew Teng, *The UMNO Drama: Power Struggles in Malaysia* (Kuala Lumpur: Egret Publications, 1989), p. 67.

36 Abdullah Ahmad, "Nexus antara PAS dan Al-Ma'unah", *Mingguan Malaysia*, 23 July 2000, p.12. An earlier disclosure of Ghazali Shafie's role had been made by S. Husin Ali in a book about his own detention, see S. Husin Ali, *Two Faces: Detention Without Trial* (Kuala Lumpur: Insan, 1996), p. 110.

37 Abdullah Ahmad, *Tengku Abdul Rahman and Malaysia's Foreign Policy, 1963–1970* (Kuala Lumpur: Berita Publishing, 1985), p. 17.

38 Husin Ali claimed that Ghazali Shafie was interested in arresting and detaining Mahathir whom he saw as "the biggest obstruction to realising his ambition" in becoming Deputy Prime Minister. Husin wrote: "Mahathir could easily be detained under the ISA, if two persons could corroborate that he had links with the communist underground. That explained why they asked Samad and I about Mahathir." Both, however, refused to play his game. See Husin Ali, *ibid.*

39 Khoo Kay Jin, "The Grand Vision: Mahathir and Modernisation", *op.cit.*, p. 50.

40 David Lim, "Malaysian Development Planning", in *The Fourth Malaysia Plan: Economic Perspectives*, ed. Jomo K.S. and R.J.G. Wells (Kuala Lumpur: Malaysian Economic Association), pp. 20–21.

41 Means, *Malaysian Politics: The Second Generation*, p. 69.

42 This was revealed by Dr Mahathir to Abdullah Ahmad, see Abdullah Ahmad, *Tengku Abdul Rahman and Malaysia's Foreign Policy* (Kuala Lumpur: Berita Publishing, 1985), p. 17.

CHAPTER SIX

1981–2001
The Changing Face of Mahathir's
Nationalism and Nation-Building

It is when every race is equally dissatisfied that one can be sure that every one is having a fair deal. Then there will be relative harmony. As has been noted it is quite impossible to ensure that every race will be satisfied. If this can be made to happen then race becomes irrelevant. At this stage racial politics would become superfluous. Until then it is better to recognize the fact of race and to provide for as much fairness as possible for all. This is what Malaysia has done.

Prime Minister Datuk Seri Dr Mahathir Mohamed
in the pamphlet *The Malaysian System of Government*
published by the Prime Minister's Office, 1995

There can be no fully developed Malaysia until we have finally overcome the nine central strategic challenges that have confronted us from the moment of our birth as an independent nation. The first of these is the challenge of establishing a united Malaysian nation with a sense of common and shared destiny. This must be a nation at peace with itself territorially and ethnically integrated, living in harmony and full and fair partnership, made up of one Bangsa Malaysia with political loyalty and dedication to the nation.

Prime Minister Datuk Seri Dr Mahathir Mohamed,
Malaysia: The Way Forward
in which he outlined his Vision 2020.

O N 16 JULY 2001, Datuk Seri Dr Mahathir Mohamed celebrated his 20 years in office — as Malaysia's longest serving and most controversial

Prime Minister. He was still firmly in control despite dwindling Malay support for his ruling party, UMNO, and growing opposition to his rule. The 75-year-old leader was still battling a slumping economy in the face of opposition calls for political reforms, amid accusations of repression, corruption, cronyism, nepotism, a weakened judiciary and press restrictions.

Known for his single-mindedness and commitment to advancing the prosperity of the Malays during his 20-year rule, he had lately become disillusioned with them. At the 21–23 June UMNO general assembly he had accused the Malays of laziness, greed, and ingratitude towards his ruling party and of squandering opportunities under a 30-year affirmative action programme, the New Economic Policy. On 30 August, on the eve of the country's 44th anniversary of independence, he said he had overdone the affirmative action programme in favour of the Malays. "We have, as a result, people who are rather laid-back and not willing to make efforts," he said.[1] His failure to change the attitude of "lazy" fellow Malays was the greatest setback of his 20-year rule.[2] "I am sad that I will leave without succeeding to change the culture of the Malays. For the Malays, working hard is a good value but in reality they do not. It is not because they can't but they don't want to." He said the Malays had failed to learn from the "good examples" of the minority Chinese. Moral decline among the Malays was so bad, he said, that the majority of "criminals, rapists, drug addicts, HIV/AIDS patients, murderers and school truants" were from the community.[3] In September he directed the Education Ministry to introduce a policy of meritocracy for *bumiputra* (the term used for Malays and other indigenous peoples). The system was to be based on qualification and merit, for certain courses at local universities to tackle the problem of *bumiputra* students lagging behind in higher education.

Dr Mahathir's own party, UMNO, regards itself as the champion of Malay rights, but in the 1999 general elections it had lost the support of the majority of Malays who coalesced around the increasingly bold Islamic opposition party, PAS, which heads an opposition front and whose long-term ambition is to create an Islamic state in multi-cultural Malaysia. Many Malays were also unhappy over the sacking, humiliation and subsequent jailing of his former popular deputy, Anwar Ibrahim, in 1998 on sex and graft charges. Since then, Dr Mahathir's efforts to engage PAS in Malay unity talks had fallen on deaf ears.

Given this rebuff, Dr Mahathir has now turned to forge stronger links with Malaysia's sizeable ethnic minorities who had propped up his ruling coalition, the Barisan Nasional, in the 1999 elections. Recently he told his coalition partners that their multi-ethnic alliance, which embraces the country's ethnic Malay, Chinese and Indian communities, will one day become a single party, but until then they had to work at it, especially to win the youth vote for the 2004 general elections. On the eve of the anniversary of the country's independence, some 2,000 representatives from 120 Chinese organizations invited him to a Chinese school, served him "ceremonial tea" and pledged loyalty to his administration.

However, his efforts to rally Chinese support have not met with unqualified success. He had a series of clashes with Chinese lobby groups, notably over education and the perpetuation of his government's affirmative action programme for Malays.[4] Fearing loss of Chinese support, he had appointed two advisors on Chinese affairs to improve communication with the Chinese community. But efforts to win over more Chinese support had soured in the months of June and July, after the controversial takeover of two independent Mandarin-language newspapers by the Malaysian Chinese Association (MCA) — the biggest Chinese party in his BN coalition. The MCA's acquisition of the *Nanyang Siang Pau*, and the *China Press*, which had been critical of the government, sparked an outcry from many Chinese groups and deepened a rift within the MCA's leadership. Most of the country's major newspapers are owned by government parties. Recently to show fairness to all communities, the government had announced measures to redress the Indian community's grievances, especially those living in the poor area outside Kuala Lumpur where ethnic clashes occurred during which several Indians were killed. The Indian leader in the coalition, Datuk Seri Samy Vellu, had asked for more financial aid, university places and civil service jobs for ethnic Indians.

However, these "give and take" policies, or policies of accommodation and compromise, of appeasing one race and then another, that he was now practicing were reminiscent of those of Tunku Abdul Rahman's policies that ironically Dr Mahathir himself used to criticize. "You can say things are going well when everyone is unhappy with his lot. You cannot give everyone everything they ask for. You can only give a portion of what they ask for. If you find that a section of the people is extremely happy with their lot, you can be sure that you have been unfair. It is very important in a multi-racial country not to be seen to be favouring one race over another — you have to compromise," he said, enunciating his "system of government".[5]

Race relations might have been shaky due to the government's "juggling" policies towards each of the races, yet they have resulted in maintaining racial harmony. But Dr Mahathir's rivals, the opposition front, the Barisan Alternatif, have even bigger problems. Ideological differences between its two biggest parties came to a head on 22 September 2001, with the secular, mostly Chinese Democratic Action Party (DAP) pulling out, charging that PAS, which headed the front, must stop pushing ambitions to establish an Islamic state. Its withdrawal came some 12 days after 10 Malays, including several PAS members had been detained under the ISA for allegedly being members of a clandestine Islamic militant group and after two commercial aircraft hijacked by Muslim Arab terrorists had crashed into the World Trade Center building in New York on 11 September, killing at least 5,600 people. The third largest partner in the opposition bloc, Parti Keadilan Nasional, headed by Anwar Ibrahim's wife, has its own problems. Six of its leaders were locked up in April under a tough security law allowing detention without trial for up to two years. They were accused of planning street protests to bring down the government. Their lawyers denied the accusations. The fourth party, the tiny Parti Rakyat Malaysia, is planning to merge with Keadilan.

Still, despite these political differences, not many other countries can match Malaysia's high-level of political stability, racial harmony and economic progress. Dr Mahathir has claimed credit for keeping the peace amid Malaysia's stark racial divisions and regarded this as his greatest achievement during his 20-year-rule[6] — despite the odd flare-up, as when six people were killed in Malay-Indian racial clashes in Kuala Lumpur in March 2001. However, six months earlier, appearing worn down by unprecedented criticism of his rule, he had told *Asiaweek* magazine[7] that he did not care what he would be remembered for. He had said:

> I don't care if people say I am a dictator, because I know I am not. If they say I practice cronyism, I know I don't…. Maybe I regret going into politics. I should have stayed a doctor. When I was practicing, I was very popular. People loved me.

Despite these negative remarks, *Asiaweek*, however, went on to acknowledge, "Under Mahathir's leadership, Malaysia has progressed from an almost exclusively agricultural economy to one largely based on technology and knowledge. He has given his nation a respected voice on the international stage and has instilled in the Malaysian people a pride in themselves and their country and its achievements."[8] This is, indeed, no small praise from an international news magazine that has frequently been critical of him.

Dr Mahathir is likely to be remembered as a great modernizer. The Malay press gave him the title of *"Bapa Pemodenan"* (Father of Modernization), apparently for creating the necessary infrastructure developments towards Malaysia's export-oriented industrialization. However, like every one of the Malaysian Prime Ministers before him, he had started his political career as an exclusivist Malay nationalist but gradually transformed himself into an inclusivist multi-racial Malaysian nationalist. He had evolved in the 1960s from an UMNO rebel in the "ultra"-Malay camp to command support from the Chinese and Indian communities and ensure peace, if not harmony in an ethnically-divided nation. As a Malay "ultra" (extremist) he was known for his outspoken remarks against the Chinese business community, his theories of racial difference and social Darwinism and his vigorous defence of ethnic Malay rights.

Dr Mahathir is also credited with Malaysia's economic recovery from the 1997 Asian financial crisis by instituting capital controls (despite this making fund managers wary about returning to Malaysia) and also for fixing the exchange rate for the Malaysian ringgit at 3.8 to the U.S. dollar.

Another part of that legacy is a near-quadrupling of GDP from US$27 billion when he came to power in July 1981 to more than US$100 billion today, and a lift in annual per capita income from less than US$2,000 in 1981 to about US$4,500 now. Malaysia also reduced poverty to seven per cent from around 50 per cent 30 years ago. Although he has made tremendous economic gains during his 20-year rule, the challenges are not getting any easier as the Malaysian economy is at the mercy of the global slow-down in information technology goods. From 1999 and into 2000, surging demand for semiconductors and other electronic components had driven Malaysia's export growth. But the slow-down in the IT sector in the United States and in Japan since the second half of 2000 stalled Malaysia's economy. Like Singapore, Malaysia may be heading towards a technical recession. But, typical of the man, he has now decided to face the economic challenge head-on by taking over the duties of Minister for Finance following the resignation of his long-time confidant Tun Daim Zainuddin from the post in June, reportedly due to their strained relations over policies.

Tun Daim had faced intense criticism and a public outcry when his ministry bought 29 per cent of the shares of Malaysia Airlines for an allegedly inflated sum of RM1.79 billion (US$856 million), more than twice the market price, from his protégé Tajudin Ramli and also agreed to take over the Light Rail Transport (LRT) STAR project owing to huge debts incurred. Ramli and another tycoon, Halim Saad, the executive chairman of the UEM-Renong stable of companies,[9] had been shining lights under Dr Mahathir's policy of developing a class of Malay entrepreneurs. They had benefited from the government's privatization policy, implemented since 1983, when it farmed out infrastructure projects to private companies. However, some of these privatized projects like MAS and the LRT Star project had encountered spectacular failures and were subsequently re-nationalized. Mahathir had blamed the failure of these privatized companies on the economic turmoil of 1997 and 1998 and because "the people involved are incompetent".[10]

The privatization process had drawn the heaviest fire from businesses and opposition, as many of the privatization projects were not carried out through an open tender system and were politically connected to UMNO.

In addition, privatized projects were monopolies, such as PLUS (which operated the North-South Highway). Because UMNO was heavily involved in business, "this kind of party capitalism gave rise to 'money politics' and then later, [to] a state of vulnerability, leading to the eventual financial crisis of 1997," commented one observer (see Ng 2001, p. 164).

After discovering workers' money had been invested by the state-run Pensions Fund and the Employees' Provident Fund (EPF), in bailing out a few debt-ridden firms, Malaysia's biggest union, the Malaysian Trades Union Congress representing half a million workers, announced it would hold a one-day picket to protest the way the EPF was being run. The opposition DAP had charged that the funds had been mismanaged and wrongfully used for purchasing TimedotCom shares which allegedly had led to a loss of RM500 million within a three-month period. The government, however, said investigations found no elements of fraud.[11]

Still, Tun Daim's approval of controversial bail-outs for both Ramli and Halim had hurt UMNO's image and alienated Malay support. Ironically, during his trials, Anwar Ibrahim had accused Tun Daim of being a prime mover in a conspiracy to frame him — a charge the authorities had denied. Observers say that any policy revisions and reversals from then on would be seen as repudiations of Tun Daim, such as the MAS, Timedotcom and Light Rail Transport bail-outs of his "cronies". Prior to Tun Daim's resignation, Dr Mahathir's son Mohkzani had divested himself of all his business interests. The 2002 Budget to be unveiled in October reportedly will push for greater domestic consumption and investment, rather than relying on foreign investment. Dr Mahathir has always sought to run Malaysia's economy on his own terms, rather than those defined by outsiders like the International Monetary Fund or U.S. pension fund managers.

Given his great ability to re-invent himself to meet challenges and changing situations, observers within and outside the party viewed the resignation of Tun Daim Zainuddin on 1 June 2001, without explanation, as a tactical ploy. He appeared to have been the fall guy.[12] It allowed Dr Mahathir to cleverly switch UMNO's attention to the next election in his speech at the party's general assembly on 23 June. The themes were vintage

Mahathir. But the tone of his message was harsh even by the feisty premier's standards: the Malays are lazy, they haven't seized or appreciated the chances given to them; the Islamic opposition misuses religion and teaches children to hate UMNO; they are willing to do anything, they are willing to sell Malay rights, religion, anything owned by the Malays to get votes from the DAP and the Chinese; Anwar's *reformasi* activists are rabble-rousing scum....[13] But media reports said despite the loud applause which greeted these remarks, there were also grumbles that Mahathir had really nothing new to say to convince fence-sitting Malays to support UMNO again; he was repeating the same old stories.

Apparently with his back pushed to the wall, he had set out on a major clean-up campaign aimed at refurbishing his image and that of UMNO. Many among the party faithful concede that the Prime Minister had to take action or risk losing the next election, which has to be called by early 2004. UMNO must serve the people, it is said, but is seen more as a party for its members to get rich quick. Both Dr Mahathir and UMNO have long been tainted with allegations of corruption, cronyism and nepotism. In May Dr Mahathir had shocked observers in a speech to an UMNO meeting, in which he said that "abundantly rich" members should be barred from holding important posts in the party. Before Tun Daim resigned, the casualties had been relatively small fry: six party divisional heads were suspended for practicing "money politics" during recent party elections. But a clear indication of Dr Mahathir's resolve will be when the party's Supreme Council decides whether or not to take disciplinary action against UMNO secretary-general Khalil Yaacob, being investigated by a party committee. Just how far he will go to distance himself from his old friends and "cronies" to carry out the reforms in UMNO is unclear, but then, Dr Mahathir is a master tactician and the great survivor of Malaysian politics.

Known for his grand ideas, Dr Mahathir's nation-building programme has involved modernization on a big scale. He managed the greatest transformation of the Malaysian economy from a commodities-based one to that of export-oriented industrialization. It turned around from the period of the recession in 1985–87 to new heights of prosperity and grew at the rate of about 9.0 per cent per year for almost a decade until another recession struck again in 1997. This recovery has been attributed to the policies of Tun Daim who was the Finance Minister before his post was taken over by Anwar Ibrahim, Dr Mahathir's former deputy whom he sacked in September 1998.

Undeniably, it was during his administration that the country embarked on a series of mega-projects — described as "prestige projects" or "monuments to his rule" by the opposition — the country's first national car, (the Proton Saga), the Penang Bridge, the North-South Expressway, the new Kuala Lumpur International Airport at Sepang, the Formula One car-racing circuit, the new administrative capital at Putrajaya, (including the RM200 million Prime Minister's residence, dubbed a *mahligai* [palace] by its critics), the world's tallest buildings, Petronas Twin Towers, and the cyber city of Cyberjaya including the Multi-Media Super Corridor. These projects, he would later claim, were to create national consciousness and put Malaysia on the international map. If it had not been for the 1997 Asian economic crisis, he would have gone ahead with the RM2.4 billion Bakun Dam Project that would have inundated a large area of Sarawak the size of Singapore island and produced enough electrical power for the Borneo territories and the peninsular states of West Malaysia. His administration reaped the fruits of Tun Razak's affirmative-action programme, the New Economic Policy, and produced its first generation of high-level Malay entrepreneurs, Malay corporate leaders, and Malay billionaires and millionaires. Malaysia entered the third millennium upbeat and determined to catch up with the developed countries in the fields of information and telecommunications technology.

In terms of national integration, his transformation into a Malaysian nationalist is best exemplified by his policy "Vision 2020" which envisaged the creation of a *Bangsa Malaysia* (Malaysian nation), in which multi-racial Malaysia would become a developed, just and egalitarian society for all races. This declaration was made in 1991 after the NEP had ended. For this reason probably the Vision 2020 was, therefore, welcomed by more non-Malays than Malays. It was all the more pronounced given his earlier profile as a "Malay *ultra*" when he had first courted and won Malay

194 • Malaysia: The Making of a Nation

popularity in the fire and smoke of the 13 May 1969 inter-racial riots. This was when he had expressed strong pro-Malay nationalist sentiments and "anti-Chinese" views. In that same year he was expelled from UMNO for his "hate" letter to Malaysia's Prime Minister Tunku Abdul Rahman, whom he had accused of being "pro-Chinese". Ironically, thirty years later, as Malaysian Prime Minister, in the country's tenth general elections in November 1999, Dr Mahathir found that like the Tunku, more than half of the Malay voters had turned their backs on him. "Must Prime Minister Mahathir Mohamed's fate be like that of the predecessor he so mercilessly tormented 30 years ago, Tunku Abdul Rahman?" asked a Malay academic resident in the United States.[14]

The personal style of his nation-building is best reflected in people's reactions to his leadership. Some loved him, while others hated him. He was often described by the Western Press as "iron-willed", confrontational and scathing in his remarks on his critics and opponents. However, he could at times be witty and was easily accessible to newsmen. Known for his zeal and dedication to work, he followed a daily workaholic schedule despite undergoing quadruple heart bypass in 1989. Dr Mahathir, whose favourite song is said to be Frank Sinatra's "I Did It My Way", has won recognition even from his local critics, especially the PAS Mentri Besar of Terengganu, Datuk Awang Hadi.

Despite his recognized achievements, he has aroused strong antagonistic feelings among his critics who have labelled him, "a dictator and an autocrat, renegade, recalcitrant and practitioner of voodoo economics".[15] Among his PAS critics he was widely derided as "*Mahazalim* (The Most Cruel) and *Mahafiraun* (The Great Pharoah).[16] In early 1999 a Malay national laureaute Shahnon Ahmad had written a satirical novel entitled *Shit* levelled at him. It became a best-seller. Shahnon's feeling of revulsion for him was not only personal but reflected partisan politics, for the novelist was a PAS supporter. In the 1999 general elections, Shahnon stood on a PAS ticket in the Sik constituency of Dr Mahathir's Kedah state and handsomely defeated his erstwhile Islamic affairs adviser and Minister, Datuk Abdul Hamid Othman.

Clearly like the Tunku, Dr Mahathir's nation-building was extremely personalized. Although his government nearly came unseated in the 1990 elections, it recovered its popularity. In 1999, although the Barisan Nasional coalition under Dr Mahathir won the general elections, his own party, UMNO, suffered a most humiliating electoral set-back. It lost four Ministers, five deputy Ministers, several parliamentary secretaries, one state Mentri Besar (Chief Minister) and several state councillors.

In contrast, the opposition Malay party, Parti Islam (PAS), emerged the biggest winner when it tripled its parliamentary seats to 27, all at the expense of UMNO. PAS regained the state of Kelantan which it had ruled since 1990 and captured the state of Terengganu from UMNO. PAS' popular vote increased spectacularly in the states of Pahang, Perak, Perlis, and Kedah. Similarly, three parliamentary seats were won by the newly-formed Parti Keadilan (Justice Party), an off-shoot of UMNO led by the wife of his former deputy, Anwar Ibrahim. The Chinese-led opposition party, the DAP, won ten parliamentary seats, while Parti Bersatu Sabah, another opposition party, won three. Dr Mahathir's ruling Barisan Nasional coalition had used the opposition pact to scare the non-Muslim minorities from voting for the DAP and PAS by telling them that a vote for these parties would be a vote for PAS' ultimate goal of an Islamic state. However, the tactics had failed to scare most of the Malay voters, especially those in the Malay heartland states.

The results gave the opposition coalition, Barisan Alternatif, a total of 45 seats in Parliament, an increase of 15 over their previous strength, but not as great as their 49 seats won in 1990. Overall, Dr Mahathir's Barisan Nasional (BN) coalition had secured 148 seats in the 193-seat Parliament, collecting 56.5 per cent of the popular vote, to its 163 seats in the 192-seat Parliament in the 1995 elections. In 1990, the BN had secured only 127 seats in the then 180-seat Parliament.

While UMNO's losses in the Malay rural areas were greater, those in many urban areas were won or lost by narrow majorities of between 1,000 and 3,000 votes. Its candidates had won on mainly non-Malay votes, a reversal of past trends when UMNO's Malay votes frequently tipped the scales in favour of the candidates of its non-Malay component parties. UMNO's narrow wins in urban areas meant urban Malay educated professionals and student voters, too, had abandoned their support of

UMNO. In the case of Dr Mahathir's own parliamentary constituency of Kubang Pasu in Kedah, his majority had been slashed by 7,088 votes. As it turned out, the voters in the two East Malaysian states of Sabah and Sarawak really saved the day for him by handing him a total of 45 parliamentary seats, which ensured his BN a two-thirds majority in Parliament.

UMNO's defeats were blamed by party stalwarts on Dr Mahathir's nation-building style and leadership. By drawing the heat and fire of politics on himself, he had deflected the interests and attention of both Malays and non-Malays away from each other and focussed them instead on himself. Unconsciously, he had become the target of national integration. National integration may be said to have been achieved when the various communities in a multi-racial society find their political attention diverted to or focused outside at a foreign enemy, or distracted to some personality or controversial major issue locally. He drew so much political fire on himself that the "Mahathir factor" and his "I did it my way" style dominated Malaysian politics for two decades.

In fact, in 1999, most Malay voters were dissatisfied with the way he had treated his former deputy, Anwar Ibrahim. "The manner in which Anwar was ousted has no parallel," says John Funston, a political scientist.[17] "He was dismissed and declared guilty of homosexuality and other sexual misdemeanors before the courts had an opportunity to hear his case. No leader before this had ever been publicly shamed as Anwar has been — contravening deeply entrenched Malay values against such behaviour." Before the elections, calls for Dr Mahathir to resign had appeared on placards and banners at pro-Anwar street protests by several thousands of youthful Malay demonstrators. This was reminiscent of the student demonstrators against Tunku Abdul Rahman's government in 1969 and against Tun Abdul Razak's government in 1974 that occurred mostly in university and college campuses. But in 1999 they were on a larger scale. It was an unprecedented sight for Malay members of the public, old men, women and children, to join Malay students and youths repeatedly in street protests against a Malay Prime Minister. At one stage, these demonstrations occurred almost every week in the urban Malay settlement of Kampung Bahru of Kuala Lumpur. They lasted for more than a month and received wide publicity in the foreign media, but were hardly reported in the government-controlled local media.

Anwar's ill-treatment at the hands of the police authorities was exposed when he appeared in his first court case with a black eye. The government had initially denied that he had been assaulted, but later a police inquiry revealed that the Inspector-General of Police (IGP) had confessed to assaulting Anwar. Dr Mahathir, however, denied that he had instructed the police chief to commit the act. The IGP was charged in court, found guilty and sentenced to two months' jail — a sentence considered by Anwar's supporters and even by the prosecutors alike as light and inadequate. When the IGP first made his admission, the street protests turned violent. Youths attacked the vehicles of the police and of the local government-owned TV station, burnt car tyres and clashed with the police. Similar angry and violent protests were held by Anwar supporters after the court announced a "guilty" verdict in Anwar's trial in April 1999. He was sentenced to six years' imprisonment on charges of having misused his authority to cover up allegations of sexual misconduct. Further street protests continued on his second court conviction for sodomy and sentence to a further nine years of imprisonment. His 15 years' imprisonment meant that he would be prevented from contesting general elections until the year 2020 unless he obtained a royal pardon. Anwar's trials were given full-length coverage in the local media. They went a long way to dent Dr Mahathir's own public image. He appeared as a national leader out to persecute and destroy his former deputy for daring to challenge him for the top leadership post of UMNO and for accusing him and other national leaders of corruption, nepotism and cronyism.

Dr Mahathir's handling of the Anwar case appears to have alienated the younger generation of Malays. At one public meeting in London, one Malaysian student called on him to resign. This open confrontation between him and the students over Anwar continued until the 29 November 1999 elections. Dr Mahathir and senior UMNO Ministers retaliated by criticizing Malay university students for being more interested in politics and street demonstrations than in their studies. Dr Mahathir even went so far as to praise non-Malay students for their diligence and studiousness.

At one UMNO meeting when he talked about the poor academic performance of Malay students, he broke down. The Mahathir-student confrontation continued till mid-July 2001 when fires had damaged properties in two universities, which were allegedly set off by students, and seditious student literature attacking him were found at one of the fire-sites. Later, two university student leaders were detained by police for interrogation over the fires. The fires broke out on the eve of Dr Mahathir's arrival to open an UMNO-organized conference on youth at the University of Malaya. Dr Mahathir, furious at the continued student opposition to his regime, announced that he would introduce new regulations for the universities which would require lecturers and students to sign contracts pledging themselves to academic pursuits and not to indulge in politics, and that admissions into universities would be strictly based on meritocracy for a trial period of one year. This was to ensure that only students who wanted to study would get in.

Clearly the Anwar factor remains the major moral issue for the Malays, especially among Malay youths and women. A significant number of them remain unconvinced about Anwar's guilt, and this issue is still one of the causes of the present split within the Malay community.[18] Most newspaper analysts, especially the pro-government ones, had viewed the 1999 elections as a humiliating defeat for UMNO in this light. Some did not mince their words of criticism at Dr Mahathir. "Quite a number of [UMNO] members and supporters turned against UMNO because of their sympathy for Anwar", said one writer of the pro-government newspaper, the *New Straits Times*.[19] Even a government Senator, the well-known journalist, Zainuddin Mydin, writing in the pro-government Malay newspaper, *Utusan Malaysia*, had come to the same conclusion. He claimed that the "liberalism" which had been practised by the UMNO leadership all these years had led to an unwritten social contract that stability, development and prosperity were more important issues than the moral quality of national and state leaders. Consequently, UMNO leaders had always shied away from the moral exposure of leaders as it would destroy rather than strengthen the party, he said.[20]

The polls over, Dr Mahathir resorted to arrests and litigious actions against several opposition Barisan Alternatif leaders — Karpal Singh

(DAP), Marina Yusof (Keadilan) and Subky Sulung (PAS). Despite the Malaysian Government's denials to the contrary, observers and opposition critics had interpreted these actions as a typically vindictive crackdown by Dr Mahathir.

Mahathir's "Tough" Image & Nation-Building

As we have seen in Chapters Two and Three, Dr Mahathir had first made his name as a Malay radical in the wake of the race riots in 1969. His "hate" letter to the Tunku had caused him to be expelled from UMNO by the party's Supreme Council. He withdrew into the political wilderness for about five years. The experience chastened him. It made him resilient.[21] He was not reinstated in UMNO until 1972 by Tun Abdul Razak who later appointed him a Cabinet Minister. His intransigent and no-nonsense image remained with the public. According to one of his biographers, J.V. Morais, his appointment as Deputy Prime Minister caused anxieties among the Chinese and Indian communities. "Mahathir had long been an ardent 'Malay-firster' ", wrote Morais, "advocating measures to bring native Malays — *bumiputras*, or sons of the soil — into economic equality with the more advanced ethnic groups". Mahathir, however, denied that he was anti-Chinese or anti-Indian, but said he had merely spoken out in favour of "Malays who have a fair share in the country's wealth, no more than that".[22] However, as he stayed on as Prime Minister, his attitude towards the non-Malays changed. He began to accommodate their demands and to recognize their rights, culture and roles in Malaysian society.

As the non-Malays warmed towards him, he began to cultivate them, especially the business and professional groups. At the same time, he encountered problems with the Malays who did not accept his leadership without challenge. In fact, within the span of 20 years as Prime Minister, he had been embroiled in contentious, acrimonious and litigious conflicts over his leadership and policies every few years either with Malay or non-Malay groups. The Malay groups included the Malay Rulers and major factions in UMNO. The most serious of these conflicts led to a Malaysian court declaring UMNO illegal in 1988. Ironically, it was the Malay groups who attacked him the hardest. He aroused the strongest feelings of dislike and hatred among them. At one stage, in 1999, there were "hate Mahathir" leaflets distributed to the public and even threats, allegedly issued by PAS members, to assassinate him. Mahathir had yearned desperately to be the great beloved leader of the Malays, but by July 2001 — when he completed 20 years in office — this dream seemed to have faded away.

To understand Dr Mahathir's nation-building process one, therefore, needs to understand his personality. The London *Sunday Times* of 28 November 1993 described him in 1993 as "prickly, vindictive and one who bears grudges". As one cynical Dutch scholar observed to this writer, "Mahathir was involved in not so much nation-building as Mahathir-building". An extremely proud, sensitive man who was prone to sulk,[23] Dr Mahathir interpreted most issues personally. At 75, he is still imbued with a personal mission. Born to a Malay mother and a Muslim Indian father, a schoolmaster, he studied medicine in Singapore. Never having gone abroad, especially to England, for his higher education unlike the previous three Prime Ministers, his home-grown nationalism is said to be intensely anti-Western xenophobic.

Before he became a full-time politician, he was a highly respected medical doctor in his Kedah state hometown of Alor Star, where he opened his clinic after a short spell in government service. He was elected to Parliament in 1964 as an UMNO candidate. In the May 1969 general elections he lost his seat to a PAS candidate for which he blamed the Tunku and was expelled from the party for his harsh criticisms of the Tunku's administration. His book, *The Malay Dilemma*, published in 1970, was immediately banned. The ban was not lifted until he became Prime Minister in 1981. It was only after he had tendered an apology to the UMNO leadership in 1972 for his misconduct over his "hate Tunku" letter that he was readmitted to the party by Tun Razak who made him Education Minister in 1974. Two years later, on the death of Tun Razak, Prime Minister Hussein Onn appointed him Deputy Prime Minister and Minister for Trade and Industry.

Supremely confident of his administrative abilities and of his own intellect, he had found his touch and mettle when he discharged his ministerial duties. As Minister for Education, he brooked no nonsense from anti-government student demonstrators in the colleges and universities. He ordered the police to enter the University of Malaya campus in Kuala Lumpur to break up demonstrations and arrest student leaders. He was also responsible for introducing the Universities and University Colleges Act that restricted students from taking part in political activities. As Minister for Trade and Industry, he broke up a strike by employees of the national airline, Malaysian Airlines (MAS), and had their leaders arrested and detained without trial under the ISA. He was also responsible for the controversial Industrial Co-ordination Act regulating foreign investments and equities in Malaysia. It was probably when he was in this ministry that his ideas for the future economic development of Malaysia were developed, including the idea to manufacture the national car.

In 1981 after becoming Prime Minister, Dr Mahathir embarked on a well-publicized campaign to reform the bureaucracy, modernize the Malays' outlook, and adopt an "open" and "liberal" style of administration. He intended to show that his new government would be driven by his personal dynamism and by his "personal style". But, as more and more of his policies encountered resistance, he took things personally. As he was repeatedly challenged within and outside his party, he began to concentrate power into his hands. By 1988 he had drawn opposition criticisms of an "authoritarian" image to himself.

"Paradoxes of Mahathirism"

Malaysian political scientist Khoo Boo Teik, in his provocative and well-written study of Dr Mahathir's political ideology, has observed that it was distinctly marked by paradoxes and contradictions. Khoo attempted to present Dr Mahathir's ideas on nationalism, capitalism, Islam, democracy and globalization, which constitute the core of what he calls "Mahathirism", as a " relatively coherent ideology".[24] Yet as Khoo readily admits, these ideas are not well-developed. They suffer from the paradoxes which he is at pains to point out. "Mahathir is no theorist", further observes Khoo,[25] so that the coherence of Dr Mahathir's views lies really in the sum total of its paradoxes, ambiguities and inconsistencies. Or, as Milne and Mauzy have rightly observed, "Mahathirism is not a guide to Mahathir's thoughts or actions. Rather, Mahathir's thoughts and actions are a guide to constructing Mahathirism. Mahathirism is an exercise in allocating his thoughts into logical categories with the aim of achieving intellectual satisfaction and understanding."[26]

For instance, the first two books of Dr Mahathir showed a shift in thinking. His first book, *The Malay Dilemma*, suggested ways for the "complete rehabilitation of the Malays". He took a critical look at the various causes of Malay economic backwardness, much of which were blamed on heredity, the environment, Malay social practices, British colonial policies, "predatory Chinese", Chinese resourcefulness and incompetent Malay leadership. Writing in a combative style, Dr Mahathir missed few opportunities to hit out at "Chinese domination of the economy". His second book, *The Challenge*, which comprises articles and speeches written in the 1970s, however, next dealt with the impact of Western imperialism and Islam on the Malay community. Khoo's study of Dr Mahathir's political ideology unfortunately ends in 1990 at the point the New Economic Policy is terminated, yet he has been able to detect important shifts in Mahathir's views prior to the first decade of his premiership.

> Between the publication of *The Malay Dilemma* and *The Challenge*, Mahathir's Malay nationalism underwent an important transmutation. Its "ultra" Malay nationalist edges of the 1960s, carried over into the pages of *The Malay Dilemma*, were blunted in the 1970s. Its direction at the Chinese was rechannelled. Mahathir's redefinition of the problems facing the Malay community in *The Challenge* turned him *inward* on to the Islamic core of the Malay community, and, simultaneously, *outward* on to the West.[27]

This merely reflects that Dr Mahathir was a shrewd politician, who was prepared to make the necessary twists and turns to suit the changing circumstances of local and international politics. Once he became Prime Minister in 1981, he realized he was no longer just a Malay leader but, as the

Tunku had never failed to remind him, he was the Prime Minister of a multi-racial society. Yet he had not yet endeared himself to the non-Malays or suspended their distrust of him or his own mistrust of them. In the 1982 and 1986 general elections, although his BN coalition won convincingly, he still appeared disappointed with the tardy non-Malay support he had obtained. In the 1986 elections, the DAP did exceedingly well, reflecting Chinese opposition in the country towards Dr Mahathir. It increased its parliamentary seats from nine in 1982 to 24, and trebling its state assembly seats from 12 to 37. Significantly, the DAP took a considerable 20.82 per cent of the popular vote, while PAS faired badly in terms of seats, winning only one parliamentary seat compared to five in 1982, and only 15 state seats compared to 18 in 1982, though it took 15.58 per cent of the popular vote. Dr Mahathir clearly equated the parliamentary opposition with the Chinese, who had not endeared themselves to him. The previous 1982 election outcome was not totally a Chinese or non-Malay endorsement of his leadership, but for the continued policies of the previous Prime Minister, Tun Hussein Onn who was quite popular with the non-Malays. But, in 1986, the non-Malays were clearly dissatisfied with Dr Mahathir's performance.

Non-Malay dissatisfaction increased in the 1990 general elections. The results were the worst for Dr Mahathir since he came to power. The elections started with the BN losing its affiliate, Parti Bersatu Sabah, which defected to the opposition front just after nomination. The final count gave the BN 127 seats, securing the two-thirds majority by merely seven seats in the 180-member Parliament. Its popular vote fell to 53.38 per cent. The DAP won 20 seats, PBS 14, the now-defunct Parti Melayu Semangat '46, a breakaway of UMNO, eight, and PAS seven. Although the 1999 general election results were better than the 1990 results, in some specific instances, they were worst than those in the 1990 and 1969 elections, particularly in the distribution of the votes and the defeat of major political figures, including Cabinet Ministers.

But it was the 1995 general elections which marked the turning-point of non-Malay support for Dr Mahathir's BN. The elections gave him the best ever endorsement — 162 seats and 65.16 per cent of the popular vote.

The opposition coalition could only secure 30 parliamentary seats. The non-Malays seemed to have been comfortable with Dr Mahathir's administration and his "Vision 2020". The BN subsequently gained more seats through crossovers and the return of Semangat '46 to the UMNO fold three years later.

This survey of electoral results does not reveal that certain political crises had occurred between these election dates that affected Dr Mahathir's popularity and leadership. The crises produced different ethnic responses towards him when the paradoxes of Mahathirism fully came into play. For instance, his decision to rely on non-Malay support began in 1988 when UMNO was split into two factions and was later declared an illegal party. Dr Mahathir was for a while a leader without a party. He was propped up mainly by the non-Malay component parties of the BN. The enunciation of his "Vision 2020" in 1991 was his *quid pro quo* or coming to terms with the non-Malays whom he now began to cultivate and to accommodate, as he needed their support for his political survival. In spite of and because of the Malay split, he won the 1995 general elections, and again the 1999 elections, when he continued to accommodate them.

Changing Policies

Hence, for his political survival, Dr Mahathir had always been prepared to indulge in paradoxes — to change his policies, to adapt to new situations, to embrace his enemies and even to drop old friends. One can, therefore, quote him on one occasion as supporting democracy, and then a while later as denouncing it. In 1968, he had supported the Malay rulers and the Malay feudal system,[28] but in 1983 and again in 1993 he had denounced them when they opposed his policies. In 1975 when he was Minister for Education, he had stepped up the use of Malay language in schools and universities, but in 1993 as Prime Minister he had ordered the re-introduction of English as the medium of instruction for science, engineering and medical subjects in institutions of higher learning. Given these paradoxes, "Mahathirism" cannot constitute a consistent ideology for posterity. It continues to stand for ambiguity and inconsistency.

Dr Mahathir's inconsistencies are best reaffirmed by a confidant, the journalist Zainuddin Mydin:

> In his early days as Prime Minister Mahathir showed extra anxiety not to lay himself open to accusations of abuse of power by not allowing guests to bring presents to his daughter's wedding. But ten years later he has laid himself open to criticism for his children's participation in the business world, and some even see similarities now between him and President Soeharto of Indonesia.[29]

And, again, Zainuddin Mydin recalls,

> Mahathir himself had to go through the same course of adaptation over a period of time since becoming a member of government. He had to make this adaptation on big things and small ones, so much so that he appeared to have shifted from his tenets and beliefs as stated in his book *The Malay Dilemma*, and had to undergo a process of reinterpretation or re-nationalisation to explain his acceptance of all those things that he had been uncomfortable with in the past...Mahathir became rather a pragmatic person, less angry, and less loud...[30]

The Liberal Phase of Dr Mahathir, 1981–87

After taking over as Prime Minister from Hussein Onn in 1981, Mahathir shocked Malaysians by asking them to rise half an hour later by putting them in the same time zone as Sabah. This time zone adjustment was later followed by Singapore, and in July 2001 Thailand announced it was thinking of following suit in order that "Thais could work an hour longer every day in order to improve their economy". Malaysian civil servants were also asked to clock in to work, and to wear name tags in an effort to improve efficiency and to show transparency, so that the public could identify and report inefficient government employees. He introduced the slogan, *"Bersih, Cekap dan Amanah"* (Clean, Efficient and Trustworthy), and a few more slogans and measures to discipline the people through *Absorption of Islamic Values*, and *Leadership by Example*.

His "open and liberal" phase of administration from 1981 to 1988 contrasted sharply to his "authoritarian" phase between 1988 and 2001. The early phase reflected a Mahathir who wanted to be loved by the public and who promoted efficiency, honesty, tolerance, accommodation and democracy. One of his first acts was to release 21 political detainees on 30 July 1981. This was two weeks after becoming Prime Minister. He also sought and obtained from the King the pardon of Datuk Harun Idris, a former UMNO ally and youth leader who, between May 1975 and December 1977, had been found guilty of various charges of corruption and sentenced to six years' imprisonment. More political detainees were released by Mahathir over a period of time. He also made a public apology to Tunku Abdul Rahman over his "hate letter" incident. He also allowed local newspapers greater freedom. He had not yet seen them a real threat. He also had not yet found political enemies at home, although he had found a few abroad. Like Don Quixote, he began to tilt his lance first at foreign windmills. It aroused in the hearts of some Malaysians a fierce spirit of patriotism, national independence and national sovereignty and hostility towards foreign powers, especially towards the former colonial master, Britain. One Singapore scholar, Joseph Liow, has observed that Mahathir's foreign policy objectives for the 1990s were framed by his personality and "idiosyncrasies" and by domestic factors to satisfy nationalist needs.[31] Locally, acts like the release of political detainees raised the people's hopes for a new era of freedom and democracy. But Mahathir's feelings and thinking began to shift differently once the political temperatures and challenges to his rule began to mount.

After nine months in office, Mahathir decided to go to the polls to win his own mandate to govern on 22 April 1982. Before making the election announcement, he pulled off a coup when he persuaded the charismatic president of the Malaysian Muslim Youth Movement (ABIM), Anwar Ibrahim, to join UMNO. This was to prevent PAS from grabbing Anwar who was rumoured to be contemplating joining the opposition party. Soon Anwar's rise was rapid. He was immediately picked to contest in the

Penang state's Permatang Pauh parliamentary constituency, and won against his PAS opponent with a majority of more than 14,000 votes. Overall, the polls endorsed Dr Mahathir's administration. It gave the Barisan Nasional 132 of the 154 parliamentary seats. It had raised its share of parliamentary seats by nine, and increased its share of the popular vote by four per cent to 61.28 per cent. For the DAP, its fifteen seats won in the 1978 election were reduced to six, while PAS' tally of five parliamentary seats remained unchanged.

Dr Mahathir next pushed his brand of Malaysian (à la Malay) nationalism by striking at Malaysia's former colonial ruler, Britain. It was a curious blend of personal slight, affront and national anger. Khoo Boo Teik observed that he had chosen to demonstrate the intensity of his nationalism "in a highly visible, curious and seemingly negative manner".[32] Some two months after becoming Prime Minister, Dr Mahathir angered the British Government with Malaysia's takeover of Guthrie Corporation in a "dawn raid" by the Perbadanan Nasional Berhad (PNB, or National Equity Corporation) in the London Stock Exchange on 7 September 1981. The British company owned some 200,000 acres of rubber estates, oil palm and cocoa plantations in Malaysia. The successful takeover meant the return of those estates to Malaysia. But it provoked the British Government under Prime Minister Mrs Margaret Thatcher to change the rules of the LSE to prevent such takeovers in future. This action was soon followed by Malaysia's official but limited boycott of British goods and services (but not direct investment) known as the "Buy British Last" policy.

What prompted this policy was the British media's and the LSE's hostile reaction to the Guthrie takeover. It was also interpreted as Dr Mahathir's retaliation after a series of frustrations at British attitudes towards Malaysia, among which was an earlier British policy to increase tuition fees for overseas students which badly affected Malaysian students in Britain among whom a large number was government-sponsored. This action was followed a year later by Mahathir reclaiming Carcosa Hill, a 7.2 acre site of real estate which had been a gift to the British Government by Malaysia's first prime minister, Tunku Abdul Rahman. Mahathir encouraged UMNO members to campaign and demand the return of

Carcosa, a move which offended the Tunku greatly. The campaign continued and did not reach a settlement until 1984. It aroused strong nationalistic sentiments only among Malays. UMNO Youth members held a huge anti-British demonstration to support the demand. To some quarters, like the Tunku, this claim was not in good taste, but for Dr Mahathir it was simply a tit-for-tat for British policies. On these two issues, Dr Mahathir obtained support mainly from Malay groups in UMNO and the UMNO-owned newspapers.

Although he had earlier made a public apology to Tunku Abdul Rahman over his conduct in the "hate letter" incident, he showed his personal angst again in 1984 at both the British Government and at Tunku Abdul Rahman, when he formally requested the British Government to return Carcosa Hill. Commenting on this incident, the Tunku said: "At one time I had been accused of selling this country to the Chinese, now Carcosa to the British, so what will remain of me after I am dead and gone, only Allah knows. I have a feeling that there will only be curses and plenty of them."[33] The British view was that it was not appropriate to hand it back while the Tunku, who gave it to the British, was still alive. On 12 May 1984, the British Government agreed to hand Carcosa Hill back to the Malaysian Government without asking for any compensation in return. In a reciprocal gesture, he offered the British an alternative site for use as official residence of the British High Commissioner. That ended the matter.

Contest with the Malay Rulers, 1983

The first direct challenge to Dr Mahathir's leadership came from the Sultan of Pahang who in 1981 had begun to interfere in UMNO politics and in state government policies. Dr Mahathir bided his time. He did not retaliate immediately. Reluctantly, he was forced to request his Pahang Mentri Besar (Chief Minister), Haji Abdul Rahim Bakar, to resign following a conflict with the Sultan over the issue of logging. The ruler wanted Rahim to be replaced with a more acceptable appointee. Apparently Dr Mahathir did not feel strong enough to act against the ruler, but before long he decided to take retaliatory action.

Problems between the sultans and the chief ministers and between the sultans and the prime ministers had been going on since the Tunku's time. UMNO leaders had repeatedly reminded the rulers not to exceed the limits of their constitutional powers, but these pleas were ignored. They interfered in the appointment of the Chief Ministers and the state executive council members. They asked for increases in their financial allocations. They indulged in extravagant life-styles and expenditures.

In 1983, in anticipation of the appointment of difficult, unco-operative and ambitious rulers who might succeed as the *Yang Di-Pertuan Agong* (the Paramount King) and his Deputy, and who might give him trouble by withholding their royal assent over legislative Bills,[34] Dr Mahathir decided to pre-empt matters by introducing in Parliament an amendment to the Malaysian Constitution which aimed, among other things, to ensure that the *Yang Di-Pertuan Agong* and other state Rulers could no longer block the passage of Bills passed by Parliament or State legislative councils.

The amendment stipulated that if for any reason a Bill which was submitted to the *Yang Di-Pertuan Agong* was not assented to within fifteen days, he is deemed to have assented to it and the Bill would accordingly become law. The Sultan of Pahang, who was then the *Yang Di-Pertuan Agong*, had earlier agreed to the amendment, but when another Malay ruler opposed it, he followed suit. The other rulers also fell in line. Dr Mahathir decided to take the issue to the people. He went on a campaign trail, during which he and UMNO leaders criticized the Malay Rulers and explained their misconduct to the people. Finally, to force the Rulers' hands, he tabled the controversial Bill and won the Parliament's approval of the amendment. The Rulers capitulated. They agreed to accept it after obtaining an amendment to allow the *Yang Di-Pertuan Agong* to be given 30 days instead of the original fifteen days' grace to consider any Bill submitted to him for his assent.

The outcome of this confrontation turned out to be Dr Mahathir's personal triumph. It also asserted the victory of constitutional government, nationalism and popular sovereignty over the royalty. What three previous Prime Ministers had failed to achieve, Dr Mahathir had accomplished. But before long, observers noted that the victory was incomplete. The Rulers seemed reluctant to give up their interference in political affairs and were expected to mount a counter-attack before long. Dr Mahathir had perforce to cross swords again with the Rulers ten years later to make the victory more decisive.

"Look East" Policy & National Car

In 1983 as a continuation of his confrontation with the British Government he introduced a "Look East" policy to re-orient Malaysians towards Japanese and Korean models of economic and socio-cultural development. Observers interpreted that this policy was directed at the Malays. Although to "Look East" could have meant looking to China and the Chinese as well, Dr Mahathir did not urge the Malays to emulate the Chinese in achieving economic success, as he was to throw caution to the winds and publicly urge them to do so in 2001, especially when he marked his 20-year-in-office. He did not do so for his "Look East" policy, according to Zainuddin Mydin, because this would have aroused the anger of the Malays then. Besides, Dr Mahathir in his book, *The Malay Dilemma*, had criticized the "Chinese economic domination" of Malaysia. Here was another glaring paradox of Dr Mahathir.

During the "Look East" campaign, Dr Mahathir launched strong criticisms of the supposed Malay "disinclination to work" and blamed the historical downfall of the Malays on a wide-spread Malay predilection for "comfort the easy way". To him, the New Economic Policy did not mean distributing wealth only to Malays, but it meant the Malays had to emulate the Japanese, the Koreans and the Taiwanese in working hard. "Look East was the policy expression of that maturation of Mahathir's nationalism," says Khoo Boo Teik. "It had come full circle in the 1980s to redirect the gaze of the Malays and Malaysians away from the West to the East but, perhaps most important of all, not inwards at its old non-Malay target [the Chinese and Indians]."[35]

But there was more to rhetoric in the "Look East" policy. Many construction projects were awarded to firms from the East Asian countries in the hope that they would provide staff training for locals and facilitate the transfer of technology to Malaysia. The government tried to inculcate the values of thrift, hard work and high productivity from these countries in Malaysian workers, but before long, critics found the results were not successful. More charitable critics said the conditions in Malaysia were not identical to the East Asian countries.

In 1985 the RM850 million 18.5 km-long Penang Bridge, the world's third longest, was completed by a Korean engineering firm. It was a project which had been planned at the instigation of the Chief Minister of Penang State, Dr Lim Chong Eu. But it was not to be funded and constructed until during Dr Mahathir's administration. To coincide with the opening of the bridge, Dr Mahathir took the opportunity to lead a parade of spanking new cars known as the Proton Saga, which were produced locally in Malaysia with the assistance of Japanese car manufacturer Mitsubishi, on the bridge.

Dr Mahathir's dream of the Proton Saga had apparently begun in 1979 when he was then the Minister for Trade and Industry. He conceived of the national car industry as the impetus to propel the nation on an industrial path. Although the local automobile industry had built up an efficient and reliant auto parts industry, it had not envisaged moving into this cost-effective and technologically innovative phase. This was a supportive role Dr Mahathir felt the Malaysian Government should play. Roundly criticized at the outset, mostly by academics, consumer groups and rival automobile companies, the project was "unashamedly nationalistic", says a Mahathir admirer who glowingly commented, "its realisation from scratch and its blazing speed between decision and implementation cumulatively make for a tale worth telling".[36] On 1 April 1985, the first Proton Saga had rolled out of its Shah Alam factory near Kuala Lumpur. Initially, the factory produced 850 units a day, but the figures kept increasing as Malaysians quickly took to the car. Its sales were partly boosted by the government's imposition of a 30 per cent tax on all imported cars, a move designed to make the Proton Saga cheaper and give it a competitive edge. These were the early triumphs in Dr Mathahir's policies of economic development.

Emboldened by such successes, he continued to tilt at foreign windmills by mocking at Western policies. He was particularly angry with the British and Australian Governments over their opposition to death sentences imposed by Malaysian courts on Britons and Australians convicted for possession of drugs. Their appeals and protests as well as those of international human rights organizations against these sentences were to no avail. In his conflict with the international media and his overseas adversaries, Dr Mahathir attempted to arouse the sentiments of the Malaysian public to his side by using local media support. As most of the local media were indirectly government-owned, it was not a difficult achievement. Internationally, Dr Mahathir began to take on the stance of a Third World critic of the Western world. His attitude was extremely confrontational. At every world forum where he had been invited to speak, he would launch attacks on Western policies, especially those of the United States, Europe, Britain and Australia. The world remembered his out-spokenness as Deputy Prime Minister in 1981 when to stem the tide of Vietnamese refugees flooding into Malaysia, he had reportedly said: "If the illegal Vietnamese refugees continue to come in, we will shoot them on sight." Nothing that was said later to explain this statement as a misquotation, such as "shoo" for "shoot", changed people's opinion of his toughness and determination.

Fighting Islamic Fundamentalism

Locally, Dr Mahathir also took on the Muslim fundamentalists, a threat that his predecessor had failed to address seriously. This was the period of the revival of Islamic fundamentalism following the Iranian Revolution in 1979. In Malaysia the *dakwah* (the return to strict, puritan Islam) movement had begun. Its message was spreading among the Muslim Malays in the cities, especially among the professional groups, in the universities and in the civil service. PAS was in the thick of the *dakwah* movement.

In 1985 one of its followers, Ibrahim Mahmud, a graduate of Al Azhar University, who was better known as Ibrahim Libya because of his connections with a Libya Islamic organization in Tripoli, had established an Islamic commune at Kampong Memali in the Baling area in Kedah state. Police attempts to arrest him and 36 others for various offences, including the possession of arms, led to an armed confrontation in which 18 people were killed. Among the dead were four police officers as well as Ibrahim Mahmud, while a number of policemen and villagers were wounded. The police arrested 159 villagers, some of whom were women and children. A curfew was imposed on the whole Baling area. Later, the Deputy Prime Minister and Minister for Home Affairs, Datuk Musa Hitam, presented a report to Parliament. PAS Deputy President Fadzil Noor said that he was shocked by the incident, regretted that it had occurred and said that the dead religious leader and the other PAS members had acted as individuals. Dr Mahathir was on an official visit to China, and had been informed of the police action. Although Musa Hitam had urged him to cancel the trip, he had refused. Later, the conduct of this incident would become one of the causes of the break-up of their partnership.

This was a time when Malaysia seemed to many Western observers and to its non-Muslim citizens to be moving towards an Islamic state. Dr Mahathir attempted to blunt the effects by not only taking on PAS on the platform of religious politics, and branding it as a dangerous extremist party but also by making concessions to these groups and by introducing Islamization policies, for which he would later be criticized for appeasing the *ulama* (the religious scholars) who threatened to engulf him.[37] In adopting these measures, he probably accepted the advice of his young Minister, Anwar Ibrahim. The introduction of the Islamic Centre, the Islamic Bank, the International Islamic University, and the Institute for Islamic Research, and the upgrading of many other Islamic institutions brought Islam into the national mainstream.

But Dr Mahathir also tried to change the Muslim Malays' attitudes. "He was unhappy with the fatalistic attitude of the Malays who did not want to accumulate wealth because they could not take it with them to their graves," says Zainuddin Mydin, referring to those whom Dr Mahathir castigated for throwing away their television sets and refrigerators.[38] There were Muslim Malays who abandoned their homes to go wandering around to spread their religion. Zainuddin Mydin adds, "He also did not expect it to go to the extent of producing a Malay woman doctor who would prod a male patient with a pencil because she was loath to touch him, but this did actually happen."[39]

He, therefore, attempted to curb Islamic extremism and militancy among some sections of Muslim intellectuals by playing an "Islamic card" — the recruitment of the President of Angkatan Belia Islam Malaysia (ABIM),

Anwar Ibrahim, into UMNO. He would later argue it was to prevent Anwar from joining PAS. Anwar's ABIM, however, had become a powerful lobby which challenged the government on issues affecting Islam, and was reportedly working with PAS. According to Zainuddin Mydin, "Mahathir saw that it would have been more dangerous to UMNO and the country if Anwar had remained on the outside and allowed to work in collaboration with PAS".[40]

As Minister for Culture, Youth and Sports, Anwar was asked to introduce moderate policies and to understand the wishes and feelings of a plural and open society as well as accommodate the aspirations of Islamization. Later, however, when he became Education Minister, Anwar adopted a policy which forced non-Muslim students in universities to take courses in Islam. Besides his strong concessions to radical Islamism, Anwar also adopted an increasingly nationalistic posture. In 1987 he attempted to change the nature of Chinese primary schools by appointing teachers who were not Chinese-educated to 153 vacancies in these schools. Despite joint protests from the MCA, the Gerakan, the DAP and Chinese educational groups, Anwar went ahead and organized UMNO Youth and Malay organizations to rally to his cause, raising inter-racial tensions which were only diffused by mass arrests of 106 people, including some of the protesters. Observers noted that Dr Mahathir condoned much of Anwar's "extremist" policies during this period, and he was regarded as "Mahathir's blue-eyed boy".

At the foreign policy level, Dr Mahathir's Islamism did not extend to supporting Iraqi leader Saddam Hussein's invasion of Kuwait in 1991, although he was aware of the strong sympathies and sentiments of Muslim Malays in his country, especially those of PAS members. Malaysia later supported a number of resolutions of the United Nations to condemn Iraq's invasion of Kuwait as well as the despatch of UN forces to liberate Kuwait. When Iraq was defeated in the Gulf War, he drew moral lessons for the benefit of the Muslim Malays. A Muslim nation, with God-given wealth, had been attacked by a greedy Muslim neighbour, he told an UMNO assembly on 8 November 1991. "In their defeat, the soldiers of this Muslim nation had to kiss the feet of their non-Muslim enemies in fear," he said.

U.S. President George Bush appreciated Dr Mahathir's support on the Kuwait issue. Malaysia's foreign policy position on the war stood out when PLO leader Yasser Arafat came to Kuala Lumpur after the Gulf War to tell Dr Mahathir of the enormous problems he was facing after the defeat of Iraq. He had lost the moral and financial support of several Arab countries, including Saudi Arabia that condemned the PLO's support of Iraq's invasion of Kuwait. Arafat was now forced by the United States to seek peace with Israel. Owing to Malaysia's continuous support of the Palestinian struggle, he felt it necessary to inform Dr Mahathir first of his plans to enter into peace negotiations with Israel.[41] By not going with the sentiments of his people, Dr Mahathir had come out strongly for a principle that no big nation could violate the sovereignty of a weak nation, and thereby even won Arafat's respect for his stand. "A leader is someone who does not drift with the current in order to seek popularity and influence, but must be prepared to be unpopular to give priority to the realities before him and the future of the people and the country," says his confidant Zainuddin Mydin.[42]

Dr Mahathir would later demonstrate his personal style of leadership over Islamic issues again when in 1994 he banned the Darul Arqam Movement and detained its leader Ashaari under the ISA. In 2001 his government took action to smash the terrorist organization Al Ma'unah, whose leader led an armed group to seize guns and ammunition from an army camp in Perak state in an abortive attempt to seize power. When Ashaari and some of his Darul Arqam followers were arrested after being extradited from Thailand, they made confessions which were carried on television. Dr Mahathir frequently castigated the local *ulama* (religious leaders) for indulging in politics, especially some *ulama* from Selangor state for their *fatwa* (decisions) banning the participation of Malay women in beauty contests and Malay men in body-building and weight-lifting competitions, even though the *fatwa* seemed to have won wide Muslim Malay support. Some observers thought he displayed great moral courage. On such issues, even Anwar Ibrahim, his Deputy Prime Minister, failed to speak out against the *ulama*.

The Authoritarian Phase, 1987–2000

As we have seen, Dr Mahathir had earlier displayed his "authoritarian" streak when he held the posts of Minister for Education and Minister for Commerce and Industry, but in 1987 he threw aside any pretensions that he was a liberal by his arrest and detention of over 100 individuals under the ISA. These repressive actions culminated after a series of events which, in Dr Mahathir's view, showed that his critics and opponents had been taking him too much for granted as a liberal, while posing serious threats to his leadership. He never returned to such a liberal stance again, even in 1999, when he agreed to the establishment of the Human Rights Commission. The Commission, which was headed by the former Deputy Prime Minister Tan Sri Musa Hitam, was frequently at loggerheads with Dr Mahathir, various Ministers and the police over alleged abuses of police power.

His popular partnership with his deputy, Musa Hitam, had ended on 16 March 1986 when Musa resigned from his post. Their partnership, which was labelled by the local Press as the "2M" administration, had foundered over personal and policy differences. One of the reasons was his refusal to accede to Musa's request that he drop Tengku Razaleigh Hamzah from the Cabinet after the former had twice defeated the latter in the contest for the post of deputy president in UMNO. It was speculated that Dr Mahathir refused to do so in order to restrain the incumbent UMNO deputy president by using Tengku Razaleigh as a counter-balance to Musa's advancing political career. Milne and Mauzy called this Dr Mahathir's "checks and balances" strategy "to make sure that holders of government posts are kept aware of the presence of a potential rival for the Prime Minister's favour".[43]

Dr Mahathir had even accused Musa of challenging his leadership and policies. He appointed Ghafar Baba, an UMNO vice-president, as the Deputy Prime Minister when Musa resigned. It is important to note that by the year 2000 four Deputy Prime Ministers have served him, the fourth being Deputy Prime Minister, Datuk Abdullah Badawi, after he had dismissed Datuk Seri Anwar Ibrahim, who was his third. In the UMNO leadership contests on 24 April 1987, Tengku Razaleigh and Musa Hitam joined forces against Dr Mahathir and Ghafar Baba, Tengku Razaleigh standing against Dr Mahathir for the post of UMNO president while Musa Hitam took on

Ghafar Baba for the deputy president's post. Both lost, Tengku Razaleigh by 43 votes and Musa Hitam by 40 votes. After his victory, Dr Mahathir acted swiftly to eliminate not only both the main contenders but all their sympathizers from his Cabinet, in spite of the fact that most of their supporters had been re-elected to their seats on the UMNO Supreme Council.[44]

As the internal struggle within UMNO raged on, Dr Mahathir launched a strong attack on the Malaysian judiciary and, according to Milne and Mauzy,[45] succeeded in the "destruction" of its independence. In 1986–87 he had been incensed by a number of important High Court decisions which went against the government. In this confrontation between the executive and the judiciary, Dr Mahathir went to great lengths to criticize the judges for acting beyond the limits of their responsibility. They were being censured outside the courtroom, he argued, when they made political statements. The Malaysian Bar Council and the highest judicial officer in the country, the Lord President, Tun Salleh Abbas, expressed their shock with the Prime Minister's view that the judiciary was a branch of the government service, instead of being apart from the legislature and the executive. Only in a totalitarian state did the judiciary serve the executive, they claimed.

Following these developments, the government decided to delineate the specific roles of the executive, legislature and judiciary. What bothered him was that the opposition parties were frequently using the courts to challenge the government's policies. After UMNO had been declared illegal and Dr Mahathir had successfully registered his new party UMNO Baru, the ousted leaders filed an appeal to legalize the old UMNO. He acted quickly by having Parliament pass, without much public notice, the Federal Constitution (Amendment) Act 1988, in which the powers of the judiciary would no longer be embedded in the Constitution, but would be conferred by Parliament through statutes. By this Act, the High Courts were stripped of the power of judicial review previously granted in the Constitution. Furthermore, the Attorney-General assumed control of instructing the courts on what cases to hear and which courts to use, and assumed responsibility for judicial assignments and transfers. "Hence, virtually overnight, the modified separation of powers was terminated and the judiciary was stripped of much of its independence and power", state Milne and Mauzy.[46]

Further attacks on the judiciary came in early May 1988 when the Lord President set the date for the Supreme Court to hear the crucial UMNO appeal by the full bench of all nine judges. But on 26 May, he was suspended for "gross misbehaviour and misconduct" over a letter he had written to the King, in which he had complained about the Prime Minister's attacks on the judiciary. His dismissal was for some breaches of protocol, especially that of by-passing the Prime Minister. A tribunal comprising local and foreign judges was appointed to adjudicate on the action against the Lord President. Four days later, five Supreme Court judges were also suspended for "gross misbehaviour" for issuing an order to block the tribunal. The tribunal submitted its report, in which it found the Lord President guilty. Tun Salleh Abbas was dismissed by the King. A reconstituted Supreme Court under the new President Tan Sri Abdul Hamid, "a school friend of Mahathir's and said to be an 'interested party' "[47] (because he was a member of the tribunal which recommended the dismissal of Tun Salleh Abbas) set aside the restraining order. These various actions including Tan Sri Abdul Hamid's appointment drew strong condemnation from local lawyers, especially from the Malaysian Bar Council, which refused to recognize his appointment. The Supreme Court later rejected the UMNO appeal, giving Dr Mahathir his critical victory. Like his battles against the Malay rulers and against his rivals in the UMNO leadership, Dr Mahathir had triumphed personally again in his battle against the judiciary.

As the Malay internal struggle in the UMNO intensified, some of its members and leaders were not averse to participate in hotly debated public issues within and without the government to win public influence and support. Some engaged in debates with opposition non-Malay politicians on sensitive issues such as Malay political primacy, the status of Tamil and Chinese education, and the "immigrant" status of non-Malays. These debates were widely reported in the local media during this "liberal" phase of Dr Mahathir, who did not approve of what he saw and read. Feeling that his leadership was seriously challenged and threatened by "democratic liberalism", he decided on the mass arrests which were carried out by the police on 28 October 1987. Those arrested and detained under the ISA came from a broad spectrum of dissent and included critics and dissidents from opposition parties, his own party UMNO Baru, religious groups, university academicians, and NGOs. It was followed by the closure of three newspapers, the English-language *Star*, the Chinese-language *Sin Chew Jit Poh* and the Malay-language weekly, *Watan*. In a statement to Parliament, he said "the government could not wait for rioting to erupt before taking action". The government's actions were criticized strongly within Malaysia and internationally by human rights groups. Although over time the detainees were released and the banning of the newspapers was lifted, the liberal atmosphere which had existed prior to these actions had not fully returned, as periodic arrests and detentions under the ISA continued. Clearly, Dr Mahathir not content with having vanquished his various rivals — the opposition in the general elections, the Malay Rulers, the dissidents in the UMNO leadership, and the judiciary — had now resorted to locking up a larger number of his opponents, critics and dissidents. For the first time, the term "Dictator" was now freely applied by his critics to Dr Mahathir.

These stresses and strains were bound to take their toll on anyone's health. Dr Mahathir suffered a heart attack on 18 January 1989 and was operated on six days later by a local team of Malay doctors, giving a big boost to local heart by-pass surgery. He made a quick recovery, and was hurtled back headlong into another decade of political crises. This was immediately followed soon after by the happy news that the Razaleigh-Musa alliance, which had always been uneasy, was formally broken up on 31 January 1989 when Musa declared himself a member of Dr Mahathir's UMNO Baru, thus bringing back his supporters from Johor and others including Datuk Abdullah Ahmad Badawi. The year was capped by Malaysia hosting the Commonwealth Heads of Government Meeting (CHOGM) in Kuala Lumpur from 18–24 October 1989. It was opened by Britain's Queen Elizabeth, and marked a reversal of Malaysia's position towards the Commonwealth in 1986–87 when Dr Mahathir had seriously considered pulling out from it, but two separate foreign policy studies had recommended against it.[48]

Mahathir's Nation-Building in the 1990s

The formation of UMNO Baru, the sidelining of his opponents in the Semangat '46 and the beginning of his "authoritarianism" now gave Dr Mahathir a freer hand at administration, in social engineering and economic development. His appointment of Daim Zainuddin as Finance Minister led to Malaysia's take-off from the economic depression in the 1987–88 period and the beginning of the country's yearly economic growth of about 8.7 per cent. As more and more government services were privatized and corporatized under the NEP, the economic development of Malays improved.

The local media was filled daily with the news and photographs of Malay business and corporate giants. In the economic boom, non-Malay business companies were also doing equally well. However, as more and more opportunities for success to many Malays in business, industry and other activities grew, criticisms of the fair distribution of the fruits of economic wealth increased and became sensitive issues. These were not only raised by non-Malay politicians, but also by opposition Malay politicians and thoses who felt they were excluded from these activities. Everyone seemed to want a share in the country's prosperity. The NEP was due to end in 1990. Consequently, the October 1990 general elections reflected both Malay and non-Malay voter disenchantment. The election results were the worst that Dr Mahathir had experienced as Prime Minister. He merely secured a two-thirds majority by just seven seats in the 180-seat Parliament, while the opposition obtained a total of 53 parliamentary seats.

Undaunted, Dr Mahathir battled on. In a working paper entitled, "Malaysia: The Way Forward", to the Malaysian Business Council on 28 February 1991, Dr Mahathir enunciated what became known as his Vision 2020, or *Wawasan 2020*. It outlined the path that Malaysian society should take to achieve the status of a "fully developed country" by 2020 when the country's Gross Domestic Product (GDP) could become eight times larger than its GDP in 1990. His winning formula included an accelerated industrialization drive, economic liberalization and further deregulation. These policies were incorporated within the new National

Development Policy (NDP) which would be promulgated in mid-1991 to replace the NEP. For Malaysia to achieve Dr Mahathir's national goal of competing equally with the advanced nations of the world, Malays and non-Malays had to play their parts in "establishing a united Malaysian nation" possessed of "a sense of common and shared destiny" and "a full and fair partnership" and "made up of one *Bangsa Malaysia*, or Malaysian nation or race".[49]

The year 1993 saw Dr Mahathir embarking on new variations of policies introduced in the 1980s. The unfinished 1983 constitutional crisis to cut down royal power and prerogatives was looming up again. It needed attending to, as one or two rulers, particularly the Sultan of Kelantan was playing politics by supporting Semangat '46, whose president Tengku Razaleigh, was related to the ruler. Tengku Razaleigh was said to have influenced the latter to support his party during the 1990 general elections. Given the successes arising from the NEP, the rulers themselves were trying to compete with UMNO leaders and members for business licences and contracts and other economic benefits. They still continued to interfere in state appointments and to indulge in various forms of improper conduct towards ordinary citizens.

It was the strategy by which Dr Mahathir handled the rulers and brought the issue to a successful conclusion that impressed most people, especially the non-Malays. This began in December 1992 when the son of the Sultan of Johor, the Tengku Bendahara Tengku Majid Idriss, had assaulted a non-Malay hockey goalkeeper. This was followed by another incident when the Sultan of Johor himself attacked a non-Malay hockey coach from Johor, Douglas Gomez. This incident was prominently reported by the English-language newspaper the *New Straits Times*. The news was immediately picked up by the vernacular press. "They convinced Mahathir of the need for swift action on an issue which had angered the people and which had transcended the bounds of politics and communalism," said his confidant, Zainuddin Mydin. "He moved in with lightning speed to tackle them."[50] The Inspector General of Police announced that the Johor police had received a report from Douglas Gomez that he had been struck on the face by the Sultan of Johor.

This incident truly shocked the nation. The Deputy Prime Minister Ghafar Baba tabled a motion in Parliament on 10 December 1992 which said the House was saddened by the incident and regarded it as an "abuse of power [which was] against the spirit of the Malaysian Constitution and ran against the aspirations of the laws of the land based on the system of constitutional monarchy and parliamentary democracy". It urged that all necessary steps be taken to ensure that such incidents would not occur again. During the debates, a Government MP exposed 23 cases of ill-treatment of the local people by the Sultan of Johor and the Johor royal family, which aroused public anger. The motion was adopted unanimously in Parliament with the MPs from the opposition parties, the DAP and PAS, supporting it.

The Parliament's move set in motion a series of events which eventually led the government to amend the Constitution to remove the immunity of the Malay Rulers from criminal prosecution and also to curb their powers and privileges. The anti-royalty campaign, the second to be mounted within a decade by Dr Mahathir has rightly been seen by some observers as a conflict between Nationalism and Monarchy,[51] leading eventually to the victory of Nationalism. This success had earned Dr Mahathir the respect and support of the people as a leader who would brook no nonsense from the Malay rulers.

Mahathir Speaks His Mind at International Forums

Until the economic crisis broke in the Southeast Asian region in 1997, Dr Mahathir had been a very outspoken champion of Third World nations and a strong critic of Western policies, especially the United States' attempts to control the world economic order. Until the CHOGM in 1989, he was critical of the Commonwealth, especially of the policies of Commonwealth member, Britain, towards South Africa, Zimbabwe and other African states. It was the CHOGM which he chaired in 1989 that succeeded in adopting economic sanctions against white-rule South Africa for its policies of apartheid. Gradually, he extended his criticisms also to some of the Third

World countries, including those in the Non-Aligned Movement, for not daring to challenge the rich and powerful countries of the West.

Although the Non-Aligned Movement attempted to promote the establishment of a New International Economic Order, their members were still burdened by foreign debt. Their policies became ineffective, smothered by protectionism and eventually they became poorer due to the high interest rates and foreign exchange imposed by economically powerful nations. The Movement has now become inactive. Dr Mahathir also continually hit out at the superpowers. He condemned the American occupation of Nicaragua and the Russian occupation of Afghanistan. Malaysia sorely bore the brunt of U.S. protectionism against its palm oil exports to the United States in 1988. The American Soybean Association (ASA) and the National Heart Savers' Association had launched a campaign against all tropical oil products — including palm and coconut oil — describing the oils as saturated fats, which make consumers prone to heart diseases. After an expensive two-year battle, the ASA finally dropped the campaign in 1989 following talks with the palm-oil industry. Although Malaysia joined the Asia-Pacific Economic Co-operation (APEC), led by Australia and the United States, Dr Mahathir attempted to counter it by setting up a rival body — the East Asian Economic Caucus (EAEC) which, however, failed to take off due to U.S. opposition and the failure of Japan to join.

It was really ASEAN which Malaysia found as the most advantageous forum for regional economic co-operation. Up to the end of the administration of U.S. President Clinton in 2000, the ASEAN Dialogues with the United States and Europe and with the East Asian giants, as well as the ASEAN Summits continued to highlight ASEAN's major role in international politics. ASEAN attempted to mediate in the regional conflict areas of Cambodia and Myanmar. In these efforts, Malaysia's diplomacy and mediating role were greatly appreciated and in great demand. Between 1995 and 1997 Third World countries had openly acknowledged Dr Mahathir as their leader. Through his personal efforts to forge South-South co-operation and the new grouping of the fast-paced newly-emergent nations in the Group 15, Malaysia and Dr Mahathir emerged as the leading spokesman, a role he continued to play until the Asian economic crisis in 1997 made it no longer feasible. Recognition came personally to him in the form of numerous international awards, honours and prizes from countries in South America, Africa and the Middle East. The only other Malaysian leader to have won such international renown was Tunku Abdul Rahman.

Closer to home, ASEAN co-operation was best seen in Singapore investments pouring into Malaysia's southern state of Johor. When Singapore announced in August 1989 that it would provide facilities for U.S. ships and aircraft, Malaysia protested that it had not been consulted. Malaysia viewed this as being against the spirit of the Non-Aligned Movement, of which Singapore was a member, and of the Zone of Peace, Freedom and Neutrality espoused by Malaysia. Malaysia calmed down only when it received assurances from the United States and Singapore. Differences between Malaysia and Singapore continued to surface throughout the 1990s and into the new millennium over several policies — immigration check-points, the Malayan Railway properties in Singapore, Singapore's request for increased supply of water from the Malaysian state of Johor, and Malaysia's objections over frequent disparaging remarks made by senior Singapore ministers on Malaysia's internal affairs.

Anwar's Rise and Challenge, 1995–98

In the intense and bitter personal rivalries that developed and continued for almost a decade in the 1980s between Musa Hitam and Tengku Razaleigh for the posts of UMNO's top leadership posts, both men became embittered and bruised, and many of their supporters suffered greatly, too. Apparently the lessons of these rivalries had not been learnt. The 1990s were to see a repeat performance in the personal rivalries, initially, between a young ambitious contender, Anwar Ibrahim, and the incumbent Deputy Prime Minister Ghafar Baba, and, later, between the former and Dr Mahathir himself.

One of the features of these heated contests was the practice of "money politics". Another was the tendency of hurling accusations and "character assassination" between the rival candidates. Leaflets would be produced and distributed, accusing candidates, especially Cabinet Ministers, of mismanagement and financial scandals. Dr Mahathir himself was a target of such attacks. "He was accused of having a small business clique which he favoured and a smaller 'kitchen cabinet' within his Cabinet, and the politics of the country were in the hands of the elite of the elites", recalls a pro-Mahathir source.[52] This same source also said, "When a company called Zenecon Bumi Sdn. Bhd., controlled by Mahathir's sister-in-law, was awarded a huge subcontracting job to build the Dayabumi forty-storey office block owned by the government-controlled Urban Development Authority (UDA), the host of accusations made by Mahathir's opponents became more credible in the eyes of UMNO members and of the general public".[53] Anwar Ibrahim's rise within UMNO took place within this atmosphere of "money politics". In the 1994 and 1995 UMNO general assemblies Dr Mahathir railed against this "money politics".

In 1993, Anwar Ibrahim decided to challenge the incumbent Deputy Prime Minister Ghafar Baba for the post of UMNO's deputy president. What was interesting was how Dr Mahathir shifted his attitude from initially asking Anwar not to challenge Ghafar Baba to one of neutrality. At first, he was convinced that when the time came, his deputy Ghafar Baba would give way to Anwar, but later he changed his mind because of his affection for Anwar. According to one source, "Anwar was not prepared to stand by and await his fate. He realized that Ghafar had a long and unique record as a political survivor. He had the feeling that he was not in Ghafar's good books, and that his political opponents were gaining ever greater influence on Ghafar", said Zainuddin Mydin.[54] When Dr Mahathir saw the waves of support for Anwar, he declared himself neutral. Ghafar Baba was defeated even before the actual day of election, as each divisional nomination was allowed to add a bonus of ten votes to each candidate. By election time, Anwar had garnered more than 200 such divisional votes, while Ghafar could only muster about four. Consequently, he withdrew from this race.

This crushing of Ghafar was not only humiliating for an old UMNO veteran, but showed the power of "money politics". Dr Mahathir remembered Ghafar's fate. When his turn came, he was determined to crush Anwar before the latter could crush him. The old fox outwitted his student. But before this happened Anwar became the new deputy president of UMNO, succeeded Ghafar as Deputy Prime Minister, and was even given an additional portfolio, Finance. This later helped him tremendously to build up his power base. Anwar was in a position to dispense favours and award business contracts.

"For Mahathir, his happiness over Anwar's victory had to be borne with a feeling of guilt for having hurt the feelings of Ghafar, a person who once did him a good turn", says his confidant, Zainuddin Mydin.[55] But in 1998, when Anwar, in turn, challenged him, and caused him to dismiss him, Dr Mahathir must have wished he had not been so enthusiastic over Anwar's victory in 1993. The ambitions of Anwar began to be evident after Dr Mahathir had publicly announced that he would be his successor on his retirement.

Critics of Anwar would later say he was impatient. He adopted the same tactics to topple Ghafar against Dr Mahathir by accusing him of corruption, cronyism and nepotism. But the same charges were later levelled at him by Dr Mahathir. In September 1998 Dr Mahathir dismissed him from the post of Deputy Prime Minister, deputy president of UMNO and UMNO member — all in one go at an UMNO Supreme Council late night meeting. When Dr Mahathir left the meeting, "Anwar supporters who threw used paper drinking cups at Dr Mahathir .... demonstrated a disrespect unlike anything seen before," said one source.[56] He was said to be a homosexual and a philanderer and therefore a person unfit for office as a potential Prime Minister. Except for one or two supporters who spoke up for Anwar in the Supreme Council, the rest accepted Dr Mahathir's proposal to dismiss him.

Economic Crisis, 1997–98

The Anwar problem surfaced immediately after the economic crisis had hit several countries in Southeast Asia, especially Thailand, Indonesia, Malaysia and Singapore, as well as South Korea. As Finance Minister Anwar Ibrahim's management of financial policies was at odds with those held by Dr Mahathir and his economic adviser, Tun Daim Zainuddin, a former Finance Minister — it aggravated their personal animosities. Due to drastic fluctuations in the foreign exchange rates, currencies like the Thai *baht*, the Indonesian *rupiah* and Malaysia's *ringgit* dropped sharply in value against the U.S. dollar. Share prices on the regional stock exchanges tumbled daily. Losses amounting to billions of dollars were incurred. Dr Mahathir blamed these losses on Western currency speculators, whom he accused of taking part in a conspiracy to manipulate the stock markets and the exchange rates. The International Monetary Fund, however, disagreed with his view. Experts seemed to agree that the real causes were high current account deficits, huge money supply in circulation and the tendency of local banks to under-regulate themselves — these views were also held by Anwar who seemed to endorse the IMF's policies. Regional governments were also accused of forcing the local banks to over-extend credit to bail out firms linked by cronyism, nepotism and corruption to those in power. Increasingly alarmed by the huge financial losses suffered by Malaysian banks and companies, Dr Mahathir said he was unsure that Malaysia could now achieve its goal of becoming a developed nation by 2020. On the other hand, Anwar as Finance Minister agreed to adopt IMF advice to tighten and reduce rapid growth in money supply and for greater fiscal transparency.

Anwar's dismissal was probably necessitated by Dr Mahathir's fears that Anwar might adopt more IMF policies and prevent the bailout of firms which were closely linked with the government. After his departure, the director and deputy director of Bank Negara (the National Bank) resigned. Dr Mahathir on taking over the post of Finance Minister, decided that the best way to protect the Malaysian *ringgit* and prevent fluctuations in the exchange rate was to fix it at RM3.80 to the U.S. dollar. Foreign investments would also earn no returns unless they remained in the country for a year. The controls would be in force for an indefinite period, but by April 1999 in the face of foreign criticisms, the Malaysian Government relaxed some of the controls by allowing foreign investors to withdraw their profits under a levy on these returns. By September 1999, the controls were removed entirely, although the *ringgit* continued to remain pegged to the U.S. dollar at RM3.80. As Malaysia possessed some $200 billion in reserves, it was speculated that it could meet demands for any losses incurred through huge withdrawals of foreign investors as well as payments for large imports of foods and heavy equipment for several months ahead. Malaysia managed to survive the crisis without obtaining any foreign loans either from the IMF or the World Bank.

Brief Assessment

By July 2001, Dr Mahathir's achievements had outweighed his deficiencies. According to Milne and Mauzy, he remained strongly entrenched in power, having defeated every threat to his rule "in a masterly fashion".[57] Among his deficiencies, however, was his failure to stem growing corruption. Another was his authoritarianism, particularly in the dismantling of the independence of the judiciary and in his continued use of the ISA to arrest and detain his opponents without trial. His arrests of political opponents in 1987, 1999, 2000 and 2001 raised international and local concerns over human rights and democracy. "In the Mahathir lexicon of politics, power has to be absolute," says the *Far Eastern Economic Review* of 11 February 1993, "and if one takes that seriously, there would be very dangerous tendencies." As one observer has commented, "The status and power of the Prime Minister in power in Malaysia under Mahathir has changed substantially. The present office of the executive is a matrix of autocracy. The constitutional processes and institutions that act as checks to prevent the Prime Minister from gaining dictatorial control over the nation are incapable of functioning effectively. Mahathir has attempted to wrest more power, and in most cases he has succeeded. Under Mahathir, authority has shifted more towards the overly political executive branch. Mahathir transformed the face of Malaysian politics while consolidating UMNO's hold on power. It is a substantial, if not necessarily a beneficial, achievement."[58] Threats to his rule seem unlikely to abate, and confrontations with his political opponents locally and abroad are likely to continue.

NOTES

1   *New Straits Times,* 31 August 2001, p. 2.
2   See report, "Sukar ubah sikap orang Melayu", *Utusan Malaysia,* 19 July 2001, p. 2.
3   *New Straits Times,* 4 August 2001, p. 2; and *Utusan Malaysia,* 4 August 2001, p. 2.
4   In May 2000 the Chinese group, SUQIU, caused a stir when it pressed the government to meet requests for a review of "special privileges" for Malays. It was forced to withdraw some of its demands after kicking up a storm of protests from Malay groups. In November the same year the government's plan for "Vision Schools" to encourage racial mixing rattled ethnic Chinese and Tamil educationalists. The Dong Jiao Zhong, representing all Chinese school boards and teachers' associations, opposed the plan on the grounds that the ultimate aim was to make the Malay language the main medium of instruction. This charge was denied by the government. In early May 2001 Malaysian Chinese parties — both inside and outside the government — attacked the country's race-based education quota system for denying high-flying students public university places because of the government's affirmative action programme. Newspaper surveys had reported that about 500 of the top non-*bumiputra* scorers, mostly Chinese, in the most recent university entrance exam had failed to win a place, despite having scored eight or more 'A' grades. The government ordered the Education Ministry to offer all of them places in public universities.
5   Robin Adshead, *Mahathir of Malaysia* (London: Hibiscus Publishing Company, 1989), p. 102. This is based on a speech he made and reproduced in a pamphlet entitled *Malaysian System of Government,* written by Dr Mahathir and published by the Prime Minister's Department in 1995.
6   *New Straits Times,* 17 July 2001, p. 1.
7   *Asiaweek,* 26 January 2001, p. 27.
8   *Ibid.,* p. 25.
9   Renong Bhd. owns 37.1 per cent of United Engineers Malaysia Bhd. (UEM), which owns 32.6 per cent of Renong. The Renong group carries a massive debt burden of US$3.4 billion (RM13 billion), making it Malaysia's biggest private borrower. Renong used to be the finance arm of Malaysia's ruling party, UMNO. Besides construction, the conglomerate's activities span oil, banks, transport and property. On 23 July 2001 the government made an offer to buy Renong and bid for a large stake in UEM, Malaysia's biggest construction company, and take over both companies' debts. See *New Straits Times,* 24 July 2001, pp. 1–2.

See also CNN report, "Government to take helm of Malaysia's Renong group", in *CNN.com/Business*, 23 July 2001.

10 See report in <www.malaysiakini.com> website, "Mahathir defends privatization policy, says it's not perfect", 27 August 2001.

11 See *New Straits Times*, 1 August 2001, p. 9.

12 See analysis by Simon Elegant, "Another Man Down? A politically cornered Mahathir takes aim at an old friend, Finance Minister Daim", in *Timeasia.com/ news magazine*, 21 May 2001, Vol. 157, No. 20.

13 See *New Straits Times*, and *Utusan Malaysia*, 25 June 2001, pp. 1–2.

14 See the letter of M. Bakri Musa in the readers' column of *Asiaweek*, 9 February 2001, p. 6.

15 See an admirer's defence of him, Hardev Kaur, "The indomitable Dr Mahathir, a man with a mission", *New Straits Times*, 4 December 1999, p. 15.

16 These terms used to appear frequently in the PAS newspaper, *Harakah*. For a pro-Mahathir journalist's point-by-point rebuttal of these criticisms, see Astora Jabat, "Dr Mahathir tidak zalim", in *Utusan Malaysia*, 6 July 2000, p. 6. For a foreign observer's comments on these terms, see William Chase, "Malaysia's General Elections in 1999: A Consolidated and High-Quality Semi-Democracy", *Asian Studies Review* 25, no. 1 (March 2001): 36.

17 John Funston, "Malaysia's Tenth Elections: Status Quo, *Reformasi* or Islamization?" *Contemporary Southeast Asia* 22, no. 1 (April 2000): 29.

18 See article by Zin Mahmud, "Anwar pecahkan orang Melayu [Anwar causes a split among the Malays]", *Utusan Malaysia*, 5 December 1999, p. 6.

19 See article, "Anwar Factor in the polls", *New Straits Times*, 1 January 2000, p. 9.

20 Zainuddin Mydin (Zam), "Menangani undi protes [Questioning the protest votes]", *Utusan Malaysia*, 2 December 1999, p. 6.

21 Zainuddin Mydin, a journalist and close aide, has recalled this period of withdrawal as follows: "Even with the Malay sentiment solidly behind him, this was a time of isolation for Mahathir, and for the first time in his life, he waited anxiously for the day of his arrest. His house had been ransacked by officers from the inland revenue, friends had remained aloof, and those who had previously beaten a path to his door were no longer to be seen. He was regarded as bad and dangerous to know. 'I felt like an outcast. People were afraid to come to my house,' he said." See Zainuddin Mydin, *The Other Side of Mahathir* (Kuala Lumpur: Utusan Publications, 1994), p. 30.

22 J.V. Morais, *Mahathir: A Profile in Courage* (Singapore: Eastern Universities Press, 1982), p. 29.

23 His propensity to sulk was first detected by UMNO leader Musa Hitam, who was his Deputy Prime Minister from 1981 to 1986. This is revealed in Zainuddin Mydin, *The Other Side of Mahathir*, pp. 143–45.

24 Khoo Boo Teik, *Paradoxes of Mahathirism* (Kuala Lumpur: Oxford University Press, 1995), p. 351.

25 *Ibid.*, p. 46.

26 R.S. Milne and Diane K. Mauzy, *Malaysian Politics under Mahathir* (London: Routledge, 1999), p. 168.

27 *Ibid.*, pp. 47–48.

28 See Dr Mahathir Mohd., MP, "In Defence of Feudalism", *Opinion* 2, no. 1 (November 1968): 183–84. See also Mahathir Mohamad, *The Malay Dilemma* (Singapore: Federal Publications, 1981), pp. 169–73.

29 Zainuddin Mydin, *The Other Side of Mahathir*, p. 221.

30 *Ibid.*, p. 134.

31 Joseph Liow, "Personality, Exigencies, and Contingencies: Determinants of Malaysia's Foreign Policy in the Mahathir Administration", in *Mahathir's Administration: Performance and Crisis in Governance* (Singapore: Times Books International, 2001), pp. 120–60.

32 Khoo, *Paradoxes of Mahathirism*, p. 54.

33 Tunku Abdul Rahman writing in his column in *The Star* of 30 June 1975.

34 An inside view of what was troubling Mahathir's mind over the rulers is revealed in an unabashedly pro-Mahathir book: "….the Prime Minister had been receiving reports that some contenders for the throne [*Yang Di-Pertuan Agong*] had been talking loosely about the way they would, if elected King, put Mahathir back in his place and uphold the position of the monarchy. One Sultan is said to have boasted that he would, with the help of the army, 'declare an emergency and throw out all these politicians who are runing the country'." See Hasan Hj. Hamzah, *Mahathir: Great Malaysian Hero* (Kuala Lumpur: Mediaparint Publications, 1990), p. 131. Clearly a ghost-written book, the author's sloppy English and poor writing style in the preface does not match the tight well-written style of the ghost-writer of the main text of the book.

35 Khoo, *Paradoxes of Mahathirism*, p. 74.

36 Hasan Hj. Hamzah, *Mahathir: Great Malaysian Hero*, p. 199.

37 See the perceptive analysis by writer and critic Farish A. Noor, "A Tale of Two Neo-Feudals: Mahathir Mohamad and Zulfikar Ali Bhutto Reconsidered" (Part 2 of 3), *From the Other Malaysia* <Malaysiakini.com>, posted 15 June 2001.

38 Zainuddin Mydin, *The Other Side of Mahathir*, p. 113.

39 *Ibid.*, p. 119.

40 *Ibid.*, p. 131.

41 See these disclosures in Zainuddin Mydin, *The Other Side of Mahathir*, pp. 232–33.

42 *Ibid.*, pp. 233–34.

43 Diane and Mauzy, *Malaysian Politics under Mahathir*, p. 159.

44 One of those surprisingly dropped from his Cabinet was his Defence Minister, Datuk Abdullah Ahmad Badawi, who was in the Razaleigh camp, despite his re-election as UMNO vice-president. "Reactions to the purge ranged from satisfaction to outright anger [in UMNO]," says Hasan Hj. Hamzah, "but the anger mainly revolved around the sacking of Datuk Abdullah Ahmad Badawi from his post of defence minister." See his *Mahathir: Great Malaysian Hero*, p. 341.

45 For a fine summary of the drastic effects which Dr Mahathir brought on the judiciary, see Milne and Mauzy, *Malaysian Politics under Mahathir*, p. 47.

46 *Ibid.*, p. 46.

47 *Ibid.*, p. 48.

48 See Hasan Hj. Hamzah, *Mahathir: Great Malaysian Hero*, p. 471.

49 For a good summary of "Malaysia: The Way Forward", see Khoo, *Paradoxes of Mahathirism*, pp. 327–31.

50 Zainuddin Mydin, *The Other Side of Mahathir*, p. 84.

51 See Roger Kershaw, "Shattered Symbiosis: The Road to Conflict between Malay Nationalism and Monarchy", *Internationales Asienforum* 24 (1993), p. 283.

52 Hasan Hj.Hamzah, *Mahathir: Great Malaysian Hero*, p. 316.

53 *Ibid.*, p. 315.

54 Zainuddin Mydin, *The Other Side of Mahathir*, p. 242.

55 *Ibid.*, p. 248.

56 See John Funston, "Malaysia's Tenth Elections: Status Quo, *Reformasi* or Islamization?" *Contemporary Southeast Asia* 22, no. 1 (April 2000): 27.

57 Milne and Mauzy, *Malaysian Politics under Mahathir*, p. 186.

58 Ho Khai Leong, "Mahathir's Administration under Siege", in *Mahathir's Administration: Performance and Crisis in Governance* (Singapore: Times Books International, 2001), p. 24.

CHAPTER SEVEN

Epilogue

Nation-Building and Leadership in Malaysia: Or, Manipulating the Social Contract and Malay Dominance

Malaysia is a modern multi-ethnic, multi-cultural nation, with a dominant ethnic Malay base. The Malaysian nation is a political community which reflects Malay political primacy; yet is not a "Malay" nation. Malaysian government policies on national unity are based on integration, not assimilation. The Malaysian nation is based upon cultural differences and is evolving a political culture that takes account of its plural culturalism.

Apart from language and education, the government's policies have been aimed at accommodation of non-Malays in the short term and at integration over a longer period, "but not to the extent of making non-Malays drastically alter their way of life or abandon their cultural heritage", observe political scientists Milne and Mauzy, who added that, "In the Borneo states integration was to be even more gradual."[1] Although the Malaysian nation has a Malay base, the ethnic and political boundaries are transcended by a Malaysian consciousness or Malaysian nationalism that consists of a nucleus of Malay nationalism enclosed by the idea of a partnership embracing Malays, Chinese, Indians and the natives of the Borneo states of Sarawak and Sabah.

There are, of course, competing notions of what kind of "imagined community" Malaysia should be among the various ethnic communities. For the Malay nationalists, Malaysia should be a "Malay" nation-state, while the non-Malay communities aspire to some kind of a multi-ethnic Malaysian nation or *Bangsa Malaysia*, as enunciated in 1991 by Prime Minister

Datuk Seri Dr Mahathir Mohamed's Vision 2020. Given the dominant position of the Malays, Malay nationalism has been most aggressive in asserting the national agendas and making its demands. The centrifugal and centripetal forces of Malaysian nationalism and Malay nationalism, respectively, are, therefore, constantly in conflict.

According to one Malay observer, as Malaysia faces the challenges and opportunities of globalization, Malay nationalism continues to safeguard Malay dominance but has been turned into "an instrument for the accumulation and concentration of corporate wealth in the hands of a few", and "i[n] the process, compromised major symbols of Malay nationalism, such as Islam, the Malay-dominated education system, and the Malay language".[2] The opposition PAS, on the other hand, conceives Islam as "borderless and beyond ethnicity: it preaches the unity of all Muslims who are principally bound by Islamic principles and values than narrow ethnic or national interests", and its objective in Malaysia is "to create an Islamic rather than a Malay state or society".[3] The Chinese-based opposition party, the DAP, however, wants Malaysia to be a more egalitarian, multi-ethnic and multi-cultural "Malaysian Malaysia".

The bonds of citizenship, the Malaysian Constitution and the sense of sharing one nation, of "my country"/"our country" among the various ethnic communities are increasingly evident in present-day Malaysia. Malaysians of different ethnic origins display the national flag, inculcate and demonstrate loyalty and patriotism, but politically they may disagree on many issues. When Malaysia's national badminton team won the Thomas Cup in 1992, the people showed tremendous support, cohesion, consensus and national pride in an unprecedented way. They also bond and are mobilized each time they choose the national leadership in general elections. Thus, the "Malaysian community of nation" develops a common sentiment and a national interest.[4]

A foreign visitor to Malaysia will discover that Malaysia has a mixed government, in which Cabinet Ministers come from different races, Malays, Chinese, Indians, Ibans, Kadazandusuns and others. In two states, the Chief Minister is a Chinese. The King is a Malay. The Prime Minister is a Malay. The bureaucracy, the police and the armed forces are predominantly

Malay. What this means is that the dominant Malays, the *Orang Asli* (aborigines) and the natives of Borneo are sharing these institutions of government with the other ethnic communities, all together are creating a Malaysian partnership and a sense of co-operation, community and identity.

In this respect, Malaysia has moved away from the Furnivallian concept of a "plural society", in which different ethnic communities merely remain separate and do not bond, mingling only in the market-place.[5]

The threads of government in Malaysia have, therefore, been held together by an astute system of power-sharing. The basis of power-sharing can be traced back to the 1955 informal "historic bargain" or "social contract" of the UMNO-MCA-MIC Alliance, representing the Malays, Chinese and Indians. It initially set out the rules or political framework within which the ethnic groups were to operate in Malaya, which obtained independence in 1957 and later became the major component of the enlarged federation of Malaysia, the other three components being Singapore, Sarawak and Sabah. Basically, the 1955 "social contract" was embodied within the 1957 Constitution of Malaya, and upheld several privileges for Malays, especially the "special position" of the Malays. This contract held good in Malaya until 1963 when Malaysia was formed, and was extended to cover new terms from Singapore, Sarawak and Sabah. Singapore's leaders challenged the old terms of the contract, especially "Malay dominance" and "Malay rule". When they failed to modify the terms towards a more egalitarian "Malaysian Malaysia", Singapore was forced to leave Malaysia in 1965.

Nation-building is, therefore, based on the theme of the making and sharing of the Malaysian nation among its multi-ethnic citizens.

The willingness of Malays and other *bumiputra* (sons of the soil, or indigenous peoples) to share their notion and membership of their "Malay land" and "native lands" in the Malay peninsula and in the Borneo states of Sarawak and Sabah, respectively, with each other and with other ethnic communities who have migrated from India, China, the Middle East and the countries of Southeast Asia is the starting-point of nation-building in Malaysia.

Achieving independence, however, was one thing, building a nation together was another; a task on which they are still embarked on.

This study is focused on Malaysia's four Prime Ministers as nation-builders. The Prime Minister wields tremendous power. He plays an important role in policy-making. Yet communal interests serve to check the extent of his power, and frequently he has to practise the art of "divide and rule". He heads a multi-ethnic coalition of political parties. He oversees overall social and economic development of the country. He determines how government funds and assistance are allocated to the various ethnic communities.

All four Prime Ministers upheld and worked the Social Contract of 1955 and 1957 and have attempted to juggle and balance the communal demands and interests of the respective communities. Every one of these Prime Ministers started off their political career as an exclusivist Malay nationalist, but ended up as an inclusivist Malaysian nationalist. In implementing the "give and take" policies towards each of the communities, each Prime Minister had been influenced, firstly, by the extent of political support he receives from his own party, UMNO. When his own position within UMNO is weak, he has had to rely on the "non-Malay" component parties in the Alliance or the Barisan Nasional (which replaced the Alliance) for support of policies to offset his lack of support within UMNO, as happened particularly to Prime Minister Dr Mahathir when UMNO was split into two factions and then was declared by the court as illegal in 1987.

Since 1957 the office of Prime Minister has been occupied by a Malay, who is the President of UMNO. However, whenever he becomes Prime Minister, the UMNO President is transformed from being the head of a Malay party to that of the leader of a multi-ethnic nation. It is how he straddles these two positions that often test the mettle of his leadership of the nation and whether he wins the support from all the communities in Malaysia and is recognized by the world community at large.

The fact that all the four Prime Ministers have been Malays have led to an unwritten accepted norm that the Malaysian leadership of the nation is biased towards the Malay community.[6] Malays have used this position as an argument to support their goal of Malay dominance *vis-à-vis* the other ethnic communities in the political, cultural and social fields. The

Malaysian Constitution is silent about the ethnic origin of the Prime Minister except that he must be a citizen by operation of law and not by registration or naturalization, that he cannot be a Senator and must be in the House of Representatives. For at least two decades after the 1969 riots, it has been almost impossible to raise the idea of a non-Malay as Prime Minister. The mood in the country has changed only slightly. In the campaigns leading to the 1999 general elections, Malay political leaders, from the ruling UMNO and the opposition PAS, in their efforts to woo non-Malay voters, who have suddenly emerged as power-brokers because of Malay disunity, have argued that the Malaysian Constitution did not bar any qualified non-Malay citizen from holding the office of Prime Minister. They said that such an appointment was possible, but it was a choice for the people to decide — a proposal that would not have been entertained at one time by any Malay politician.

The two central issues on which nation-building and national leadership have been evaluated in this study, are (a) the "social contract" of the UMNO-MCA-MIC formulated in 1955 in relation to the Malay, Chinese and Indian communities and its extension to the other communities in Sarawak and Sabah after the formation of Malaysia in 1963; and (b) *ketuanan Melayu* or Malay dominance, the relentless cry of Malay nationalism in Malaysia, and how the national leadership has handled it in the context of power-sharing among the various ethnic communities.

Ketuanan Melayu or Malay Dominance was accepted by the various Alliance parties and formed part of the informal "bargain" of the 1955 Alliance Election Manifesto and Malaya's 1957 Constitution. Ethnicity became politically emphasized and a charged issue when the UMNO-MCA-MIC Alliance Government under the leadership of Prime Minister Tunku Abdul Rahman began to make a distinction and channel the various ethnic communities into two politically-constructed ethnic groups — *bumiputra* and *non-bumiputra*. The moral claim of *bumiputra* or indigeneity is legitimacy. Malays, once labelled as "indigenous", had claim to special consideration over others who were "non-indigenous".

In tracing the history of race relations, it was shown that during the Tunku's regime, Malay political primacy was not publicly promoted nor proclaimed as an acknowledged fact, because the Tunku preferred instead to juggle and accommodate the demands of the respective communities. Given the fragile years of a newly-independent country like Malaya, his immediate priority was to maintain peace and inter-racial harmony among the various races.

However, after the 1969 inter-racial riots, the Tunku's successor, Tun Abdul Razak, changed the "rules of the game" for the various communities. He believed that Malay economic dissatisfaction was behind the riots, while non-Malays who were already economically dominant were having high political expectations. He decided to remove ambiguity and make it clear to the public that the Malays would be politically dominant. He began to accommodate the demands of Malay nationalism. The Malay language was used as the main medium of instruction in the educational system. More jobs were created in the public service and filled by Malays. The economy would be restructured under the New Economic Policy to allow Malays to advance in areas previously dominated by the non-Malays (including foreigners) until they had achieved 30 per cent of the wealth of the country. This would be done within the framework of a rapidly expanding economy that would allow for reasonably large non-Malay economic growth and even for increased activity by foreign-owned enterprises.

Some of these goals were reached by the time of his death in 1976, but the rest were certainly achieved during the regime of his successor Tun Hussein Onn and the regime of the fourth Prime Minister, Dr Mahathir Mohamed. The policies of Tun Hussein Onn and Datuk Seri Dr Mahathir reinforced and extended Malay political primacy.

Malay political primacy, however, rests on the assumption that the Malays are united and that Malay unity and Malay political strength would continuously reinforce Malay superiority and Malay dominance. Political differences and factionalism that frequently break out within the Malay community, however, belie this assumption. The UMNO-PAS split in 1976 and the UMNO split in 1987 reveal that Malay political dominance was undermined through serious divisions within the Malay community itself and by the effects of globalization.

The dialectics of Malay nationalism and disunity are to be found within the UMNO-PAS rivalry and the perennial competition for power and wealth among UMNO politicians. Increasingly, given Malaysia's rapid economic development and Malay advancement under the New Economic Policy, competition for power has been motivated by economic and material ambitions among the rising rich and middle class Malays who are represented within UMNO and whose aspirations and claims are manifested in the intra-party rivalries of UMNO.

Similarly, the material dialectics of unity and disunity also operate within the non-Malay communities. It is often assumed that they, too, could promote and safeguard their own communal interests and ethnic unity. But in the context of Malaysian politics, however, the dispersal of their community members in different political parties and along class and linguistic lines has made them as unsuccessful as the Malays in achieving ethnic unity within their respective communities. Frequently, they do not speak with one voice.

Given this background of communal divisions and politics in Malaysia, the "social contract" and Malay dominance have become more problematic than ever. If we briefly chart the responses and roles of the various Prime Ministers towards the various ethnic groups in Malaysia since 1957, it is possible to say that the Tunku tried to be even-handed towards the various ethnic communities, Tun Razak was inclined more towards the Malays, Tun Hussein Onn continued this policy but Datuk Seri Dr Mahathir first adopted "pro-Malay" policies and then latterly reached out to the non-Malays, each time largely determined by his need for political support and for his own political survival.

During the Tunku's regime, however, Singapore was forced to leave Malaysia because it questioned the terms of the informal "social contract" of 1955 and 1957. For the *bumiputra* of Sarawak and Sabah, the contract has not been very relevant, as they have been more concerned with safeguarding their respective state rights and their own status as *bumiputra vis-à-vis* the other local *bumiputra* . While they generally accept Malay dominance at the Federal level, they contest it at the state level in Sarawak and Sabah. The local *bumiputra* of Sarawak and Sabah are in the anomalous position of being able both to enjoy *bumiputra* rights and to categorize themselves either with the Malays or the "non-Malays".

In 1991 while enunciating his Vision 2020 Dr Mahathir firmly accommodated the non-Malays as co-partners with Malays in the task of transforming Malaysia into a modern, highly-developed, "just and equal" *Bangsa Malaysia,* or Malaysian nation. More non-Malays than Malays however, welcomed his idea. Chinese social organizations, while accepting Dr Mahathir's Vision 2020, have argued that to make the vision a reality, differences between *bumiputra* and non-*bumiputra* ought to be removed. The ensuing debates showed that Malays generally were not yet willing to give up their special privileges. Until the Malays themselves were willing to do this, said Dr Mahathir, the government would not take them away. Until then, *ketuanan Melayu* will remain part of the Malaysian political system and *Bangsa Malaysia* seems remote.

However, since 1999, religion has become another contentious element in the making of the Malaysian nation-state. It has figured prominently in the debates on the making of Malaysia as an Islamic state. As most Muslims in Malaysia are Malays, an Islamic state is actually another form of a "Malay nation" except that Islamic principles become the basis of its administration, as in Iran.

When Dr Mahathir declared in September 2001 that Malaysia was already an "Islamic state", this was contested by the opposition PAS leaders, who said that until the Islamic *syariah* and criminal *hudud* laws were wholly incorporated into the Malaysian Constitution, Malaysia remains a secular state.

It is clear that in the making of the Malaysian nation-state, the interests of both ethnicity and religion would continue to compete for the attention of the multi-ethnic population in which the role of the Prime Minister would be crucial.

****

NOTES

1   R.S. Milne and Diane K. Mauzy, *Politics and Government in Malaysia* (Singapore: Federal Publications, 1978), p. 368.

2   Halim Saleh, "Globalization and the Challenges to Malay Nationalism as the Essence of Malaysian Nationalism," in *Nationalism and Globalization East and West*, ed. Leo Suryadinata (Singapore: Institute of Southeast Asian Studies, 2000), pp. 132–74.

3   *Ibid.*, p. 154.

4   I am grateful for the above insights from Dr Mansor Mohd. Nor of the Centre for Policy Research, Universiti Sains Malaysia. He has conducted several studies on ethnic harmony and ethnic polarization among USM students between 1996 and 2002. See Mansor Mohd. Nor, "Cohesion and Consensus: The Prevalence of Ethnic Harmony in a University Campus", *Jurnal Pendidik dan Pendidikan* 17 (2000/2002), pp. 91–111; and also Mansor Mohd. Nor, "Social Conflicts in Indonesia and Malaysia: Could the Cause be Religious?" in *Conflict and Conflict Management in Southeast Asia*, (Special Issue), *Kajian Malaysia* XVIII, nos. 1 and 2 (June/December 2000): 188–206.

5   See J.S. Furnivall, *Colonial Policy and Practice: A Comparative Study of Burma and Netherlands India* (Cambridge: Cambridge University Press, 1948).

6   Some studies reveal that Malays and Chinese would choose "a good quality leader, but often an ethnic Malay, to lead the country". See Mansor Mohd. Noor, "Crossing Ethnic Borders in Malaysia: Measuring the Fluidity of Ethnic Identity and Group Formation", *Akademika* 55 (July 1999): 61–62.

Chronology

3 September	1945	British forces reoccupy Malaya and the British Administration is set up
10 October	1945	Details of the Malayan Union Policy announced and the following day the British Government's representative Sir Harold MacMichael arrives to negotiate with the Malay Rulers
23 January	1946	White Paper on the Malayan Union published
1 March	1946	The All-Malay Congress proposes the formation of the United Malays National Organization (UMNO) to mount opposition to the Malayan Union
1 April	1946	Malayan Union inaugurated. UMNO and the Malay Rulers boycott inauguration ceremony
11 May	1946	UMNO formally set up in Johor Bahru
1 February	1948	Federation of Malaya (Persekutuan Tanah Melayu) inaugurated
23 June	1948	State of Emergency declared in Malaya followed soon after by communist armed rebellion and ban on the Communist Party of Malaya
	1951	Datuk Onn Jaafar resigns as UMNO president and is succeeded by Tunku Abdul Rahman
January	1952	UMNO-MCA Alliance contest municipal elections
	1954	UMNO-MCA-MIC Alliance formed

17 July	1955	Alliance wins 51 of the 52 contested seats in the general election for the Legislative Council. Tunku Abdul Rahman becomes Chief Minister
28 and 29 December	1955	'Peace' Talks at Baling between Tunku Abdul Rahman and the Communist Party of Malaya
May	1956	Razak Education Report published
31 August	1957	Malaya achieves independence
	1959	Alliance is returned to power in general elections in Malaya, but Kelantan state falls to PMIP
	1960	State of Emergency in Malaya ends
	1962	The Tunku dismisses his controversial Minister for Agriculture Aziz bin Ishak
4 April	1963	Indonesia announces "Confrontation" of Malaysia
16 September	1963	Federation of Malaysia comprising Malaya, Singapore, Sarawak and Sabah inaugurated
April	1964	Alliance is returned to power in general elections
9 August	1965	Singapore leaves Malaysia
	1965	Chief Minister of Sabah, Donald Stephens, is removed from office following disagreement with the Federal Government over Singapore's withdrawal from Malaysia
	1966	Chief Minister of Sarawak, Stephen Kalong Ningkan, is removed from office following disagreements with Federal Government over state rights
8 August	1967	ASEAN formed. Comprises Malaysia, Singapore, Thailand, the Philippines and Indonesia
12 May	1969	Alliance returned to power in general elections but without two-thirds majority

13 May	1969	Inter-racial riots break out in Kuala Lumpur
15 May	1969	The *Yang di-Pertuan Agong* declares a national state of emergency. The Parliament is suspended. The National Operations Council formed under Tun Abdul Razak
31 August	1970	The *Yang di-Pertuan Agong* promulgates the *Rukunegara* or state ideology
21 September	1970	Tunku Abdul Rahman retires as Prime Minister and is succeeded by Tun Abdul Razak
February	1971	Malaysian Parliament reconvenes and approves "Sensitive Issues" Bill
July	1971	Malaysian Parliament approves the New Economic Policy
	1971	The Kuala Lumpur ASEAN Summit Declaration of ZOPFAN (Zone of Peace, Freedom and Neutrality)
2 August	1973	Tun Hussein Onn is appointed Deputy Prime Minister on the death of Tun Dr Ismail
14 January	1976	Tun Abdul Razak dies and Tun Hussein becomes Prime Minister. Datuk Seri Dr Mahathir Mohamed becomes his Deputy
	1976	Industrial Co-ordination Act is enforced and meets with opposition from foreign and Chinese businesses
	1976	Datuk Mustapha Harun steps down as Chief Minister of Sabah after his party USNO is defeated by Berjaya party in Sabah elections
	1978	At UMNO General Assembly, Education Minister Musa Hitam rejects Chinese proposal to establish Chinese-medium Merdeka University

	1977	Barisan Nasional is returned to power in general elections
	1979	Datuk Samy Vellu becomes MIC President on the death of Tan Sri Manickavasagam
1 February	1981	Tun Hussein Onn steps down as Prime Minister owing to ill-health and is succeeded by Datuk Seri Dr Mahathir
	1982	Barisan Nasional under Dr Mahathir returned to power in general elections
	1983	Dr Mahathir adopts "Look East" Policy
	1983	Parliament approves Bill to ensure that the *Yang di-Pertuan Agong* can no longer block Bills passed by Parliament
1 April	1985	The first Proton Saga, Malaysia's national car, rolls out of its Shah Alam factory
16 March	1986	Musa Hitam resigns as Deputy Prime Minister citing differences with Dr Mahathir
	1986	Barisan Nasional under Dr Mahathir returned to power again
24 April	1987	Tengku Razaleigh contests UMNO's presidency against Dr Mahathir, but loses
	1988	Parliament approves Federal Constitution (Amendment) Act to curb powers of judiciary
26 May	1988	Lord President Tun Salleh Abbas suspended from office
October	1990	Barisan Nasional returned to power in general elections and Dr Mahathir again becomes Prime Minister
28 February	1991	Dr Mahathir announces his Vision 2020 and the Concept of *Bangsa Malaysia*

	1991	Tunku Abdul Rahman dies and is given state funeral
10 December	1992	Parliament adopts motion criticizing Sultan of Johor for his high-handed action against a hockey coach
	1992	Anwar Ibrahim defeats Ghafar Baba in the contest for Deputy President of UMNO
18 January	1993	Malay Rulers accept the Constitution (Amendment) Bill passed by Parliament removing their immunity from criminal prosecution
	1995	Dr Mahathir and Barisan Nasional returned to power in the general elections
	1997	Financial crisis hits Malaysia and several countries
September	1998	Dr Mahathir sacks his deputy Anwar Ibrahim on charges of committing sexual misconduct
September	1999	SUQIU announces its demands
November	1999	Barisan Nasional under Dr Mahathir's leadership is again returned to power in general elections, but Kelantan and Terengganu states fall to PAS. Majority of Malay votes swing to PAS
5 January	2001	SUQIU and UMNO Youth reach agreement under which SUQIU agrees to "put aside" seven of its claims
16 July	2002	Dr Mahathir celebrates 20th anniversary in office as Prime Minister

Bibliography

Articles and Books

Abdullah Ahmad. *Tengku Abdul Rahman and Malaysia's Foreign Policy, 1963–1970*. Kuala Lumpur: Berita Publishing Sdn. Bhd., 1985.

_____ . "Nexus antara PAS and Al-Ma'unah". *Mingguan Malaysia*, 23 July 2000, p. 12.

Adshead, Robin. *Mahathir of Malaysia*. London: Hibiscus, 1989.

Allen, James de V. *The Malayan Union*. New Haven: Southeast Asian Studies Council, Yale University, 1967.

Anderson, Benedict. *Imagined Communities: Reflections on the Origin and Spread of Nationalism*. London: Verso, 1983.

Ardizzone, Michael. *A Nation is Born*. London: Forum Books, 1946.

Aziz Zariza Ahmad. *Mahathir's Paradigm Shift*. Kuala Lumpur: Firma Malaysia Publishing, 1997.

Batson, Benjamin. *The End of Absolute Monarchy in Siam*. Kuala Lumpur: Oxford University Press, 1984.

Bendix, Reinhard. *Nation-Building and Citizenship*. Berkeley: University of California Press, 1964.

Campbell, Bill. *Berjaya's Success Story*. Kota Kinabalu: Chief Minister's Department, n.d. (1987?).

Chandra Muzaffar. "Islamic Resurgence: A Global View (with illustrations from Southeast Asia)". In *Readings in Malaysian Politics*, ed. Bruce Gale. Kuala Lumpur: Pelanduk Publications, 1987.

Cheah Boon Kheng. "The Erosion of Ideological Hegemony and Royal Power and The Rise of Postwar Malay Nationalism, 1945–46". *Journal of Southeast Asian Studies* 19, no. 1 (March 1988).

_____ . *Red Star Over Malaya: Resistance and Social Conflict During and After the Japanese Occupation, 1941–1946*. Singapore: Singapore University Press, 1983.

_____ . "Asal-Usul dan Asas Nasionalisme Malaya [The Origins and Basis of 'Malaya' Nationalism]". In *Nasionalisme: Suatu Tinjaun Sejarah*. Kuala Lumpur: Fajar Bakti, 1985.

249

_____. "Malayan Citizenship and the Citizenship Issue, 1945–1948". *Review of Malayan and Indonesian Affairs* 12, no. 2 (December 1978): 1–25.

_____. "The Japanese Occupation of Malaya, 1941–1945: Ibrahim Yaacob and the Struggle for Indonesia Raya". *Indonesia* 28 (October 1979): 85–120.

Crouch, Harold. "Authoritarian Trends, the UMNO Split and the Limits to State Power". In *Fragmented Vision: Culture and Politics in Contemporary Malaysia*, ed. Joel S. Kahn and Francis Loh Kok Wah. Sydney: Allen and Unwin, 1992.

Esman, Milton J. *Administration and Development in Malaysia*. Itahaca: Cornell University Press, 1972.

Enloe, Cynthia H. *Multi-Ethnic Politics: The Case of Malaysia*, Research Monograph Series, Centre for South and Southeast Asia Studies. Berkeley, California: University of California, August 1970.

Faaland, Just et al. *Growth and Ethnic Inequality: Malaysia's New Economic Policy*. Kuala Lumpur: Dewan Bahasa dan Pustaka, 1990.

Fan Yew Teng. *The UMNO Drama: Power Struggles in Malaysia*. Kuala Lumpur: Egret Publications, 1989.

Gale, Bruce. *Musa Hitam: A Political Biography*. Kuala Lumpur: Eastern Universities Press, 1982.

Goh Cheng Teik. *The May Thirteenth Incident and Democracy in Malaysia*. Kuala Lumpur: Oxford University Press, 1971.

Gullick, J.M. *Malaya*. London: Ernest Benn, 1967.

Harper, T.N. *The End of Empire and the Making of Malaya*. Cambridge: Cambridge University Press, 1999.

Hanafi Dolah. "Nasionalisme Malaya: Satu Versi Yang Defektif". *Ilmu Masyarakat* 5 (Jan.–June 1984): 71–76.

Hasan Hj. Hamzah. *Mahathir: Great Malaysian Hero*. Kuala Lumpur: Mediaprint Publications, 1990.

Heng Pek Koon. *Chinese Politics in Malaysia: A History of the Malaysian Chinese Association*. Kuala Lumpur: Oxford University Press, 1988.

_____. "Chinese Responses to Malay Hegemony in Peninsular Malaysia (1957–1996)". In *Cultural Contestations: Mediating Identities in a Changing Malaysian Society*, ed. Zawawi Ibrahim. London: Asean Academic Press, 1998.

Hill, Michael and Lian Kwen Fee. *The Politics of Nation Building and Citizenship in Singapore*. London: Routledge, 1995.

Ho Khai Leong. "The Political and Administrative Frames: Challenges and Reforms under the Mahathir Administration". In *Mahathir's Administration: Performance and Crisis in Governance*, ed. Ho Khai Leong and James Chin. Singapore: Times Books International, 2001.

Ismail Kassim. *Race, Politics and Moderation: A Study of the Malaysian Electoral Process.* Singapore: Times Books International, 1979.

Jayasuriya. *Dynamics of Nation-building in Malaysia.* Colombo: Associated Educational Publishers, 1983.

Jawan, Jayum A. *Iban Politics and Economic Development: Their Patterns and Change.* Bangi: Penerbit Universiti Kebangsaan Malaysia, 1994.

Jomo, K. S. *A Question of Class: Capital, the State and Uneven Development in Malaysia.* Singapore: Oxford University Press, 1986.

Kamaruddin Jaafar, ed. *Dr Burhanuddin Al-Helmy: Politik Melayu dan Islam.* Kuala Lumpur: Yayasan Anda, 1980.

Kaur, Hardev. "The indomitable Dr Mahathir, man with a mission". *New Straits Times,* 4 December 1999, p. 15.

Kershaw, Roger. "Shattered Symbiosis: The Road to Conflict between Malay Nationalism and Monarchy". *Internationales Asienforum* 24 (1993).

Khoo Boo Teik. *Paradoxes of Mahathirism.* Kuala Lumpur: Oxford University Press, 1995.

Khoo Khay Jin. "The Grand Vision: Mahathir and Modernisation". In *Fragmented Vision: Culture and Politics in Contemporary Malaysia,* ed. Joel S. Kahn and Francis Loh Kok Wah. Sydney: Allen and Unwin, 1992.

Kohn, Hans. *The Idea of Nationalism* Toronto: Collier Books, 1969.

———. *Nationalism: Its Meaning and History.* New York: Van Nostrand, 1965.

Lau, Albert. *A Moment of Anguish: Singapore in Malaysia and the Politics of Disengagement.* Singapore: Times Academic Press, 1998.

Lee Kam Hing. "Three Approaches; in Peninsular Chinese Politics: The MCA, the DAP and the Gerakan". In *Government and Politics of Malaysia,* ed. Zakariah Haji Ahmad. Singapore: Oxford University Press, 1987.

Lee Kuan Yew. *The Singapore Story: Memoirs of Lee Kuan Yew.* Singapore: Times Editions, 1998.

Lim, David. "Malaysian Development Planning". In *The Fourth Malaysian Plan: Economic Perspectives,* ed. Jomo K.S. and R.J.G. Wells. Kuala Lumpur: Malaysian Economic Association, 1982.

Lim Hong Hai. "Sabah and Sarawak in Malaysia: The Real Bargain, or What have they gotten themselves into?" In *Sabah and Sarawak: The Politics of Development and Federalism,* ed. Francis Loh Kok Wah. Published by *Kajian Malaysia* XV, nos. 1 and 2 (Jan./Dec. 1997): 15–56.

Lim Teck Ghee. *Social and economic integration of different ethnic groups in Southeast Asia, with special reference to Malaysia: A review of the literature and empirical material.* Geneva: International Institute for Labour Studies, 1995.

Liow, Joseph. "Personality, Exigencies and Contingencies: Determinants of Malaysia's Foreign Policy in the Mahathir Administration". In *Mahathir's Administration: Performance and Crisis in Governance*, ed. Ho Khai Leong and James Chin. Singapore: Times Books International, 2001.

Loh Kok Wah, Francis. "Modernisation, Cultural Revival and Counter-Hegemony: The Kadazans of Sabah in the 1980s". In *Fragmented Vision: Culture and Politics in Contemporary Malaysia*, ed. Joel S. Kahn and Francis Loh Kok Wah. Sydney: Allen and Unwin, 1992.

_____. "Understanding Politics in Sabah and Sarawak: An Overview". In *Sabah and Sarawak: The Politics of Development and Federalism*, ed. Francis Loh Kok Wah. Published by *Kajian Malaysia* XV, nos. 1 and 2 (Jan./Dec. 1997): 1–14.

Mahathir, Mohamad. "In Defence of Feudalism". *Opinion* 2, no. 1 (November 1968): 183–84.

_____. *The Malay Dilemma*. Kuala Lumpur: Federal Publications, 1981.

Malaysian Chinese Association. *The Future of Malaysian Chinese*. Kuala Lumpur: MCA, 1988.

Mauzy, D.K. *Barisan Nasional: Coalition Government in Malaysia*. Kuala Lumpur: Maricans, 1983.

McIntyre, Angus. "The Greater Indonesia Idea of Nationalism in Malaya and Indonesia". *Modern Asian Studies* 7, no. 1 (1973): 75–83.

McVey, Ruth T. *The Calcutta Conference and the Southeast Asian Uprisings*. Ithaca: Cornell Modern Indonesia Project, 1958.

Means, Gordon P. *Malaysian Politics: The Second Generation*. Kuala Lumpur: Oxford University Press, 1991.

Miller, David. *On Nationality*. Oxford: Clarendon Press, 1995.

Milne, R.S. and K.J. Ratnam. *Malaysia — New States in a New Nation: Political Development of Sarawak and Sabah in Malaysia*. London: Frank Cass, 1974.

Milne, R.S. and Diane K. Mauzy. *Malaysian Politics under Mahathir*. London: Routledge, 1999.

_____. *Politics and Government in Malaysia*. Singapore: Federal Publications, 1978.

Mills, Lennox A. *Malaya: A Political and Economic Appraisal*. Conn.: Greenwood Press, Westport, 1973.

Morais, J.V. *Mahathir: A Profile in Courage*. Singapore: Eastern Universities Press, 1982.

_____. *Hussein Onn: A Tryst With Destiny*. Singapore: Times Books International, 1981.

Nagata, Judy. "Islamic Revival and the Problem of Legitimacy among Rural Religious Elites in Malaysia". In *Readings in Malaysian Politics*, ed. Bruce Gale. Kuala Lumpur: Pelanduk Publications, 1987.

Nam, Tae Y. *Racism and Nation-building in Malaysia and Singapore*. India: Sadha Prakashan, Meerut, 1973.

Ng Beoy Kui. "Vulnerability and Party Capitalism: Malaysia's Encounter with the 1997 Financial Crisis". In *Mahathir's Administration: Performance and Crisis in Governance*, ed. Ho Khai Leong and James Chin. Singapore: Times Books International, 2001, pp. 161–87.

Ong, Pamela. *One Man's Will: A Portrait of Dato' Sir Onn Jaafar*. Penang: published by author, 1998.

Ongkili, James P. *Nation-building in Malaysia, 1946–1974*. Kuala Lumpur: Oxford University Press, 1985.

_____. "Perkembangan Nasionalisme". *Jebat* I (1971/1972): 24–43.

_____. "The British and Malayan Nationalism, 1945–1946". *Journal of Southeast Asian Studies* V, no. 2 (September 1974).

Paridah Abd. Samad. *Tun Abdul Razak: A Phenomenon in Malaysian Politics*. Kuala Lumpur: Affluent Master, 1998.

Pluvier, Jan M. "Malayan Nationalism: A Myth". *Journal of the Historical Society, University of Malaya*, 1867/18, pp. 26–40.

Puthucheary, Mavis. *The Politics of Administration: The Malayan Experience*. Kuala Lumpur: Oxford University Press, 1978.

Puthucheary, Dominic and K.S. Jomo. *James Puthucheary: No Cowardly Past*. Kuala Lumpur: Insan, 1998.

Raja Aziz Addruse. *Conduct Unbecoming: In Defence of Tun Mohd. Salleh Abbas*. Kuala Lumpur: Walrus Publications, 1990.

Ramachandran, Selvakumaran. *Indian Plantation Labour in Malaysia*. Kuala Lumpur: Institute for Social Analysis, 1994.

Ramlah Adam. *Dato Onn Jaafar: Pengasas Kemerdekaan*. Kuala Lumpur: Dewan Bahasa dan Pustaka, 1992.

Ratnam, K.J. and R.S. Milne. *The Malayan Parliamentary Election of 1964*. Kuala Lumpur: University of Malaya Press, 1969.

Ratnam, K.J. *Communalism and the Political Process in Malaya*. Kuala Lumpur: University of Malaya Press, 1967.

Roff, Margaret. "The Rise and Demise of Kadazan Nationalism". *Journal of Southeast Asian History* 10, no. 2 (1969): 326–43.

S. Husin Ali. *Two Faces: Detention Without Trial*. Kuala Lumpur: Insan, 1996.

Searle, Peter. *Politics in Sarawak, 1970–1976: The Iban Perspective*. Singapore: Oxford University Press, 1983

Seton-Watson, Hugh. *Nations and States: An Inquiry Into the Origins of Nations and the Politics of Nationalism*. Boulder, Colorado: Westview Press, 1977.

Shaw, W. *Tun Razak and His Times*. Kuala Lumpur: Longmans, 1977.

Sheppard, Mubin, *Tunku: His Life and Times (The Authorized Biography of Tunku Abdul Rahman Putra al-Haj)*. Kuala Lumpur: Pelanduk Publications, 1995.

Sheridan, L.A. *Federation of Malaya Constitution*. Singapore: University of Malaya Law Review, 1961.

Silcock, T..H. and Ungku Abdul Aziz. "Nationalism in Malaya". In *Asian Nationalism and the West*, ed. W.L. Holland. New York: Macmillan, 1953.

Simandjuntak, B. *Malayan Federalism, 1945–1963*. Kuala Lumpur: Oxford University Press, 1969.

Singam, S. Durai Raja, ed. *Tribute to Tunku Abdul Rahman*. Kuala Lumpur: published by author, 1963.

Sinnadurai, Visu. "The Citizenship Laws of Malaysia". In *The Constitution of Malaysia: Its Development, 1957–1977*, ed. Tun Mohamed Suffian et al. Kuala Lumpur: Oxford University Press, 1978.

Smith, Anthony D. "Nations and Their Past". In *Nations and Nationalism* 3, no. 3 (November 1986).

Stockwell, Anthony, ed. *Malaya: Part III The Alliance Route to Independence, 1953–1957*. London: British Documents on the End of Empire Series B, Vol. 3, HMSO, 1995.

Tan Chee Khoon. *Without Fear or Favour*. Singapore: Eastern Universities Press, 1984.

Tan Liok Ee. *The Politics of Chinese Education in Malaya*. Kuala Lumpur: Oxford University Press, 1996.

_____. "Descent and Identity: The Different Paths of Tan Cheng Lock, Tan Kah Kee and Lim Lian Geok". *Journal of the Malaysian Branch of the Royal Asiatic Society*, LXVII, part I (1995).

Tan, T.H. *The Prince and I*. Singapore: Mini Media, 1979.

Tunku Abdul Rahman Putra. *Looking Back*. Kuala Lumpur: Pustaka Antara, 1977.

Tunku Abdul Rahman. *Viewpoints*. Kuala Lumpur: Heinemann, 1978.

_____. *As A Matter of Interest*. Kuala Lumpur, 1981.

_____. *Lest We Forget: Further Candid Reminiscences*. Kuala Lumpur: Heinemann Educational Books, 1983.

Tun Salleh Abbas. *May Day for Justice*. Kuala Lumpur: published by K. Das and Tun Salleh Abbas, 1989.

Ungku Abdul Aziz. "Co-operative the Key to rural success". *Straits Times*, 17 October 1963.

Vasil, R.K. *Politics in a Plural Society*. Kuala Lumpur: Oxford University Press, 1971.

Von Vorys, Karl. *Democracy Without Consensus: Communalism and Political Stability in Malaysia*. Princeton, New Jersey: Princeton University Press, 1975.

Wang Gungwu. *Community and Nation: Essays on Southeast Asia and the Chinese*. Singapore: Heinemann, 1981.

Williams, Peter Alderidge. *Judicial Misconduct.* Kuala Lumpur: Pelanduk Publications, 1990.

Zainal Abidin bin A. Wahid. *Glimpses of Malaysian History.* Kuala Lumpur: Dewan Bahasa dan Pustaka, 1974.

Zainuddin Maidin (Zam). "Menangani undi protes" [Questioning the protest votes]. *Utusan Malaysia*, 2 December 1999, p. 6.

Zainuddin Mydin. *The Other Side of Mahathir.* Kuala Lumpur: Utusan Publications, 1994.

Zin Mahmud. "Anwar pecahkan orang Melayu" [Anwar causes a split among the Malays]. *Utusan Malaysia*, 5 December 1999, p. 6.

Government Publications

General Report. Population Census of Malaysia, 1970. Vol I, 1977.

Report of the Federation of Malaya Constitutional Commission, Kuala Lumpur: Government Press, February 1957.

Report of the Working Committee Appointed by a Conference of the Governor of the Malayan Union, The Rulers of the Malay States and the Representatives of the United Malays National Organization, (Revised up to 19 November 1946). Kuala Lumpur: Malayan Union Government Press, 1946.

Report of the Education Committee, 1956. Kuala Lumpur: Government Printing Office, 1956.

Second Malaysia Plan 1971–1975. Kuala Lumpur: Government Printing Office, 1971.

Index

THE AUTHOR

Cheah Boon Kheng retired in 1994 as Professor of History at the Universiti Sains Malaysia in Penang and is presently a Visiting Fellow at the university's Centre for Policy Research. He has written extensively on Malaysian social and political history. His books include *The Masked Comrades* (1979); *Red Star Over Malaya* (1983); and *The Peasant Robbers of Kedah* (1988).